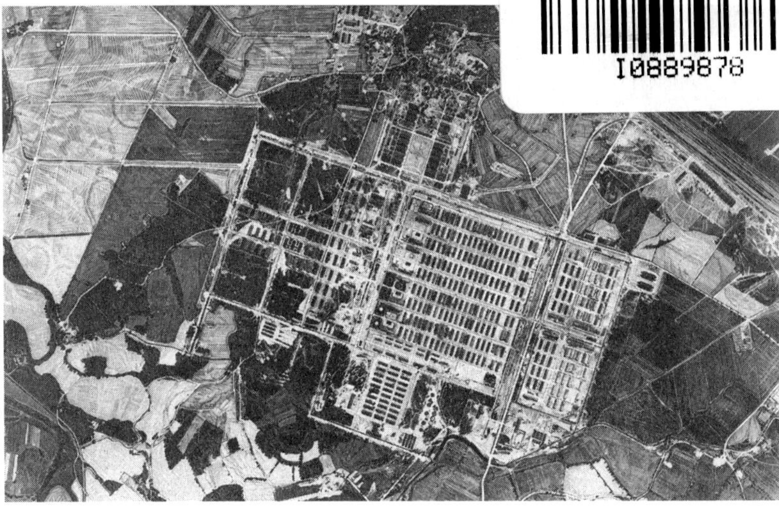

THE PASTORA GOLDNER SERIES
in Post-Holocaust Studies

The Pastora Goldner Series in Post-Holocaust Studies explores questions—ethical, educational, political, spiritual—that continue to haunt humanity in the aftermath of Nazi Germany's attempt to destroy Jewish life and culture. Books in this series, addressing the most current and pressing issues of our post-Holocaust world, proceed from scholarship undertaken by the Pastora Goldner Symposium, whose membership—international, interdisciplinary, interfaith, and intergenerational—is committed to dialogue as a fundamental form of inquiry. The symposium and the series are generously supported by Pastora Campos Goldner, who has devoted much of her life to working toward *tikkun olam,* the healing of our world, and whose vision and courage inspire the participants in the symposium who contribute to this series.

THE PASTORA GOLDNER SERIES
in Post-Holocaust Studies

After-Words: Post-Holocaust Struggles with Forgiveness, Reconciliation, Justice
Edited and Introduced by David Patterson and John K. Roth

AFTER-WORDS

Post-Holocaust Struggles with Forgiveness, Reconciliation, Justice

Edited and Introduced

by David Patterson and John K. Roth

UNIVERSITY OF WASHINGTON PRESS

Seattle and London

Printed in the United States of America
Designed by Pamela Canell
10 09 08 07 06 05 04 6 5 4 3 2 1

University of Washington Press
P.O. Box 50096
Seattle, Washington 98145–5096
www.washington.edu/uwpress

Library of Congress Cataloging-in-Publication Data
can be found at the back of this book.

The paper used in this publication is acid-free and recycled from 10 percent post-consumer and at least 50 percent pre-consumer waste. It meets the minimum requirements of American National Standard for Information Sciences—Permanence of Paper for Printed Library Materials, ANSI Z39.48–1984. ♾ ♻

Illustration (jacket, pp. i, 3, 81, 167): *First Station: Auschwitz-Birkenau,* by Arie Galles (1998, 47 1/2" x 75", charcoal and white Conté on Arches with barbed wire–impressed wrought-iron frame), from the suite of fifteen drawings *Fourteen Stations/Hey Yud Dalet (Hashem Yinkom Daman),* the latter phrase meaning "May God avenge their blood." The title of the suite refers both to the Stations of the Cross and to the fact that the Nazi concentration camps and killing centers were near railroad stations. Galles's drawings are based on Luftwaffe and Allied aerial photographs of those sites. Within this drawing and all the others are invisibly embedded, hand-lettered phrases from the Kaddish, the ancient Jewish prayer for the dead.

TO THE MEMORY OF

DAVID HIRSCH AND CLAIRE NUER

In memory, you are not alone.

You are surrounded by people. . . .

And you hear them and you speak to them,

and when you need a presence,

it's their presence.

—Elie Wiesel, *Conversations with Elie Wiesel*

After? Did you say: after? Meaning what?

—Elie Wiesel, *One Generation After*

CONTENTS

Prologue: "Did you say: after? Meaning what?"
DAVID PATTERSON AND JOHN K. ROTH xiii

Part One: Forgiveness

1 / Forgiveness, Reconciliation, and Jewish Memory after Auschwitz
PETER J. HAAS 5
In Response
RACHEL N. BAUM 16
LEONARD GROB 20
PETER J. HAAS 24

2 / The Face of Forgiveness in a Post-Holocaust World
HENRY F. KNIGHT 28
In Response
BRITTA FREDE-WENGER 41
DAVID PATTERSON 45
HENRY F. KNIGHT 49

3 / Forgiveness after the Holocaust
DIDIER POLLEFEYT 55
In Response
PETER J. HAAS 69
JUERGEN MANEMANN 73
DIDIER POLLEFEYT 75

Part Two: Reconciliation

4 / Useless Experience: Its Significance for Reconciliation after Auschwitz
JOHN K. ROTH 85
In Response
RACHEL N. BAUM 99
DIDIER POLLEFEYT 103
JOHN K. ROTH 108

5 / Anthropological Remarks on Reconciliation after Auschwitz
BRITTA FREDE-WENGER 115
In Response
JUERGEN MANEMANN 128
DIDIER POLLEFEYT 132
BRITTA FREDE-WENGER 137

6 / Struggles for Recognition in an Era of Globalization: The Necessity of a Theology of Reconciliation from a Political-Theological Perspective after Auschwitz
JUERGEN MANEMANN 142

In Response
PETER J. HAAS 154
DAVID PATTERSON 158
JUERGEN MANEMANN 162

Part Three: Justice

7 / G-d, World, Humanity: Jewish Reflections on Justice after Auschwitz
DAVID PATTERSON 171
In Response
BRITTA FREDE-WENGER 182
JOHN K. ROTH 187
DAVID PATTERSON 192

8 / The Israeli-Palestinian Conflict: Just Reconciliation in the Shadows of the Holocaust
LEONARD GROB 197
In Response
HENRY F. KNIGHT 210
JOHN K. ROTH 214
LEONARD GROB 219

9 / The Post-Holocaust Jewish Heart
RACHEL N. BAUM 224
In Response
LEONARD GROB 236
HENRY F. KNIGHT 240
RACHEL N. BAUM 244

Postscript: An *After* That Is *Yet to Be*
DAVID PATTERSON AND JOHN K. ROTH 249

Bibliography 255

About the Editors and Contributors 267

Index 271

PROLOGUE

"Did you say: after? Meaning what?"

I know the difference between before and after.
—Charlotte Delbo, *Auschwitz and After*

"OCTOBER 1944" IS one of the chapters in *Survival in Auschwitz,* Primo Levi's classic Holocaust memoir. As autumn's light and warmth retreated, Levi knew that the devastation of another Auschwitz winter had arrived. "It means," he said, "that in the course of these months, from October to April, seven out of ten of us will die. Whoever does not die will suffer minute by minute, all day, every day."[1] *Winter,* Levi went on to suggest, was not the right word for that dreadful season. Nor could words such as *hunger* and *pain* do justice to the realities of Auschwitz. Those words, it seemed to him, were "free words, created and used by free men who lived in comfort and suffering in their homes."[2] After making that point, Levi then added one of his most telling sentences: "If the Lagers had lasted longer," he contended, "a new, harsh language would have been born: and only this language could express what it means to toil the whole day in the wind, with the temperature below freezing, wearing only a shirt, underpants, cloth jacket and trousers, and in one's body nothing but weakness, hunger and knowledge of the end drawing near."[3]

Although it may not have lasted long enough to produce in full the new, harsh language of which Levi spoke, the Holocaust continues to leave survivors, historians, philosophers, theologians, novelists, and poets groping for words to describe and reflect upon, let alone explain, the immensity of that watershed event in which Jewish life was targeted—root and branch—for utter annihilation. The inadequacy of words, however, is only part of the struggle to express the Holocaust's realities and implications. Those efforts stretch language to the point where it is unavoidably silenced, and yet the silence, too, evokes responses. Dialogue—sometimes halting, often fragmented, but dialogue nonetheless—is one result of that give-and-take between speech and silence. Deepening awareness, post-Holocaust dialogue can show how the Holocaust affects—*upsets* and *reorients* are two more verbs that come to mind—our understanding of the most ordinary concepts.

This book, for example, has an epigraph, one of those brief quotations that introduces a governing theme or mood. Used in the title of this prologue, it comes from Elie Wiesel, another Auschwitz survivor. His versatile writings sometimes include Holocaust-related dialogues—spare and lean, they often consist of just a few hundred words or less. These dialogues are distinctive not only for their minimalist quality but also because their apparent simplicity, their unidentified settings, unnamed characters, abrupt and open endings raise fundamental questions in moving ways. In Wiesel's *One Generation After,* one partner in a dialogue—it could involve two persons or a single person's self-interrogation—tries to pull the other from a downward-spiraling sadness. "Look around you," says the upbeat voice. "The trees in bloom. The shop windows. The pretty girls. What the hell, let yourself go. I promise you that after. . . ." *After*—not allusions to spring's new life—that's the word, the problem, that gets the other's attention. "After?" asks the downcast voice. "Did you say: after? Meaning what?"[4] With that question the dialogue ends, but far from being over, it has only begun.

After—that word is ordinary because human life is thick with time. Encountering what is present, anticipating what lies ahead, our living is always *after,* whose meanings denote a subsequent or later time and a seeking or questing for something one does not have. In either case, the question " after? Meaning what?" has its place. What was it that came before so that we could and must say "after?" What is it that our seeking after is trying to get or find? For many people—not only Americans but especially them—*after* now directs attention back to September 11, 2001, a grisly day when terrorists turned hijacked jetliners into missiles that leveled the World Trade Center in New York City. At least in the foreseeable future, that complacency-shattering destruction is likely to keep the world at war.

Having lost her life to cancer in 1985, Charlotte Delbo knew nothing about the attack on the World Trade Center, but she wrote, "I know the difference between before and after."[5] Primo Levi was deported from Italy to Auschwitz on February 22, 1944. A year earlier, on January 24, 1943, Delbo had been deported to that same place from her native France. Of the 230 women in her convoy—most of them, like Delbo herself, non-Jews who had worked in the French Resistance—only 49, including Delbo, survived.[6] For Delbo, *after* irrevocably referred to Auschwitz. Its reality, she emphasized, was "so deeply etched in my memory that I cannot forget one moment of it."[7] Like Levi's, her Auschwitz experiences left her acutely aware of how the Holocaust and its aftermath had fragmented the meaning of words. "There are people," she observed, "who say, 'I'm thirsty.' They step into a café and order a beer."[8] Those words are her ironic conclusion to a chapter entitled "Thirst." It attempts to describe what the "free word" *thirst* can never capture, an experience ungrasped even when Delbo writes that it took her to "the point of losing my mind." The parching that she found no words to describe was so all-consuming that it could only be relieved by drinking and drinking from a pail, as she was finally able to do, "like a horse, no, like a dog."[9]

Perhaps after September 11, 2001, but certainly after Auschwitz, even simple words such as *after* cannot mean what they did before. What happens, then, to words whose meanings were already fragile, problematic, and contested before terror struck and the Holocaust raged? What about words such as *forgiveness, reconciliation,* and *justice*? As its title suggests, this book identifies them as "after-words." They remain after Auschwitz; they persist after September 11. The fact that they have not been silenced, that they are still spoken and heard, indicates that these words are needed. Yet these after-words are also wounded words. The horror unleashed by human hands makes it unclear whether justice can be achieved, and to the extent that justice cannot be achieved, the credibility of that ideal is jeopardized as well. The suffering that people have inflicted on one another, and the memory of that suffering, makes it hard to glimpse how reconciliation and forgiveness are possible, no matter how necessary they may be to curtail revenge, hate, and the violence that both ignite. In a post-Holocaust world, which unfortunately remains one where human beings fall prey to terror, mass murder, and genocide, how should forgiveness, reconciliation, and justice be understood? What, if anything, can be retrieved from philosophical and religious traditions to restore the integrity and credibility of those ideals? Why is it so important to keep working at these tasks? This book focuses on those questions. As its contents show, the issues surrounding forgiveness, reconciliation, and justice form minefields that must be explored and disarmed with care lest hasty inquiry, insensitive judgment, or premature closure set off explosions that enlarge harm's way.

The nine contributors to *After-Words* are members of the Pastora Goldner Holocaust Symposium. Led by Leonard Grob and Henry Knight since its founding in 1996, the symposium's thirty-five Holocaust and genocide scholars—a group that is interfaith, international, interdisciplinary, and intergenerational—meet biennially in Oxfordshire, England, at the Wroxton College campus of Fairleigh Dickinson University. The symposium stimulates small working groups. Committed to writing in a dialogical, give-and-take style, the team that created this book came together at Wroxton College not only because its members shared concerns about forgiveness, reconciliation, and justice, but also because we knew that our particular religious traditions and philosophical perspectives entailed differences and disagreements that would be fruitful to investigate. Our writing began in earnest after June 2000. As we exchanged and revised our post-Holocaust reflections, current events—especially but not only those of September 2001—gave our deliberations about forgiveness, reconciliation, and justice added intensity, relevance, and anguish. In the autumn of 2001, through the kindness of the Samuel Rosenthal Center for Judaic Studies, Peter Haas invited us to Case Western Reserve University to advance the book's development. When September's violence intervened, our European colleagues were unable to participate in that meeting, which became one in which the absence of justice in the world as well as the absence of friends was keenly felt.

This book's reflections on "after-words" are not complete, let alone final. We met, worked, and wrote to learn, to open our minds and hearts, and to help each other in that process. When critical, as scholars have to be, we tried hard to do justice to each other's thinking. When in disagreement, as scholars tend to be, we tried not to attack or defend but to clarify and understand so as to produce reconciliation that emphasized the importance of respect for differences. When we failed, as scholars often do, and especially when we discovered that our efforts at dialogue had created misunderstanding and hurt, we tried to admit our shortcomings and to change. Invariably those efforts were met with hospitality that helped us to see, at least in part, what forgiveness requires and means.

These experiences are mentioned not for self-congratulation, but to indicate that our working together helped us to glimpse more fully some of the concerns and prospects that are most important *after* the brokenness and the fragmentation of the human condition are confronted. Our readers will be the judges, but we hope that the after-words we have written will communicate what we have discerned and encourage others to participate in similar inter- and intrafaith inquiries.

We would like to acknowledge, with gratitude, the excellent work of copy editor Jan Spauschus. Special thanks are due to Pastora Goldner, whose dedication and generosity sustain the work of the Goldner Symposium and its writing projects, including this book, in particular, and to Naomi Pascal and Xavier Callahan, our supportive editors, and their superb staff at the University of Washington Press. We are also indebted to the artist Arie Galles, a member of the Goldner Symposium, who generously allowed us to use his image of Auschwitz-Birkenau. The memory of David Hirsch and Claire Nuer, good Wroxton friends whom death took too soon, informed our work profoundly by helping us feel and know the difference between before and after.

DAVID PATTERSON AND JOHN K. ROTH

NOTES

1. Primo Levi, *Survival in Auschwitz: The Nazi Assault on Humanity,* trans. Stuart Woolf (New York: Macmillan, 1976), p. 112.

2. Ibid., pp. 112–13.

3. Ibid., p. 113.

4. Elie Wiesel, *One Generation After,* trans. Lily Edelman and Elie Wiesel (New York: Avon Books, 1972), pp. 72–73.

5. Charlotte Delbo, *Auschwitz and After,* trans. Rosette C. Lamont (New Haven: Yale University Press, 1995), p. 258.

6. After the Holocaust, Delbo gathered as much information as she could about every woman who was on her Auschwitz transport. Their stories are told in Charlotte Delbo, *Convoy to Auschwitz: Women of the French Resistance,* trans. Carol Cosman (Boston: Northeastern University Press, 1997). The book was originally published in 1965 as *Convoi du 24 janvier.*

7. Charlotte Delbo, *Days and Memory,* trans. Rosette C. Lamont (Marlboro, Vt.: Marlboro Press, 1990), p. 2.

8. Delbo, *Auschwitz and After,* p. 145.

9. Ibid., pp. 142, 144.

AFTER-WORDS

Post-Holocaust Struggles

with

Forgiveness,

Reconciliation,

Justice

Part One
FORGIVENESS

Relatively few people have never felt the need for forgiveness, asked to receive it, and found relief when it was granted. Forgiveness is important, but as an after-word, *forgiveness* also poses problems and raises questions. For example, do reconciliation and justice depend on forgiveness? Opening these post-Holocaust struggles with issues about forgiveness might create that impression, which, in turn, might imply that *forgiveness* is the most basic of the three fundamental after-words before us. Peter J. Haas shows, however, that such assumptions may not hold. His essay "Forgiveness, Reconciliation, and Jewish Memory after Auschwitz" begins this book's dialogues by questioning key terms and by contending, in particular, that Christians cannot expect Jews to embrace ideas that are alien to Jewish thinking. He argues that attempts to impose the burden of forgiveness on Jews—if such attempts ignore issues of repentance and the action it entails—serve only to widen the gap between the post-Holocaust Jewish and Christian communities. The questions that haunt both Haas and his respondents include the following: How can that gap be bridged, if indeed bridging it is possible? Is it enough to work side by side, if not hand in hand? Finally, can the gap serve dialogue rather than threaten it?

In "The Face of Forgiveness in a Post-Holocaust World," Henry F.

Knight takes up the task of bridging. He seeks to recover a face-to-face relation between Christians and Jews, whom he describes as the Christians' "significant other." Just as Haas challenges the concept of forgiveness from his Jewish standpoint, Knight does so from his Christian perspective. However, unlike Haas, who wonders whether forgiveness is even intelligible in post-Holocaust Christian-Jewish relations, Knight retains the category of forgiveness by redefining it as that which must be at once sought and refused. In a bold move, he maintains that confession is an important element in the dialogical relation; it must be heard and responded to, but not allayed by an automatic granting of the forgiveness it seeks. Thus, Knight refuses premature closure, for only when such fundamental matters remain unsettled can the dialogical relation—and the mutual hospitality it implies—be sustained. Here, too, Knight raises a crucial question, as Britta Frede-Wenger points out in her response to him: Is there a connection between the divine-human reconciliation process and the interhuman reconciliation process, and, if so, how are they connected? Knight suggests that they might be connected through the Eucharist, but David Patterson's response keeps the inquiry open by wondering how Jews can really have a place of their own in that setting.

Taking yet a different approach, Didier Pollefeyt's "Forgiveness after the Holocaust" finds that reconciliation is impossible without forgiveness. Thus, one may gather from Pollefeyt's reflections, the cooperation that Haas calls for and the interrelation that Knight longs for are impossible without forgiveness. But that is not necessarily so, as Pollefeyt explains. He underscores that forgiveness is a matter of releasing oneself from resentment, anger, and hatred, and not one of letting bygones be bygones; it is a recognition of the perpetrator's repentance, inasmuch as that repentance is genuine. And, as if anticipating Peter Haas's response, Pollefeyt insists that forgiveness cannot be extorted from the victim. Here too, however, questions remain: Does the very concept of forgiveness make an imposition on the victim? And will returning meaning to this after-word in fact mend the broken relation? As indicated by these issues and the authors' dialogues about them, *forgiveness* may not be the most important after-word, but scarcely any are likely to be more so.

1

Forgiveness, Reconciliation, and Jewish Memory after Auschwitz

PETER J. HAAS

AS WE ENTER the twenty-first century, the Holocaust is moving from the realm of actual experience to the realm of memory. Fewer and fewer people alive today were actual participants in, or witnesses of, the Holocaust. As this process matures, the questions of repentance, forgiveness, and reconciliation are thrown into a new context. We now have to ask not how victims and their victimizers are to establish a new relationship with each other, but how the post-Shoah Jewish community and the post-Shoah Christian community are to relate to each other. While there has been considerable activity in this regard coming from the Christian community, the response from the Jewish community has been hesitant. While many individual Jews have come to their own personal terms with Christians, and Germans in particular, there has been little in the way of a communal gesture of forgiveness and reconciliation. In what follows I want to look at the theological reasons for this lack of resolution in Jewish communal responses. As I shall show, the reason for this hesitancy is that the dynamics of repentance, forgiveness, and reconciliation as understood by the Judaic tradition are different from what has emerged in Christianity. The result is that the statements and acts of contrition and repentance put forth by various Church bodies do not resonate within the semantics of the Jewish tradition.

To get at the classical Jewish notions of repentance, forgiveness, and reconciliation, I propose to turn first to the great medieval compendium of the Jewish tradition, Moses Maimonides' *Mishneh Torah,* which was compiled around the year 1154. In this collection, Maimonides dedicates a particular treatise, *Hilchot Teshuvah* (Laws of repentance), to the issues under discussion here. After adducing the central theory, logic, and structure of forgiveness and repentance as these emerge from the *Mishneh Torah,* I want to look at some contemporary responsa dealing with reconciliation and forgiveness as regards the Holocaust in particular. While most of these come from the Orthodox community, they nonetheless articulate a view of repentance, forgiveness, and reconciliation that is widespread in the broader Jewish religious community. These various texts raise the question not only of what form repentance and forgiveness should take, but also of whether these are even possible in the absence of the actual victims and perpetrators. I will close with a brief reflection on how we might understand the statement of Jewish response to Christian expressions of penance, "Dabru Emet" ("speak truth," from Zechariah 8:16), in light of the traditional literature.

I

A reading of Maimonides' treatise on repentance shows that it is based on the assumption that, just as sin sets into motion a chain of consequences, so must repentance set off a chain of events that will cancel out, as it were, the effects of the misdeed. Although not stated explicitly, the mechanism for repentance parallels that for dealing with what the Bible calls *me`ilah* (often translated into English as "sacrilege"). *Me`ilah* occurs when one takes something that belongs to the Deity, say a calf dedicated to the altar, and uses it for personal gain. Overturning the *me`ilah* requires three steps: a sincere sense of regret *(teshuvah)* on the part of the miscreant, confession (sometimes accompanied by a sacrifice), and repayment of the misbegotten gain. A major consequence of the parallel Maimonides adduces is that the initiative for repentance must come, logically enough, from the offender. As Maimonides himself puts matters, "For just as a person sins with his cognizance and with his will, so does he make repentance with his cognizance and with his will" (6:2).[1] So setting repentance into motion depends in the first instance on the transgressor. It is of course understood that once the proper acts of *teshuvah,* confession, and repayment have been executed, forgiveness should directly follow, just as the Deity forgives *me`ilah* once *teshuvah,* confession, and repayment have been accomplished. The bulk of the discussion in *Hilchot Teshuvah* is devoted to elucidating what precisely constitutes true repentance in various situations.

Maimonides begins his discussion of this topic, as is his wont, with general principles and works his way down to specifics. The opening paragraph says that

> as regards all of the commands in the Torah, whether positive or negative, if one transgresses any one of them either intentionally or unintentionally, when this one would repent and turn away from the misdeed, he must make confession before God. . . . Thus even those who owe guilt or sin offerings, at the time they bring their offerings for their unintentional or intentional deeds, are not atoned for through their offerings until they have repented and made explicit confession. . . . Likewise for those whose punishment is death by the courts or flogging, their deaths or floggings do not effect atonement until they have repented and made confession, and so also for one who harms his fellow or damages his property—even if he has paid what he owes, he is not atoned for until he makes confession and turns back from doing the like again forever. (1:1)

By the same token, once the sinner has in fact repented and made confession and paid damages, the prerequisites for atonement are deemed to have been completed. Thus we find in the next section the statement that "nowadays, when the Temple is not in existence and we have no atoning altar, there is nothing but repentance, and this repentance atones for all transgressions; even for one who was evil all his days but made repentance at the end we no longer mention any of his evil doings" (1:2). Yet, while such an act of repentance is necessary, it may not in itself be sufficient. Maimonides goes on to point out that for more heinous crimes, full atonement may not be effected until the punishment, suffering, or even death of the evildoer is carried out.

With this background in place, Maimonides turns to fleshing out his scheme. Thus he continues in chapter 2 of the *Mishneh Torah,* "What is complete repentance? The case in which one has the opportunity to commit the sin again and refrains from doing so because of remorsefulness and not because of fear or lack of power" (2:2). This is true even if one feels true remorse and repents in the absence of the ability to repeat the transgression—in one's old age, for example, or even on one's death bed. This means that in the case of the Nazi who committed crimes of genocide during the Holocaust, it is possible for repentance to occur even after the war, when the possibility of carrying out such acts is no longer available. While not a complete act of repentance, the perpetrators' sense of remorse and act of confession would nonetheless be deemed efficacious if they were heartfelt and done with the firm determination never to commit such acts again should the opportunity ever present itself. Yet even such feelings of remorse and a determination not to commit the acts again are not in themselves sufficient for full atonement. In 2:9 Maimonides asserts that

> neither repentance nor Yom Kippur effect atonement except for transgressions committed between a person and the Omnipresent . . . but for transgressions that are between a person and his fellow, such as one who injures his fellow or curses his fellow or steals from him and the like, there is never forgiveness for this one until he gives his fellow what he owes him and appeases him; even if he gives him back payment for what he owes him he must appease him and ask that the victim forgive him. Even if he only hurt his fellow through words, he must mollify him and entreat him until he forgives him.

Only when all this has been done can we say that the act of repentance on the part of the perpetrator has resulted in some sort of closure. The ball, as it were, is now in the court of the victim. The remaining passages in this chapter stress that once the perpetrator has repented in this way, the victim is bound morally, if not legally, to offer forgiveness, thereby completing the process of reconciliation.

So far, Maimonides has stressed direct confrontation and reconciliation between the perpetrator and the victim. This mechanism clearly will not work if the victims are no longer available, as is mostly the case for the Holocaust. Maimonides' reading of the Jewish tradition does deal with a version of this eventuality. At the end of chapter 2 he notes that "as for the one who sins against his fellow and his fellow dies before he asks forgiveness of him, he is to bring ten people and stand at the grave of the victim and say in front of them, 'I have sinned against the LORD, God of Israel, and against so-and-so by doing such-and-such.' And if he owes him recompense, he returns it to his heirs and if he does not know who the heirs are, he gives the recompense to the court and makes confession" (2:11).

A further variation on this difficulty occurs when the transgressor does not even know the identity of the victim, a situation much more like what we face in the mass-produced death of the Shoah. Maimonides addresses something of this situation in chapter 4: "There are five [deeds] such that if one does one of these, it is impossible for him to repent with complete repentance because they are sins against one's fellow but he [the perpetrator] does not know against whom he committed the sin so that he might recompense him or ask forgiveness of him" (4:3). But even in these situations, Maimonides points out at the end of the chapter (4:5), remorse and confession are efficacious enough to at least allow the penitent entry into the world to come.

Yet this still leaves open the question as to whether or not there are sins so heinous that even partial penance is precluded. Maimonides' answer appears to be yes. Consider his remark in 6:3 that "it is possible that one will commit such a great sin, or so many sins, that the judgment comes to the Judge of Truth for the requital of this sinner, for the sins which he committed with his cognizance and with his will are such as to prevent him from repentance and do not give him leave to repent from his evil—the result being that he will die and be lost through his sin." The one situation that Maimonides does not and, given his assumptions, cannot deal with is that of the perpetrator who fails to go through any act of repentance. In this case the process of closure never even begins.

The above paragraphs outline the main points in Maimonides' classic articulation of the Jewish view of repentance and forgiveness, a view that has remained more or less definitive within the traditional Jewish community down to our own day. It is clear from all this that, except for the most unusual cases, there is no way for the actual process of repentance and forgiveness to occur between the perpetrators and the victims of the Holocaust, let alone between their descendants. Jewish law assumes that the offense in question was the act of a particular perpetrator and was aimed at a specific victim. The process of repentance and forgiveness is set in motion only when the perpetrator directly faces the victim, expresses his remorse, and makes restitution as appropriate. Needless to say, this scenario is impossible as regards the Shoah since there is no possibility of direct confrontation between an individual victim and his or her victimizer. This raises a significant question as to how the Jewish community, within the parameters of its own legal and moral (and theological) tradition, is to deal with matters of forgiveness and reconciliation as regards the Shoah.

II

One possible alternative is to ask whether the structure laid down by Maimonides can work not only on an individual level but also on a communal level. That is, can we take the apologies of Church representatives, for example, or the payment of restitution by German industries to constitute an act of repentance that is in effect a sort of vicarious *teshuvah?* On the one hand, surviving victims are being approached with expressions of repentance, and payment of some sort is being made to compensate for their losses. The acceptance by the victims of these apologies and payments would, on the face of matters, appear to constitute an acceptance of the acts of *teshuvah* made by the heirs of the perpetrators, the people who presumably would have "benefited" from the crimes. But at least two important elements are missing. First, the vast bulk of the victims are no longer alive, and so not able to accept apologies or recompense. Second, it is not the perpetrators themselves who are proffering these acts of contrition. Further, it is not even clear that one corporate entity (the Germans) can effect reconciliation with another corporate body (the Jewish people). So crucial elements of the mechanism of repentance and reconciliation are lacking. Nonetheless, there are some discussions along these general lines in contemporary legal rescripts (responsa) of Orthodox authorities. As we shall see, however, for most of these writers the whole matter of forgiveness and reconciliation with the heirs of the perpetrators is not even considered a viable possibility.

One of the outstanding authorities who has addressed these kinds of issues is Isaac Halevy Herzog, former chief rabbi of Israel. In his *Heichal Yitshaq (Orach Hayyim)* #61, published in Jerusalem in 1972, Herzog is asked whether or not it would be legitimate to establish a special annual memorial day for victims of the Holocaust. The establishment of such a day poses a problem because the Torah specifically decrees that we are not to subtract from or add to what the Torah has already decreed. Would not adding such a day to the Jewish liturgical calendar be an addition and so prohibited? My interest in this responsum is not with the calendrical issue per se but with Herzog's characterization of the Holocaust. After discussing the precise legal definition of the prohibition against adding to the holiday calendar, as found in R. Moshe ben Nahman's commentary to the Torah portion *Ve-etchanan,* Herzog continues:

> But the point, in my view, is that we have no fear here of transgressing the opinion of R. Moshe ben Nahman (may his memory be a blessing) insofar as the intention is to evoke repentance . . . there are days when all the people of Israel fast because of the troubles that have occurred on them, so as to encourage our hearts to open up to the ways of repentance and so that this might act as a reminder of our evil deeds, and the deeds of our ancestors that were like ours until they caused them and us those troubles. For it is through memory of those things that we return to the good. . . . For no destruction like this has come upon the people of Israel since the days of the Temple (may it soon be restored) and there is a need to awaken ourselves to repentance each year on account of that terrible and horrendous destruction that came upon us because of our transgressions.

According to Herzog, then, the Holocaust was not so much a criminal act perpetrated by individual Nazis or their sympathizers against individual Jews as it was a divine punishment brought upon the Jews for their sins. The perpetrators here are not visualized as human moral agents capable of reflective choice but rather as passive instruments of the divine will, much like the biblical Amalekites or Babylonians. This is not then an event in which repentance of the perpetrators is even called for. If there is to be repentance at all, it is from the side of victims whose sins brought about this divine chastisement in the first place.

That this sentiment is not an isolated one is shown by a comment by Moshe Feinstein, one of the leaders of American Orthodoxy. In his responsa collection *Iggeret Mosheh,* published in New York in 1964, he takes up the same question. In a section entitled "As to why we did not establish a set day of fasting and prayer in memory of the killed of the Shoah," he states:

> As to the evil decrees according to which, for our many sins, approximately [six million] were killed by the evil ones, Hitler and his comrades—may their names be blotted out—would it not seem to be necessary to have some set day for fasting and prayer? In fact, there is astonishment that this has not already been done. But [we learn that we should not establish such a special day] from the lamentations that all Israel says on Tisha b'Av [the traditional day in late summer for mourning the destruction of the Temple]. For [our ancestors] expressly did not establish a special day for fasting and crying for the evil decrees of the Crusades—during which the evil decree fell on all the countries of Europe where most of the Jews lived, and many cities and towns were destroyed—but [rather, lamentations for the Crusades] are read [on Tisha b'Av] in memory of the year 1096, even though in the Land of Israel also many Jews were killed, because [they were of the opinion that] we do not establish additional days for fasting and crying. Therefore we must remember [all such catastrophes] in the lamentations that are said on Tisha b'Av for the destruction of the Temple. And for that very reason we do not establish a special day for the evil decrees of our time, and this is the case for all of the evil decrees that have occurred during this whole long time of Exile. (IV:4:57)

Even more explicitly than Herzog, Feinstein presents the Holocaust not as a unique matter, but as part of a divine pattern of punishing visitations upon the Jewish people. Just as for Herzog, the implication is that Hitler and his cohorts are not really individual transgressors who can effect repentance and be accorded forgiveness, but rather are mere tools for God's chastisements. Not only are the Nazis and their allies not in a position to ask for repentance, but it would be a real theological problem, according to this view of matters, for the Jewish people to accept such *teshuvah* from them or to forgive or reconcile with them.

Not all Orthodox thinkers agree that no special day for Holocaust memorial is needed. There are opinions among rabbis in the Orthodox community that the Holocaust does merit a special place in the Jewish liturgical cycle. Yet even among these rabbis we find that there is no willingness to accept the possibility of the perpetrators' being able to repent. They are held, as above, to be simply the mythic evildoers. A good example is found in *Sheridei Esh,* published in Jerusalem in 1962 by Rabbi Yehiel Jacob Weinberg, former head of the Hildesheimer Rabbinical Seminary in Berlin and himself a Holocaust survivor. In this responsum, Weinberg states:

> In my opinion it is fitting to establish a special day of mourning and memory to remember our rabbis and the holy ones of Israel that were killed, slaughtered, and burned for the sanctification of the Name, and to bring to mind on this day the souls of these saints. We should do so not because of the honor of the sanctified alone but also for the sake of generations to come, that they should not forget what was lost to our people during the time when the darkness of murderous wickedness covered the land of Europe. And as for those who preach forgiveness and solidarity, I say, "It is sufficient for you to preach to the accursed evil ones that they should do what the executioner did at the time of [the death of] R. Hanania ben Teradion, for [this executioner, knowing his own evil] jumped and fell into the fire [as told in B. Avoda Zara 18a]." (II:30)

Orthodox Judaism represents only about 15 percent of the Jewish population, both in Israel and in North America. One might conclude, then, that the view sketched out above is only a minority or marginal opinion, yet a review of responsa from the Liberal community reveals a similar attitude. In fact, the only recent responsum I could find from the Reform movement (the Conservative movement of American Judaism does not issue responsa) dates from 1989 and, like the Orthodox rescripts, does not even raise the question of reconciliation. Like its Orthodox counterparts, it deals with memorialization, in this case the building of Holocaust memorials. The author, Rabbi Walter Jacob, notes that the construction of memorials to Jewish victims of wars and attacks has a long history. In the Middle Ages this usually took literary form—elegies, special prayers, or historical chronicles, for example. Only in the modern period have Jewish soldiers killed in battle been memorialized "in fountains and statues as well as whole buildings."[2] This is so because only nowadays in the West is it possible to build such memorials in the general community. While these "facilities could take many forms all of which would be appropriate as memorials," he goes on to ask what is to be accomplished by all this: "On the one hand it is necessary for us and for the entire Western world to remember the Holocaust so that nothing like it will occur again to us or to any other group of people. However, we certainly do not wish to look upon ourselves as primarily survivors of this tragedy. . . . There is a great deal which is positive which we have accomplished in the modern world."[3] In this ending, the issue of forgiveness and reconciliation has simply been sidestepped with the reference to all the good that has come to the Jewish people in the modern world. If there is to be a rapprochement with Christians, the responsa implies, it is only so that we can work together to prevent another Holocaust from happening.

It seems fair to say, from this very brief survey of the literature, that in terms of the ideational structure of the post-Shoah Jewish community, such notions of repentance and forgiveness as those being put forth by Christian communities have little meaning. There is no mechanism within Jewish law for extending forgiveness to perpetrators who did not, and now cannot, repent. This does not mean, of course, that joint work and friendly relations cannot exist today between Jews and Christians. As Walter Jacob himself notes, there is much good that has come out of the Jewish relationship with the modern world. But the gap opened by the Holocaust simply cannot be bridged, any more than "forgiveness" can be granted the Romans for destroying the Second Temple, or the Babylonians for destroying the First Temple, or the Amalekites for harassing the tribes coming out of Egypt.

III

In light of this conclusion, I want to turn briefly to the recently published statement "Dabru Emet," a proclamation dealing with Jewish-

Christian relations signed by more than 150 rabbis and Jewish scholars from the United States, Canada, the United Kingdom, and Israel. It was published in the *New York Times* and *Baltimore Sun* in late September 2000 in response to apologies put forth by various Church leaders. The statement notes at one point that many Protestant and Catholic religious leaders have "made public statements of their remorse about Christian mistreatment of Jews and Judaism. These statements have declared, furthermore, that Christian teaching and preaching can and must be reformed so that they acknowledge God's enduring covenant with the Jewish people." The signers felt that measures like these taken by the Christian community toward reconciliation deserve some positive response from the Jewish community. To this end, the document expressed the view of its authors that "we believe it is time for Jews to learn about the efforts of Christians to honor Judaism. We believe it is time for Jews to reflect on what Judaism may now say about Christianity." In the paragraph on the Holocaust, the document notes, "We applaud those Christians who reject this teaching of contempt, and we do not blame them for the sins committed by their ancestors."

It is important to note what the document says and what it does not say. Despite its cautious and circumscribed language, a number of Christian correspondents to Internet discussions have interpreted "Dabru Emet" as a statement of Jewish forgiveness. In light of the discussion above, it should be clear that no document can authentically offer forgiveness on behalf of Jewish victims, although it could take a step toward reconciliation. This very point is made by one of the scholars behind the text, Michael Signer, professor in the Department of Theology at the University of Notre Dame. He put matters this way: "I would not use the term forgiveness, but reconciliation. In order to reconcile, Christians have to do an accounting of what they have done wrong and what attitudes they have had that have been harmful to Jews. As they engage in these discussions they will find their way to a more profound understanding of their own faith. Only God can forgive the sins of the past. Jews need more time to see if Christian *teshuvah* is real."[4]

The question of what repentance, forgiveness, and reconciliation might mean after the Holocaust is a complicated one. Not only is the Holocaust an infinitely complicated set of phenomena, but it involves religious communities with different notions of what repentance, forgiveness, and reconciliation are, even at their most basic levels. From the perspective of the Jewish community, there is a strong sense that the transgressions committed in the Holocaust are beyond the realm of human repentance and forgiveness. What happens between the individual penitent perpetrator and God is another matter, of course. But expecting forgiveness, especially forgiveness in a Christian sense, from the Jewish community is to ask the Jewish community to do what its tradition simply is not equipped to do. This does not mean that reconciliation between the two religious communities and dialogue among peoples of different faiths is impossible. In fact, there is growing interest in just that in virtually every segment of the Jewish community. But such relationships and dialogue do not and cannot, in the terms supplied by the Jewish tradition, amount to an acknowledgment of repentance on the parts of the perpetrators or of forgiveness on the parts of the post-Shoah Jewish community.

NOTES

1. All the translations of the *Mishneh Torah* and the responsa are my own. I have added my own explanatory material in brackets.

2. Walter Jacob, ed., *Questions and Reform Jewish Answers: New American Reform Responsa* (New York: CCAR, 1992), pp. 323–24.

3. Ibid., p. 324.

4. From Victoria Barnett, "Provocative Reconciliation: A Jewish Statement on Christianity," *The Christian Century* (Sept. 27–Oct. 4, 2000).

In Response to Peter J. Haas

RACHEL N. BAUM

IN HIS CONTRIBUTION to this volume, Peter Haas offers a learned and articulate explication of the concept of forgiveness in the Jewish tradition. His essay helps explain why Jews and Christians find themselves at such an impasse over Christian expressions of repentance after the Holocaust, for the two traditions have irreconcilable understandings of the nature and possibility of forgiveness. I deeply appreciate Haas's essay, particularly because I am not well versed in the Jewish sacred texts. It is instructive to see the current issue of forgiveness after the Holocaust in the context of Judaism's approach to history, repentance, and forgiveness. What is striking to me is that, as a Jew, I share so many of my tradition's attitudes toward forgiveness, even though I am unfamiliar with their textual underpinnings. As Haas points out, I am not alone; the traditional texts have shaped the modern Jewish understanding of forgiveness, even among liberal and secular Jews.

This is significant, given the claim Haas makes that the Jewish understanding of forgiveness has not stood in the way of friendly relations between Jews and Christians. He writes: "There is no mechanism within Jewish law for extending forgiveness to perpetrators who did not, and now cannot, repent. This does not mean, of course, that joint work and friendly relations cannot exist today between Jews and Christians. . . . But the gap opened by the Holocaust simply cannot be bridged, any more than 'forgiveness' can be granted the Romans for destroying the Second Temple, or the Babylonians for destroying the First Temple, or the Amalekites for harassing the tribes coming out of Egypt." Thus, it is not simply that Jewish law does not allow for forgiveness in this context; Haas's further suggestion is that the wide assumption of this perspective among Jews has not stood in the way of interfaith work between Jews and Christians. History would seem to bear out Haas's claim, for interfaith efforts do indeed go on, despite the Jewish rejection of forgiveness after the Holocaust.

Yet I sense that Haas moves too quickly to affirm "joint work and friendly relations," eclipsing the sheer effort at the heart of these relationships. For surely there is *something* that is withheld in the Jewish attitude toward forgiveness. While this something may not be essential for interfaith work, withholding it may make interfaith relations difficult. Thus, my response to Haas's essay focuses on the possibility of reconciliation—of "joint work and friendly relations"—in light of the Jewish conceptions of forgiveness.

For Haas, part of what Jews refuse to offer Christians is a sense of closure. Indeed, he writes that working together requires Jews and Christians to accept that the gap opened by the Holocaust cannot be bridged. This is undeniably true, for surely interfaith efforts cannot smooth over the rupture of the Holocaust. But here too, I seek specificity: what precisely is the gap that must forever haunt relationships between Jews and Christians?

This, it seems to me, is the central question that must be the cornerstone of any Jewish-Christian dialogue after Auschwitz. What has changed? What has changed for us individually, as Jews and Christians, and, most crucially, what has changed between us? Is the post-Holocaust gap one of trust between Jews and Christians? Can Jews trust Christians, even if they do not forgive them? Is the gap one of commonality? Can Jews and Christians ever stand again under the same sign of humanity? If the irreparable rupture of Auschwitz is one that exists between Jews and Christians, then it throws doubt on Haas's claim that joint work and friendly relations are possible. Or, more to the point, it throws doubt on the extent to which these efforts can succeed in being meaningful.

These are significant issues, for they dig beneath the soil of the word *forgiveness.* Obviously, *forgiveness* has particular resonance, particularly to Christians, but beneath this single word lie others—*trust, commitment, faith.* To say we forgive someone is presumably to say that we no longer hold their acts against them, that we believe that they have changed, that we can open ourselves to them again and trust that we will not be hurt. Even if we understand that Jews are theologically unable to forgive Christians for the Holocaust, or even after it, we are still left with the difficulties of post-Holocaust trust.

Haas places the issue of forgiveness after the Holocaust in the context of atrocities committed by the Romans, Babylonians, and Amalekites. Significantly, though, Jews were not engaged in cross-cultural work and coexistence with the Romans, Babylonians, or Amalekites. The historical atrocities committed by these groups are marked by contemporary Jews through mourning and drowning out the name of the enemy. Clearly, the Holocaust is different precisely because Jews and Christians must live together.

Thus, while forgiveness after the Holocaust may be impossible for Jews, we are left with the question of how to live together. Even the phrase *live together* does not adequately describe the connection between Jews and non-Jews. With the exception of the Orthodox sects that segregate themselves from the non-Jewish world, most Jews today not only live with Christians, but also have lives that are fully intertwined in profound and abiding ways with those of non-Jews. We cannot, therefore, rest in our tradition's denial of forgiveness after the Holocaust but must continue to search for the possibilities for closeness and connection between Jews and Christians.

Unlike Haas, I am not a scholar of the Torah, but as a Jew, I want the sacred texts of my tradition to offer me some guidance about how to draw closer to people—all people. Is there a way of understanding the gap that has opened after Auschwitz as a gap of humanity, something we all share, rather than a gap between Jews and Christians? This is particularly challenging after the Holocaust because we know that Christian doctrine did not save the Jews. While we may expect religion at its best to advocate for the divinity and sacredness of all human beings, we know all too well that this is not always the case. Thus, in some sense, it seems wrong to ask Judaism to do what Christianity could not—embrace the essential divinity of all humans. The burden of reconciliation cannot fall on Jewish shoulders.

But if we are to live after the Shoah as whole human beings, we must push a bit, perhaps, beyond what is comfortable for us. Perhaps we Jews are too comfortable in our resistance to Christian theology. Rather than rest on our tradition, perhaps it is time to challenge it—not to embrace forgiveness, but to provide us an adequate guide for how to live with Christians after the Holocaust. Mere tolerance is not enough for me; I want to learn how to love my neighbor. Can the sacred texts teach me how to love after the Holocaust?

This is all rather optimistic on my part. It belies my own cynicism about many Christian expressions of contrition. I know many faithful Christians who authentically struggle with the legacy of the Holocaust, but, like many Jews, I am wary of institutional expressions of contrition, which often seem self-serving at best. So my thoughts here are not to suggest that Jews must simply let down their guard and embrace all Christian efforts at reconciliation. We may choose to embrace those efforts that seem to us sincere, profound, and complex; we need not accept those that seem anything less. But it is to suggest that reconciliation—at minimum, to be reconciled to the coexistence of Jews and Christians after the Holocaust—requires pushing beyond the limits of what is comfortable for us.

This will take work on the part of Christians as well, who must also push against the comfort zones of their own traditions. Perhaps Christians have been too comfortable in their sense that repentance can heal the wound of Auschwitz. If Jews are to imagine the unredeemable gap of Auschwitz as one of humanity itself, we must see that acknowledgment reflected in Christian theology and doctrine. We must have a sense that Christians can let go of their expectation of forgiveness from Jews, and work actively on what it means to live and trust in the shadow of the destruction.

I want to be clear that I do not fault Haas for writing the essay he did—on forgiveness—rather than the one I am asking him to consider—on reconciliation, or what I might call simply *connection.* Haas's essay provides a vital step in the process of reconciliation between Jews and Christians, and his work has significantly advanced my own thinking about this issue. My comments are intended to continue the conversation, to ask how the traditional texts can help us think about reconciliation between Jews and Christians, and how we might be able to forge meaningful connections after the Holocaust.

In Response to Peter J. Haas

LEONARD GROB

PETER HAAS OFFERS us a cogent analysis of traditional Jewish thinking throughout the ages on questions of repentance, forgiveness, and reconciliation. In his exposition of the application of this thinking to the post-Holocaust period, Haas leaves little doubt in the reader's mind that basic Jewish understandings of forgiveness make it well nigh impossible for "statements and acts of contrition and repentance put forth by various Church bodies" after 1945 to find complete resonance within normative Judaism. The thorny issue of forgiveness, to which Maimonides devotes so much attention, fails to be addressed—indeed, Haas argues, *cannot* be addressed as a legitimate concern—in contemporary legal responsa to issues surrounding the Holocaust. After reading his well-crafted chapter, we are in a better position to grasp the nature of Jewish responses to those in-depth queries regarding forgiveness put forward by many Christian leaders, as well as responses to the more popular forms such questions have frequently taken, such as "Why can't the Jews just forgive?" and "Why can't they just let it alone?" Haas makes it clear why Jews can't "just forgive" their Christian brothers and sisters and "get on with life."[1]

Although I am cognizant of the limitations of space imposed on all contributors to this anthology—limitations that necessarily restrict the scope of an author's thesis—I nonetheless wish that Haas had probed in greater depth those issues, briefly alluded to at the conclusion of his chapter, surrounding what *might be possible* in post-Auschwitz interreligious dialogue. Given the fundamental differences between Jews and Christians on issues of repentance and forgiveness, what is the nature of that "reconciliation between the two religious communities and dialogue among peoples of different faiths" which Haas claims is not "impossible" in the post-Holocaust world? It is clear from Haas's account that such dialogue does not include "an acknowledgment of repentance on the parts of the perpetrators or of forgiveness on the parts of the post-Shoah Jewish community." But what *does* such dialogue include? What is the nature of that move toward rapprochement which Haas finds implicit in the paragraph dealing with the Holocaust within "Dabru Emet"? If reconciliation is to be more than resignation, more than mere tolerance or "settling for," what might constitute the essence of dialogue between the two traditions regarding the issues at hand after Auschwitz?

Haas gives us some indication of what such rapprochement might mean when he cites Michael Signer's comments to the effect that any form of reconciliation demands that Christians acknowledge what they have done to Jews. Assuming responsibility for two millennia of anti-Jewish attitudes and acts is most certainly a necessary condition for any form of post-Holocaust reconciliation. Yet I wish Haas's exploration of reconciliation had gone further. It goes without saying that the Holocaust represents a watershed event for Christian-Jewish relations. Although, with regard to issues surrounding repentance, the burden of radical change falls squarely on Christians, *each* tradition in the post-Holocaust world is faced with an unprecedented moment of crisis in its history; each must come to grips with raw extremity.[2] The murder of two-thirds of European Jewry summons Christians to face the culmination of two thousand years of anti-Jewish attitudes; it demands that the Church address the question of just how integral to Christianity is enmity toward Jews. Jews, for their part, face both the unprecedented destruction of life and the attempt by the Nazi regime (under the watch of Christians) to eradicate the very essence of Judaism itself. If genuine reconciliation between Jews and Christians is ever to be achieved, it must be forged in the fires of such extremity.

For Christians, this means rethinking the central category of forgiveness as a mode of relating to Jews after Auschwitz. Christian forgiveness, as Haas has argued, cannot be the vehicle for understanding Jewish experience in the post-Holocaust world. As long as Christians hold to traditional understandings of forgiveness as an alleged absolute, meaningful post-Holocaust dialogue between the two traditions is *not* possible. What is called for, in the face of burning children, is a new and radical humility. Indeed, the Holocaust renders suspect not merely Christian forgiveness, but *all* totalizing categories of understanding in which the experience of the other—in this case, the Jewish other—is comprehended within one's own (unquestioned) frames of reference. Without humility, the hegemonic thrust of dogma casts doubt upon the possibility of that genuine turning-toward-the-other which lies at the heart of authentic dialogue.

Genuine dialogue is not to be confused with superficial interfaith conversation. Fundamental to all instances of dialogue is heeding the other—with his or her radical alterity squarely before us—in the fullness of his or her personhood. Such alterity is not to be overcome in any surface attempt at unity. Yet, according to Martin Buber, although the distance between Judaism and Christianity constitutes "a gulf which no human power can bridge," acknowledging such a gulf does not at all prevent—indeed, I would add, it paradoxically *opens the path to*—meaningful dialogue: "Uniqueness and dialogue are corollaries," according to Buber.[3]

Respecting the basic differences between them, both traditions can be empowered to say "something as yet unsaid to each other," something beyond "all the creedal truths of the earth."[4] Buber concludes that such respect is not to be confused with mere tolerance: if they are to be partners in authentic dialogue, Judaism and Christianity "must acknowledge the real relationship in which both stand to the truth."[5]

Although I had by no means expected Haas, in a brief chapter devoted to Jewish attitudes toward forgiveness, to articulate a vision of the full range of possibilities of post-Holocaust interfaith dialogue, it is nonetheless the case that his few allusions to the possibilities of such dialogue may well call for elaboration. The Buberian understanding of reconciliation which I have sketched above appears to me to add substantially to Haas's reference to future dialogue in terms of "joint work and friendly relations" between Christians and Jews. Haas's analysis of the reasons for Jewish hesitancy to accept a Christian call for forgiveness can well serve as the *point of departure* for an examination of what—given the new parameters just discussed—might now constitute authentic Christian-Jewish dialogue. While preserving the core of uniqueness within each tradition—in this instance, the integrity, in particular, of the Jewish understanding of repentance and forgiveness—meaningful dialogue must be created from the ashes of that limit case of inhumanity which is the Holocaust. Haas clears the path toward authentic dialogue by articulating that impasse with regard to the concept of forgiveness which, if allowed to continue, would bar the door to any serious quest for meaningful encounter.

A final consideration: I have addressed the tasks which Christianity might well assume in the face of the unprecedented evil of the Holocaust. How might Jews relate to a transformed post-Holocaust world in general and to the beginnings of transformative thinking on the part of their Christian brothers and sisters in particular? Here I would agree with the authors of "Dabru Emet" to the effect that "it is time for Jews to learn about the efforts of Christians to honor Jews." Yet I believe more needs to be said: Jews must address post-Holocaust changes in the Christian world as part of the more profound endeavor *not to give up on a world which has given ample cause for total despair.* Refusing despair, identifying the work of "repair of the world"—these are modes in which Jews might respond meaningfully both to Christians struggling to overcome centuries of anti-Judaism and to a world at large whose very habitability has been cast into doubt. As Haas implies, the business at hand is not to dwell any longer on what sometimes appears to have become a fixed, and fruitless, Christian-Jewish debate on issues of repentance and forgiveness, but rather for Christian and Jew to work together, in authentic dialogue, to address in-the-doing the myriad lessons to be learned from the Holocaust.

NOTES

1. These questions, among others, are described by Eugene J. Fisher in his response in the "Symposium" section in Simon Wiesenthal, *The Sunflower: On the Possibilities and Limits of Forgiveness,* ed. Harry James Cargas and Bonny V. Fetterman (New York: Schocken Books, 1997), p. 132.
2. Conversation with Professor Ernest Sherman of Pace University, July 20, 2001.
3. Martin Buber, "The Two Foci of the Jewish Soul," in *Israel and the World: Essays in a Time of Crisis* (New York: Schocken Books, 1963), p. 40.
4. Ibid.
5. Ibid.

In Response to Rachel N. Baum and Leonard Grob

PETER J. HAAS

RACHEL BAUM DID a fine job of bringing to the surface some of the deeper implications of my study of the traditional Jewish approach to forgiveness. In so doing, it seems to me, she has laid bare one of the operative assumptions of this book, namely that somehow forgiveness is a necessary precondition for reconciliation. This is obviously an issue of considerable philosophical complexity and one, unfortunately, that is not taken up in traditional Judaic literature. This is due in good part to the fact that the question never really came up. In traditional Jewish discussions, the assumption was always that the encounter was one-on-one and that the perpetrator either repented or did not. It was beyond their wildest imagination that an entire Christian community would perpetrate a massacre against the Jewish community and then sincerely repent and seek forgiveness and reconciliation.

In this regard, the Holocaust really has brought in its wake something quite new. For the first time there has been a sincere attempt on the part of significant segments of the Christian community to confront its Judeophobia and to seek ways of repentance. At the same time, it should be noted, this change in the Christian community has occurred at a time in Jewish history when the vast bulk of Jews have made the decision to abandon Jewish exclusivity and to engage as partners in the larger society. So we find ourselves at the particular and unprecedented point in history in which both Jews and Christians have an interest in building a future as partners rather than as antagonists. This is of course all occurring in the wake of an unprecedented evil. So even if Jews out of their own tradition cannot forgive the individual and unrepentant Christians who perpetrated the Holocaust atrocity, they still have an interest in forging some way to move forward. But this is a move for which, as I said, the Jewish tradition offers no precedents. In moving from the impossibility of forgiveness to some sort of reconciliation, whatever that might be, we really are on our own. In some sense, we are being challenged to reconsider our understandings of what forgiveness and reconciliation mean, and how they relate to each other.

Baum is of course correct in noting that in having to contemplate reconciliation without forgiveness, a gap seems to have opened, so that there is a sense of business left undone. I cannot deny that. There simply is a gap in our past that cannot go away. I think it is a given that all future relationships between Jews as Jews and Christians as Christians will have to take place in the shadow of that reality. It cannot be swept away by pious formulas of forgiveness. But this does not mean that future relationships cannot be constructed. In some sense, we really have no choice but to learn to trust each other and live together, even as we always feel a horrid past breathing over our shoulders.

It is precisely this point that Grob addresses. He, like all of us who are contributing to this volume, is aware that it cannot be business as usual after the Holocaust. Even on the Christian side there is a clear recognition that there must be changes beyond repentance and forgiveness. So what is clear, regardless of whether or not one thinks forgiveness is possible, is the conviction that the relation of Jews and Christians will be of an entirely new and unprecedented sort. In fact, Grob's remarks make me wonder if in some sense this whole volume is an answer to the question of precisely what such a post-Shoah reconciliation should look like. In that case, my sense that the Jewish tradition at this point is unable to find grounds for offering forgiveness does not prevent our communities from moving ahead—it only highlights how unfamiliar is the territory we are proposing to enter.

Baum also asks about how Scripture (or *Tanakh*) can guide her in the search for such post-Shoah reconciliation. My answer, I suppose, is that the Bible is a record of just such caesuras and reconciliations, mostly between the Jewish people and the Deity. We have in the *Tanakh* a history full of pain, suffering, and feelings of abandonment. Even post-biblical Jewish history is replete with examples of the Deity feeling betrayed by the Jewish people, on the one hand, and of the Jewish people feeling abandoned by the Deity, on the other. This is a constant theme of deliberation in Jewish theological thinking. Yet in spite of this turbulent history, the relationship between the Deity and Israel goes on and reconciliation, if even with a bit of wariness on both sides, is always achieved. Certainly Jewish tradition has taught us that while a messy past cannot be erased, it can be transcended as each side reaches a new maturity. That maybe is the model we must now follow in Jewish relationships with Christianity.

In a sense, of course, this is just what Grob foresees. His citation of Buber asserts explicitly that the gap between Judaism and Christianity is not to be bridged, but it is, paradoxically, just that unbridgeability that opens the way for real dialogue (as opposed to the exchange of theological pleasantries). And he ends on the same note, as it were, as the *Tanakh,* stating that in spite of all this tangled and twisted history, we must not despair. It is all too easy in this world of hijacked airplanes and anthrax scares to simply resign ourselves to a world beyond hope and redemption. There is a real temptation to throw everything on the shoulders of the Messiah and to wait for the final redemption to come down upon us. But the *Tanakh* points to the possibility that maybe in the end the way to a true and good relationship can only be found in ourselves and our efforts. And so our struggle goes on. If, despite the howling gaps in our shared history, we can find a way to achieve a real and authentic reconciliation between Christians and Jews in the post-Shoah world, then maybe we can give the world a good measure of the hope it now so desperately needs.

2

The Face of Forgiveness in a Post-Holocaust World

HENRY F. KNIGHT

THE POST-SHOAH SITUATION

The name Auschwitz signals a threshold in Christian history. Marked by a long night of wrestling with the violence in our own confessional traditions, we Christians cross the boundary of "after Auschwitz" informed by the tragic knowledge of complicity and shame regarding our covenantal siblings. Hereafter we cannot do theology, whether in the pulpit or at the computer, in the assembly or alone, without asking if the dark shadows of our own violence have not been once more incorporated into our most precious truths.

In recognition of this watershed character of the Shoah for Christian theology, Roman Catholic theologian J. B. Metz has declared that responsible post-Shoah Christians must do their theology as a dialogical act, with Jewish companions, every step of their confessional way forward. For too long, Christians have done their theological work as if the covenantal heritage of Jesus were meant to displace the very people he came to serve. The disdain and contempt that have been incorporated in the heart and depths of Christian tradition cannot be healed or removed without help from our estranged siblings. Jews remain the significant other of Christians even if and when they are dismissed or hidden from view.

In a now well known essay, "Cloud of Smoke, Pillar of Fire: Judaism, Christianity, and Modernity after the Holocaust," Irving Greenberg framed a principle that has been seared into the consciousness of nearly every theologian, Jew or Christian, who attempts to address the post-Holocaust situation responsibly: "No statement, theological or otherwise, should be made that would not be credible in the presence of the burning children."[1] These words have become constant companions for anyone making serious statements about how life proceeds in our time after Auschwitz. Greenberg's criterion of the burning children challenges every syllable we utter—to ourselves, to others, to the Eternal One we serve. If we are not careful, it paralyzes our speech, rendering us mute. But we dare not stop speaking and professing our faith. So we continue on the way, walking with a profound limp, more clearly identified as Abraham's grandchildren than we ever dared imagine. As we proceed after Auschwitz, we do so carefully, rethinking every previously embraced truth, knowing that none of our ways is free of the violence that has shaped our lives with others. We make our way accompanied by those we have previously wounded. They are our significant others, now reclaimed in more positive relation, as partners in our covenantal way. Thus we proceed, but limping. And in this way, limping, we dare walk in critical faith, embracing the psalmist's plea: "May the words of our mouths and the meditations of our hearts be acceptable in your sight, *Adonai* / O LORD, our strength and our redeemer" (Psalm 19:14).

Our wounded walk with others is the confessional preface that distinguishes responsible post-Shoah faith and modifies our most fundamental relationships to the sacred. Identifying this approach as a confessional preface anticipates a critical reconfiguration of the face of every other, which is now viewed through the prism of my Jewish other. This outlook defines the way I have come to hold my Christian faith as I move forward in the twenty-first century. The image of limping, rooted for me in Jacob's anguished night at the Jabbok (Genesis 32:22–33), accompanies my theological musings about the great issues and the mundane ones. The language and images of that biblical story inform the ways I shape essential expressions of my sacramental ministry as a member of the Christian clergy.

FACING THE CHALLENGE

As a United Methodist pastor, I am guided by a liturgical practice that links confession and pardon as a single act following or preceding the proclaimed word of Scripture. Whether as preparation or response, the movement of confession and pardon is seen as an appropriate way for Christians to express their identity before God and neighbor in the light of God's Word. Most typically, the format is represented by a call to confession, a shared prayer of confession, silence for specific prayers, then biblical words of pardon and assurance that affirm the gift of forgiveness offered in the name of Christ.

For those following the format suggested in our denominational publications, the readings of Scripture and the commentary of sermon are followed by a time of confession and pardon. Typically a unison prayer of confession is offered, gathering together a general litany of sins for participating worshipers to express in penitential identification. A period of silence follows in which individuals may pray more particularly as they are moved. Then the celebrant recites assuring words from Scripture to express the forgiveness that is offered in Christ to the participating persons. For example:

CONFESSION AND PARDON

Gracious God, we confess that in ways devious and hard hearted, subtle and pretentious, we have worked against your purposes for an open and loving world. We have gained at the expense of others and glossed over the immoralities around us. We have claimed rights and privileges that we have denied others. We have forgotten history. Surely we have need of repentance. Therefore, we beseech your pardon and the blowing of your spirit through our lives that we may be set free from sin to live our days in freedom and fidelity. In Jesus' name, we pray. Amen.

All Pray in Silence

If we confess our sins, God is faithful and just, and will forgive our sins and cleanse us from all unrighteousness. In the name of Jesus Christ, you are forgiven.

In the name of Jesus Christ, you are forgiven. Glory to God. Amen.

The intentionality in this liturgical act reflects studied attention to a number of theological issues that beat in the heart of historic Protestant spirituality. Using a form like the one above, confession follows, as a response (or precedes, as preparation), the preached word. It embodies the words of Paul: "All have sinned and fall short of the glory of God" (Romans 3:23). None is without need of confession. Moreover, the sin confessed in this fashion is directed not simply to private attitudes of misdirected piety but also to failed as well as committed actions toward others—personal, economic, individual, and corporate. And in the spirit of post-Shoah sensitivities, even the failure of memory may be confessed. Furthermore, the assurance that follows is first biblical, then dialogical. But given what we have learned about theology after Auschwitz, are these qualifications sufficient? Have we declared more than we have the right to declare, and in the process declared much less than we thought we did?

As I examine the typical liturgical practice of my own tradition and view it in the light of the burning children of Auschwitz, its credibility is challenged. The automatic format so easily practiced on a Sunday-by-Sunday basis obscures the promissory nature of grace and promotes what Dietrich Bonhoeffer would surely be able to call an easy or cheap grace. If the biblical words of assurance are repeated too automatically and without the nuance of mediating an unfinished promise that Christians experience in a proleptic way, then the reality of forgiveness is reduced to an automatic pronouncement that in the eyes of the burning children must be resisted, if not actively challenged. To put it boldly, forgiveness is not a form of spiritual entitlement. Neither is it an automatic response to authentic penitence and confession.

Consider another liturgical setting. In 1972, following the breakdown of negotiations between the United States and the North Vietnamese and the renewal of massive bombing of Hanoi and Haiphong, a small interdenominational congregation gathered in Milwaukee for a service of reconciliation. Their liturgy included a corporate prayer for forgiveness and a plea for absolution of the sin they confessed with regard to the war effort. The story is related by Herbert Anderson and Edward Foley:

> "We beg for forgiveness," they prayed, "for our sin against humanity, and for the violence our country perpetrates in our name." A lone minister . . .

> garbed in alb and stole, answered back from the sanctuary, "Your words are empty; your actions betray you; the murdering continues."
>
> "We are truly repentant," the assembly continued, "for our national arrogance, for our reliance on bombs rather than God, and for our thirst for war rather than peace." The minister replied, "Your words are easy, but they are hollow to the thousands of innocents you have savaged in the name of democracy."
>
> "We ask for absolution," the people prayed. "Absolve us for the pain and destruction we rain on the people of North Vietnam, and for our inability to stop the leaders who commit these crimes in our name." A pause . . . and then frightful, unexpected words from the minister: "I deny you absolution; I withhold the consolation of the church from you; I refuse to collaborate in your search for spiritual comfort, for though you may be repentant, you have not been reconciled with your enemies."

Anderson and Foley explained their recollection of this incident succinctly: "This story . . . is remembered because it raises poignant questions about the nature of reconciliation in the broadest sense of that term and because it suggests that reconciliation is not as easy or as accessible as we would like it to be. The story shatters our expectations that absolution is automatic, even when repentance is authentic."[2]

In other words, we are not entitled to forgiveness simply because we confess our sin, even when we do so with great remorse. As this example explains, reconciliation has yet to occur. Perhaps more importantly, where confessions of complicity are concerned, forgiveness may not be the most theologically appropriate response. If the liturgical withholding of absolution is appropriate, perhaps it was not appropriate to seek forgiveness in the first place. Perhaps what should be sought instead, by way of confession, is an enlarged sense of human connection and responsibility. Lawrence Kushner has put it well: "Each apology must involve this retreat from some territory thought conquered by the self. Only now we understand that it does not belong to us and never did. And we 'return' to our place."[3] That is, confession can be more than the simple acknowledgment of a wrongful deed or attitude toward another as a step forward on the way to responsibility. It can also be an act in which responsibility is relocated in a reconfigured identity that is given new and more responsible shape in the full expression of confession.[4]

RETHINKING CONFESSION AND PARDON

In confession we face the other from whom we are estranged, either because of some action we have taken or failed to take or because we have become a person whose identity is fundamentally challenged by the presence and identity of that other. Confession becomes a way of facing the other in deed and in introspection that can restore a more authentic relationship with the other, both in terms of one's identity and in the dynamics of differentiating the self from the other. Whether or not such a healing quality in confession obtains depends upon how one confesses the previous violation. Such a confession must not only acknowledge the violence but also let go of the violating self/other configuration, either in one's identity or in one's behavior and attitude toward the other, in order to reconfigure a more positive relationship between one and the other.

Confession can, in this regard, be restorative and healing. But it often needs acknowledgment from a significant other who by his or her signification is able to restore the promise of relation with a whole face. In some cases, this may lead to the gift of forgiveness as relation is restored in its wholeness. In other cases, it may lead not to forgiveness but to the promise of reconciliation. In any case, the determining factor is not some abstract theological principle but the nature of the relationship itself.

The movement is toward relational wholeness. Some situations call for continued wrestling with the nature of shared responsibility, and the restored relationship calls for sustained engagement with matters of responsibility. Other situations may summon a shamed or guilty party to turn away from self-preoccupation and embrace his or her acceptance in a relationship that is not asking for perfection but full engagement, one with another. But the dynamics of relation and responsibility guide the movement toward wholeness. Forgiveness, then, is not automatically the answer for the estrangement or brokenness that might be present; neither is shared anguish. Rather, the answer may more nearly resemble a movement toward increased engagement with the other and a fuller embrace of life.

Elie Wiesel recounts a pair of stories from an earlier century that capture another dimension modifying how we express or withhold forgiveness. He describes two contrasting Hasidic teachers, Elimelekh and Zusia, brothers and disciples of the Baal Shem. In the first instance, Elimelekh is attending the ritual baths and meets a Jew who has come from Hungary to spend Shabbat in his presence. Unrecognized, Elimelekh challenges his guest: "You took the trouble to come from so far away for this idle faker, this liar, this make-believe Rebbe?"

The guest replies angrily in defense of his unrecognized host: "How dare you? How dare you slander a saint and a sage of Israel?" In the evening, when they meet in Elimelekh's house, with his disciples gathered in his presence, the visitor begins to weep and asks for forgiveness. "Rebbe, I didn't know," he sobs. But Elimelekh interrupts his confession, saying, "Dry your tears. You told me your truth, and I told you mine."

Then Wiesel continues, citing a similar anecdote regarding Zusia: "Once in an inn somewhere, a wealthy guest mistook Zusia for a beggar and treated him accordingly. Later, when he learned Zusia's true identity, the guest sought him out and proclaimed his remorse: 'Forgive me, Rebbe. Forgive me. You must—for I did not know.' But Zusia replied, 'Why do you ask Zusia to forgive you? You have done nothing to him. It is not Zusia you insulted,' said Zusia, shaking his head. 'Rather, you insulted a poor beggar. Go and ask him to forgive you. Ask the beggars you meet.'"[5]

In Wiesel's anecdotes, we are given two examples of situations where the forgiveness being requested may not be the forgiveness that should be sought. Each confession needs work, as does the distorted or myopic vision that has not yet been fully faced. The estranged other is not the other who is recognized in the act of confession—a factor both Elimelekh and Zusia confront by asking for further work by their supplicant students.

In Anderson and Foley's story, a sacred penitential ritual is turned parabolically on itself to reveal the temptation that lurks in the shadows of forgiveness and grace. The priest has determined that the wholeness of the Gospel requires the suspension of an easy absolution. Even though its specific context—the Vietnam War—is different, the issue of complicity is forthrightly focused in its narration. And by facing the complicity, confession is invited in a more forthright, holistic fashion. In other words, following this litany of confession, the withholding of forgiveness leads to a larger holding of reality than its easier alternative. More life is embraced. A greater engagement with life is fostered as the priest enacts a parabolic role instead of the expected sacerdotal one. Still, the sacramental mediation of God's rule and realm of life is served. And in this case, confession without forgiveness serves to invite the recovery of relation and responsibility.

Though none of the stories is about the Shoah, each reveals a mature insight into the nature of theological truths after the loss of theological innocence. They are never simply what they appear and, to use the language of one of Paul's letters, "we have this treasure in earthen vessels" (2 Corinthians 4:7).

There is another quality embedded in the 1972 case from Milwaukee that remains unexamined, but that in the light of the Shoah requires probing as well. The problematic character of forgiveness is framed within an unquestioned, sacramental system that pairs authentic confession with the sacramental authority of a priest to pardon a penitent congregation. The parabolic nature of the story turns on the withholding of pardon. But the authority to pardon lies unquestioned. What assumptions about power and representative agency must we examine now? The authority to pardon is the authority of one with hierarchically encompassing power. It is the power of monarchs and presidents, supreme commanders of a people or corporate entity—and their representatives. Whether they derive that power democratically, as in the U.S. system of government, or by so-called divine right or birth in monarchical systems, or by force when power is won by conquest, the exercise is monolithic. In short, it is the power of empire.

The power to exercise pardon has been questioned before, of course. In Jesus' time, the religious leaders of his day questioned the right of human beings to usurp this power. Jesus challenged the status quo by telling parables about the empire of God / heaven, undercutting a number of issues. My own midrashic work has enabled me to see that Jesus, when speaking in parable of the rule and realm of God, radicalizes the reality of empire in more than one way.[6] Many read his parables about forgiveness and God's grace as ways to undercut the social structure of empire by casting the status of human relations in terms of inverted power relations. The low are lifted up; the marginalized are given central status; the left-out are included. Power is inverted. Indeed, liberation theology has made this dynamic a central issue on which it stands in reading the Gospel message of new life. Jesus is leveling the least with the greatest, reconfiguring their roles to expose injustice and to restore lost dignity.

In his parables, one may also read Jesus undercutting the notion of empire. His parables challenge the very structure of empire that his social world, and ours, takes for granted. The way of God seeks always the one not yet included, the one not yet blessed. As long as one is missing, the whole gestalt of God's way is incomplete. The structure of have-and-have-not that the empire presumes is an either / or configuration of life that is undercut by his stories of inverted power.

In the same spirit, one may also read otherwise the biblical witness wherein Jesus grants the power of heaven to forgive, which his traditional hearers resist because it signals a human being usurping divine authority. The notion of empire presumes the hierarchical structuring of the authority to pardon and forgive. But if one reads his declarations about the power to forgive in the indicative voice, and not as a prescriptive charge, one may see these transactions not as a granting of an authority Jesus either has been given by divine right or presumed in arrogance, but as Jesus acknowledging the power all human beings have in each other's lives—whether they realize it or not. In this case, Jesus would be calling his followers and any others who heard him to use the power they have in each other's lives with much more discretion, for whatever they bind on earth extends farther than they realize, and whatever they set free is freed beyond their comprehension. In this way, Jesus would be calling for covenantal responsibility to be practiced wisely and with great care, declaring that there is far more at stake than we realize. He would not be granting a presumptuous authority but summoning his disciples to increased responsibility.

In the light of Greenberg's call for increased covenantal responsibility after Auschwitz, such a reading offers an important option too often overlooked. That is, how one frames the matter of forgiveness and its agency is critically related to the reconciliation that forgiveness seeks. Forgiveness can, however unintentionally, diminish its desired covenantal connection and responsibility. Whether or not it enhances or diminishes that partnership depends on how forgiveness is framed and expressed.

RECONFIGURING RELATION

More than confession and pardon are at stake here. As Miroslav Volf seeks to show in *Exclusion and Embrace,* the relational character of creation, and more particularly the relational character of each individual self that the dynamics of confession and pardon express, is at stake. He uses the figure of embrace, viewed dialectically, to capture its complex ecology. In the full experience of embrace, we open ourselves—our bodies and our worlds—to others; we wait for them to respond in kind; we hold them as they hold us in mutual regard and care, and we let go of any attempt to keep them in our grasp and control.[7]

For Volf, embrace is embodied in the biblical notion of covenant life. When covenant is rooted in the steadfast will of God for relation, one of the essential features of that relation is that its covenanted character cannot be undone even though the covenant can be broken: "Every breach of the covenant still takes place *within* the covenant; and all the struggle for justice and truth on behalf of the victims of the broken covenant takes place *within* the covenant."[8]

David Ford, in reflecting on the complex ecology of relationships in which the Christian life is embodied, identifies the Eucharist as the primary context in which the realities of confession and forgiveness serve the larger ecology of hospitality and generosity that Volf addresses through the metaphor of embrace.[9] This is a helpful reminder. While one may argue that confession and forgiveness are necessary prerequisites for participating in this sacramental act, the biblical witness and practical experience remind us that the table fellowship that embodies the divine generosity and hospitality of God manifests a hospitality for others that welcomes sinners without qualification. Some may have confessed before coming; some may have sought forgiveness; some may find there a grace that invites subsequent confession. Indeed, in the prayerful thanksgiving that sets this table apart, another table is recalled in which its guests were reminded that they would deny, and betray, the very relationships being sustained there. Still, the table welcomed them.

The fellowship is not without boundaries, of course, but these boundaries are articulated as expressions of hospitality and generosity and vary from congregation to congregation as they do among denominations. They serve open relationships that respect others and the gifts that others bring to their relationships *as others.* In just this spirit, the June 2000 gathering of the Goldner Symposium, under whose auspices these reflections have been undertaken, was faced with how to embody very similar concerns. Our gathering is an intentionally diverse group of Holocaust scholars, Jews and Christians, as well as secular humanists. Meeting over the Shavuot / Pentecost holiday weekend, we chose to celebrate the Jewish Sabbath and the festival of Shavuot in appropriate Jewish ritual on Friday night and Saturday morning and the Christian Eucharist on the following Pentecost Sunday. I accepted responsibility for celebrating the Eucharist. The challenge was to celebrate the heart and soul of the Christian faith sacramentally in the full presence and awareness of our Jewish siblings without denigrating their identity as Jews. We sought a way to articulate the boundaries of Christian identity that confessed that identity while also affirming the larger, covenantal ecology that others might choose to honor and serve differently.[10] The Eucharistic prayer and all parts of the service were framed with a sense of open hospitality rooted in Christian particularity, which itself was rooted in the steadfast generosity of God. The earlier sacramental act of corporate confession turned to ancient liturgical chant of the *Kyrie,* with individuals invited to add their own statements of contrition if they were so moved. The invitation to the table was rooted in penitent humility. Furthermore, the table was identified as an open table where welcome and presence were articulated as essential features, even for those who chose not to receive the bread and wine.

CONCLUDING REVIEW

As I review my initial offering in this extended conversation, I am aware that I have perhaps generated more questions than I have answered—certainly for myself. Forgiveness and confession are much more complexly woven into the fabric of our covenantal ecology than we might wish to admit. While we may be more limited in what we can say about these sacramental actions, we know that neither of them is a panacea we can apply to solve the problems of creation. But we also know, as Jesus reminded his followers, that what we do with regard to forgiveness and confession is extraordinarily, if not ultimately, significant. What we bind in our worlds we bind for others and for time to come. What we set loose, we unbind in similar fashion. The gift of creation and its ongoing welfare are truly in our hands.

These reflections remind us that both confession and forgiveness fit in a larger framework, a covenantal ecology of relationships. The self is relational at the core. Forgiveness and confession serve that relationality and bring healing when significance and place are restored to the displaced and estranged other / Other. When they are tainted by deeper estrangements or abused in the service of selfish ends, the relatedness of every self is diminished. And those violated boundaries and structures need responsible articulation if healing is ever to follow. Volf is right to insist that forgiveness is not an end in itself.

To be sure, after Auschwitz, Christian theology limps, but its limp is more than the manifestation of a wounded condition afflicting our attempts to be faithful. It is part of our fidelity, the full story of our covenantal walk with life. It is no accident that the biblical story of that covenantal way so often includes the failures and betrayals along the way. The hospitable host of life with whom we dwell in covenantal regard remains faithful even as we stumble along in our walk. We preserve that memory in our traditional identity as an essential aspect of who we are as people of faith. After Auschwitz that is more important than we ever realized. What does God require of us but to act justly, love steadfastly, and walk humbly with the Eternal One?

NOTES

1. Irving Greenberg, "Cloud of Smoke, Pillar of Fire: Judaism, Christianity, and Modernity after the Holocaust," in Eva Fleischner, ed., *Auschwitz: Beginning of a New Era?* (New York: KTAV, 1977), p. 23.

2. Herbert Anderson and Edward Foley, *Mighty Stories, Dangerous Ritu-*

als: Weaving Together the Human and the Divine (San Francisco: Jossey-Bass, 1998), p. 171.

3. Lawrence Kushner, *River of Light: Spirituality, Judaism, Consciousness* (Woodstock, Vt.: Jewish Lights Publishing, 1991), p. 130.

4. For a more expanded reflection on these dynamics, see my essay "From Shame to Responsibility and Christian Identity: The Dynamics of Shame and Christian Confession Regarding the Shoah," *Journal of Ecumenical Studies* 35, no. 1 (Winter 1998): 41–62.

5. See Elie Wiesel, *Souls on Fire: Portraits and Legends of Hasidic Masters,* trans. Marion Wiesel (New York: Simon & Schuster, 1982), pp. 125–26.

6. See Henry F. Knight, *Confessing Christ in a Post-Holocaust World* (Westport, Conn.: Greenwood Press, 2000).

7. Miroslav Volf, *Exclusion and Embrace: A Theological Exploration of Identity, Otherness, and Reconciliation* (Nashville: Abingdon, 1996), pp. 141–43.

8. Ibid., p. 156.

9. See David F. Ford, *Self and Salvation: Being Transformed* (Cambridge: Cambridge University Press, 1999).

10. The Great Thanksgiving included the following affirmation of this covenantal heritage:

> You created all things and called them good.
> You created us in your image.
> And even though we rebelled against your love,
> you did not desert us.
> You walked with our forebears—Abraham and Sarah,
> Isaac and Rebecca, Jacob and Leah and Rachel;
> you spoke through Moses and Aaron and Miriam,
> and through all the prophets.
> You called all Israel your people,
> binding yourself to them in covenant.
> Even when they stumbled, you kept faith with them,
> bearing witness to your steadfast commitment to them
> and to all your creation.
> Through them you bound yourself to us.
> Therefore we join our voices to theirs, and to all your people
> on earth, as we join the unending chorus of heaven, singing
> your praise.

The Face of Forgiveness in a Post-Holocaust World

In Response to Henry F. Knight

BRITTA FREDE-WENGER

HENRY KNIGHT ADDRESSES what at first sight seems to be a clearly definable problem: the "face of forgiveness in a post-Holocaust world." He roots his understanding of forgiveness in the liturgical act of confession and pardon, more precisely in the liturgical practice of the United Methodist Church. His reflection on this practice is guided by Irving Greenberg's paradigmatic hermeneutical axiom that challenges (not only) theologians to ask whether their statements are credible "in the presence of the burning children." Taking this approach, Knight can reflect on the possibility of forgiveness *after* Auschwitz without ignoring the context of a world in which Auschwitz has been real.

Knight is challenged by the worshiper's confession of sin and the pastor's absolution that he feels to be an "automatic format so easily practiced on a Sunday-by-Sunday basis." If we really reflect on what people have done and continue to do to their fellow human beings, he asks, doesn't pardon come too easily and quickly? A consideration of a reconciliation service held in Milwaukee during the Vietnam War leads Knight into the wider discussion. In that service the pastor refused the congregation's plea for absolution and thereby broke with the "automatic format" (while at the same time revealing it as an automatism). Thus Knight's question begins with a liturgical focus and then grows into a larger question of the nature of forgiveness among people. As Knight concludes, "[F]orgiveness is not an end in itself."

In my reply, I want to point out that Knight's question can be dealt with only within a terminological framework that includes more consistent definitions of three elements that play into one another: confession, forgiveness, and atonement / reconciliation.

Let us return to the liturgical setting. In the liturgical confession the individual and the community of worshipers address God in prayer and express where and how they have sinned. Sins here include both transgressions against the world and against God: "We have worked against your purposes for an open and loving world." In other words, by failing to work toward a certain way of living as a community, people have failed in the face of God, and thereby stand in need of God's pardon. The horizontal and the vertical dimensions come together here. In the sacramental act God grants his pardon through the priest's words of assurance. With the completion of the liturgical dialogue of confession and pardon, reconciliation with God is believed to be actually achieved, since, more than a promise, a sacrament is a speech act. It results in a renewed relationship between God and the worshiper. Confession and pardon are elements in a relationship. Knight's theological question is, Does this speech act not result in cheap grace? Doesn't God forgive too quickly?

Knight approaches this question by turning toward the dynamic of interhuman reconciliation processes. He finds no automatic format of confession and forgiveness between people. People live in relationships that can be violated and stand in need of restoration. This restoration requires a renewed practice. At this point, Knight's terminology becomes inconsistent. He writes, "Confession must not only acknowledge the violence but also let go of the violating self-other configuration." In a confession we admit to the other that we have failed, and we may *promise* to change. A changed practice must precede and follow a confession if reconciliation is to be achieved; however, confession and renewed practice are to be distinguished. So it is not that the "confession needs work" but that the confession is an element within a larger process of renewal.

A similar argument holds for the term *forgiveness.* As Theodor Schneider has said, forgiveness "is part of the nature of specific words, sentences, and expressions that I can never say to myself, that I have somebody else say to me."[1] One of these sentences is "I forgive you." I am aware that the term *forgiveness* can and does also refer to a relation between two partners that is achieved through an act of forgiving. In fact, this is the meaning Knight starts to use. He stresses that confession "often needs acknowledgment from a significant other who by his or her signification is able to restore the promise of relation with a whole face. In some cases, this may lead to the *gift of forgiveness* as relation is restored in its wholeness. In other cases, it may lead *not to forgiveness* but *to the promise of reconciliation*" (my italics). In this passage Knight seems to use *forgiveness* and *reconciliation* almost interchangeably. Both serve to characterize the process of healing and the relation to be achieved through it. Similarly, he calls forgiveness "a *movement* toward increased engagement with the other and a fuller embrace of life" (my italics). Since Knight's interest is to reflect on a renewed liturgical practice, it might be helpful to keep more strictly to the meaning of forgiveness as an act, that is, as the speech act "I forgive you." Why?

At the core of Knight's argument lies the insight that in the process of reconciliation between people there is no automatism of confession and forgiveness. However, both confession and forgiveness are necessary *acts,* mostly but not exclusively speech acts (can we not imagine an embrace to be an act of forgiveness?) in a *process* called reconciliation. What Knight shows is that all three elements—confession, forgiveness, and a renewed relationship—must come together to form a *successful* movement toward reconciliation.

It is now possible to see more clearly what Knight finds disturbing in the liturgical practice of confession and pardon. I stated earlier that what is at stake here is reconciliation with God, or better, atonement. However, when theology is centered on a reconciliation that *has been fulfilled once and for all* through Jesus' death and resurrection, atonement *might* be understood to require nothing but the speech acts of confession and forgiveness. The format seems to work without renewed practice; a truly penitent heart and public confession are seen to be enough.[2] The three elements seem to be reduced to two. That, however, is not acceptable in the presence of the burning children.

Knight ends his consideration of his liturgical examples by saying, "Though none of the stories is about the Shoah, each reveals a mature insight into the nature of theological truths after the loss of theological innocence." But into which theological truth have we gained a more mature insight, and what insight have we won? Knight has touched upon a point that is crucial for his question of a renewed practice of sacramental forgiveness without formulating it. The question that needs to be addressed is, Is there a connection between the divine-human reconciliation process and the interhuman reconciliation process, and if so, what kind of connection?

Interhuman reconciliation cannot be achieved without a process of healing. In light of the Holocaust, can atonement for human sins before God be independent of a process of healing? No. But what does this process that is the underlying dynamic of divine-human reconciliation look like? Knight himself spells out the answer. It can be found in the practice of Jesus: "If one reads his declarations about the power to forgive in the indicative voice, and not as a prescriptive charge, one may see these transactions not as a granting of an authority Jesus either has been given by divine right or presumed in arrogance, but as Jesus acknowledging the power all human beings have in each other's lives—whether they realize it or not." More than that, "[W]hat we do with regard to forgiveness and confession is extraordinarily, if not ultimately, significant." In Jesus' practice lies the key to the question of what the *process* of atonement looks like. It is impossible to theologically or liturgically set atonement apart from interhuman reconciliation: the reconciliation process between God and humankind is connected to the striving of humankind toward reconciliation in the world. Just as in interhuman relationships, however, in the reconciliation process between God and humankind, the sentence "I forgive you" is important.

Finally, it might be possible to formulate one question regarding liturgical practice—one of the questions Knight raises between the lines. We have seen that speech acts of confession and forgiveness form a necessary element of the interhuman reconciliation process. The liturgical practice relies strongly on such speech acts. In a world after Auschwitz, we know that God's granting of forgiveness cannot result in cheap grace and a flight from a world full of suffering. At the same time, as Christians we believe that God has not withdrawn his forgiving love. While we know that sacramental actions are not "a panacea we can apply to solve the problems of creation," they are not placebos either. Can the affirmation of forgiveness give hope for a reconciliation that continues to be worked toward in this world? Can the promise of forgiveness be celebrated as a sacrament of hope against despair in a world in which Auschwitz was real? J. B. Metz speaks of the necessity that theology let go of "strong" categories and think in "weak" categories. For Metz, "weak" categories do not universalize faith but make the believer's historical context of guilt, suffering, and pain seen and felt. The paradigmatically "weak" religious category, therefore, is the remembrance of suffering, especially the suffering of the other.[3] What could a "weakened" liturgical practice of confession and pardon look like?

To speak of divine forgiveness in the presence of the burning children will not only require a limping *theology* but, first and foremost, limping believers who, while wrestling with evil in the world, also wrestle with God, saying, "I will not let you go, unless you bless me" (Genesis 33:26).

NOTES

1. Theodor Schneider, *Zeichen der Nähe Gottes* (Mainz: Grünewald, 1992), p. 195 (my translation).

2. I want to emphasize that atonement *seems* to work like this because theology across denominational borders has always stressed that the penitent heart and the public confession are not enough for true reconciliation, which must also include *deeds* of atonement.

3. See Johann Baptist Metz, "Im Eingedenken fremden Leids," in *Gottesrede* (Münster: LIT-Verlag, 1996), pp. 3–20.

In Response to Henry F. Knight

DAVID PATTERSON

HENRY F. KNIGHT'S essay "The Face of Forgiveness in a Post-Holocaust World" is written with eloquence and courage. For here Knight raises some very difficult questions that continue to haunt post-Holocaust Jewish-Christian relations. The questions he raises run so deep, in fact, that Knight himself perhaps has not yet realized all their implications. His insights and inquiries, however, do have their troubling aspects.

Before going into the difficulties, I would like to underscore one of Knight's most crucial claims, namely that "where confessions of complicity are concerned," neither forgiveness nor "shared anguish" may be "the most theologically appropriate response." Knight is not suggesting that one should not ask for forgiveness, but rather that one must ask and then *must be refused.* His example of forgiveness refused in the Vietnam War story taken from Anderson and Foley's *Mighty Stories, Dangerous Rituals* is a good one, and it drives home the matter of why forgiveness must be sought and must be refused: because "confession without forgiveness serves to invite the recovery of relation and responsibility." And relation and responsibility—more than harmony or good feelings—are precisely what is needed in a post-Holocaust world ridden with strife.

Responsibility in this instance is not the opposite of innocence—it is the opposite of isolation, smugness, retreat, silence. It is a stance of listening and attending, not of lecturing or proselytizing. It is a stance taken by one whose redemption is not settled because his forgiveness is not complete, by one who has *not* been washed clean, despite the blood of the Lamb. Knight's position here is extremely courageous because it is extremely heretical. For if Knight is right, then neither the cross nor faith settles the matter of redemption, so that whosoever believes in Christ does not necessarily have everlasting life. When in his concluding remarks Knight says that he has generated more questions than he has answered, he is quite correct. For he has shaken to the core the Christian covenant of redemption, without which there is no Christianity, just as without the covenant of Torah there is no Judaism.

Which brings me to a troubling aspect of Knight's essay, his view of the "covenantal" relation between Christians and Jews. In his opening paragraphs, for example, he refers to Jews as the Christians' "significant others," "covenantal siblings," and "partners," declaring that after Auschwitz "we make our way accompanied by those [that is, the Jews] we [that is, the Christians] have previously wounded. They are our significant others, now reclaimed in more positive relation, as partners in our covenantal way." But it is hardly clear that for Jews, Christians are significant others or covenantal siblings, and some explanation is needed with regard to the "covenantal way" that is shared by the two. There is very little in the covenantal missions of the Christian and Jewish traditions that would suggest any sort of partnership. Among the chief missions of the Christians, for example, is to bring the Gospel to the world; a primary aim for the Jews lies in embracing the *mitzvot* or commandments of Torah. Each of these projects is utterly alien to the other. Even the task of mending the world, viewed in *covenantal* terms, has to be seen differently by Christians and Jews *as* Christians and Jews, inasmuch as Christians take Jesus to be essential to rectifying the world, while Jews take Torah and *mitzvot* to be the key. Here what is crucial to one is superfluous to the other.

Essential to the Christian notion of covenant, moreover, is the notion of a *new* covenant (see, for example, Hebrews 8:13).[1] Essential to the idea of covenant transmitted to the world through the Jews is that the covenant of Torah is set and eternal *as it stands* and that there can be no new covenant (see, for example, Deuteronomy 4:2).[2] Essential to the covenantal teaching of Torah is the principle that the *mitzvot* or commandments are humanity's *only* link to G-d, a view that is alien to the teachings of the Christian "new covenant," with its emphasis on the faith in Jesus Christ that *alone* justifies the human being (see, for example, Galatians 2:16).[3] If Christians and Jews join together to feed the hungry, make peace where there is strife, and resist the moral collapse of society—as they certainly should—they may be acting as partners, but they are not acting as *covenantal* partners.

A more serious matter in Knight's statement is the "our" in "our covenantal way," since it appears to refer to Christians, as the "our" in the rest of the citation does, meaning the covenantal way of Christians. A partnership in the covenantal way of Christians, however, is both impossible and offensive to an adherent of Judaism because the covenantal way of Christians lies in the covenant of Christ, which is the covenant of blood and faith expressed in John 3:16.[4] Jews surely do not wish to be partners in *this* covenantal way, and the suggestion that Christians should "reclaim" Jews for such a covenant is especially offensive in the post-Holocaust era. If by this reclaiming Knight means that Christians should embrace the covenant of Abraham, then is he calling for mass circumcisions and an observance of the laws of Torah on the part of Christians? Surely not. But if not, where is the *covenantal* partnership?

Knight's confusion over covenants parallels a certain confusion about the audience he addresses when making his very important point concerning the need for confession in the process of seeking and being refused forgiveness. "All have sinned and fall short of the glory of G-d," Knight quotes Paul (Romans 3:23), and adds, "None is without need of confession." But is the need of the Jew the same as the need of the Christian? Or is Knight addressing his remarks here only to the Christians? He is quite correct when he indicates that neither forgiveness nor shared anguish is the answer, but what he suggests as an answer—"a movement toward increased engagement with the other and a fuller embrace of life"—also has its problems, if the "other" here is the Jew. What must be determined is why the Jew should be interested in an increased engagement with the Christian *as* Christian. Do the same issues of confession, forgiveness, and shared anguish apply from the standpoint of the Jew?

In a reference to Miroslav Volf's book *Exclusion and Embrace* Knight writes, "In the full experience of embrace, we open ourselves—our bodies and our worlds—to others; we wait for them to respond in kind; we hold them as they hold us in mutual regard and care, and we let go of any attempt to keep them in our grasp and control." But why should Jews open their bodies and their world to Christians, who, in accordance with Christian doctrine, have to regard Jews as "unredeemed," since Jews have consciously rejected salvation in Jesus Christ? And is a Jew to respond *in kind* to the Christian's quest for forgiveness? Should the Jew confess to the Christian his sins against Christians and thereby seek a mutual forgiveness? If not, what is the basis for a *mutual* regard and care?

Knight further associates the metaphor of embrace with the Eucharist, which he sees as "as the primary context in which the realities of confession and forgiveness serve the larger ecology of hospitality and generosity." Here, it seems, the Christian embraces his "covenantal partner," the Jew, by inviting him to participate in the Eucharist. If, however, the Eucharist *is* the Eucharist, it means joining oneself with Jesus Christ, eating in remembrance of the sacrifice and resurrection that comes only through Jesus Christ, affirming one's faith in redemption through Jesus Christ, and so on. Is *that* what the Christian now invites the Jew to do? In a post-Holocaust world there could be nothing more offensive to the Jew nor more scandalous to the Christian. If this Eucharist is to work—if the hospitality and embrace are to affirm a mutual regard—then Christ has to be taken out of the Eucharist. Which means this Eucharist is no Eucharist.

Thus, in responding to Knight's essay, we go from the confession that the blood of the Lamb does not quite wash the sinner clean to the realization that the Eucharistic hospitality offered to the Jew requires the removal of Jesus Christ from the Eucharist. It appears that if the Jew and

Christian are to have the covenantal relation that Knight describes, one of them will have to abandon his covenant. The alternative is to abandon the business of covenantal partnership, respect each other's covenantal difference, and enter into a human-to-human relation, rather than a Christian-to-Jew relation.

NOTES

1. Commenting on Jeremiah 31:31, Paul asserts, "In speaking of a new covenant he treats the first as obsolete. And what is becoming obsolete and growing old is ready to vanish away" (Hebrews 8:13 RSV).

2. "You shall not add to the word which I command you, nor take from it; that you may keep the commandments of the Lord your G-d which I command you" (Deuteronomy 4:2 RSV).

3. "A man is not justified by works of the law but through faith in Jesus Christ" (Galatians 2:16 RSV).

4. "For G-d so loved the world that he gave his only Son, that whoever believes in him should not perish but have eternal life" (John 3:16 RSV).

In Response to Britta Frede-Wenger and David Patterson

HENRY F. KNIGHT

BRITTA FREDE-WENGER, in her response to my essay, calls for "more consistent definitions" of confession, forgiveness, and reconciliation. In doing so, she draws on systematic distinctions between forgiveness and reconciliation that grow out of the once-and-for-all quality of the atonement brought about by Jesus. Typically, Christian theologians distinguish between the theological fact of one's forgiveness, which they know "in Christ," and the process of reconciliation, which is not yet complete, except in the promise of new life experienced by individual believers. Forgiveness is viewed as the theological given, reconciliation as the process that is not yet complete. One could just as easily distinguish between justification and sanctification in the life of a single individual, as my own Wesleyan tradition has done.[1]

But these distinctions are products of theological reflection that have not known the reorientation occasioned by the Shoah. Frede-Wenger identifies forgiveness as an act oriented toward the individual believer as he or she stands before God and reconciliation as having to do with the relationship between that believer and others as well as that believer and God. But if the self is relational at the core, then forgiveness may refer to a moment in a process of forgiveness that is relational in a different way than reconciliation. For example, forgiveness for issues rooted in shame may unfold over time before it ever moves toward actual others, since it involves the healing of relationships with internalized others in one's own identity. In other words, the view of forgiveness as a single gift may be too simple. In this case, the ambiguity between forgiveness and reconciliation may not be a failure to distinguish theological truths but an attempt to recognize an ambiguity inherent in the very issues we are facing.

The traditional distinctions Frede-Wenger seeks to maintain may not provide for a view of the self in need of reconceiving itself in such fundamental ways. In the reconfiguration of the self / other relationship we do not promise to maintain or pursue a changed relationship as much as we indwell an altogether new self / other gestalt that bears promise for a new way of relating each to the other. Because this reconfiguration unfolds in moments of recognition of problematic configurations that give way to new ways of relating, we should not view this as a single epistemological breakthrough, even if we grant each moment ontological significance. It is much more processual in character. Likewise, the speech act of forgiveness that fosters this growth may similarly be viewed as a series of speech acts or moments in an unfolding relationship.[2]

For me, as a Christian theologian who lives and works in an interfaith environment, posing these questions in the context of my sacramental responsibilities raises in turn the question of whether Jews and Christians are prepared to let each other wrestle with fundamental matters of identity that bear on how they view themselves in relation to each other. Facing up to the Shoah forces me to question my own actions in using the performative language of ritual. To be sure, a Roman Catholic theology of sacramental action will differ significantly from my Protestant take. As a Protestant Christian, albeit with a strong sacramental sensibility, I do not see myself as a passive vessel of divine grace granting forgiveness by my representative speech act. Rather, I view my role as one of participating in a reality that my speech acts call forth, even as my speech acts pledge my commitment to that reality; most importantly, that reality transcends any particular action. I am an actor in a gestalt of promise and grace in which I participate and which I represent in my words and deeds. But I do not pronounce it into reality; I announce its aborning presence as I participate in it.

Similarly, I am using the word *promise* as meaning more than a pledge or a performative act of the will. Like a symbol, a promise may participate in a larger reality to which it also points. I intend the promise of forgiveness to have this dynamic quality. It participates in the generosity and grace of God and therefore embodies that grace. But as promise it is not a consummated reality. Still, it is often, though not always, a speech act, participating, albeit incompletely, in the reality to which it points.

Frede-Wenger asks which theological truths are glimpsed with increased insight after the loss of theological innocence. To paraphrase Irving Greenberg, every theological truth is challenged by the criterion of the burning children. For me, that is precisely the motivating factor for wrestling with the matter of forgiveness, particularly as it is focused in my responsibilities as a sacramental person. But we may be operating with different epistemologies here.

As I turn to the response of my colleague David Patterson, I must confess some confusion. In one sense I wonder whether he has read the essay I intended to write. He reads my description of denied forgiveness in the example from the Vietnam War as a prescription to deny forgiveness in the face of genuine confession. That was not my intent. I was citing these ritual occasions to indicate situations in which the usual relation between forgiveness and confession did not follow. In some circumstances, forgiveness is the wrong response because confession stands as an act with its own integrity. In other circumstances, confession points to unfinished work that must continue. Work dedicated to healing will confront these jagged features of broken relationships with honesty and compassion. Nevertheless, in some cases, forgiveness is the proper, liberating, and restorative response to confession. After Auschwitz, we must learn to recognize the alternatives and when to honor them.

In my attempt to account for a larger covenantal framework / ecology of life intended by God for all creation, I spoke of a covenantal partnership with God that Jews and Christians could each honor. They need not share the same covenant to do that. But in order for us to move beyond competing covenantal identities in which the other is displaced in the gestalt of one's identity, there needs to be some larger covenantal framework that the individual covenants are called upon to honor and embody. Until we find language to articulate how the particular covenants can relate to the covenantal intention of God for creation, we will be stuck in what Richard Rubenstein calls disconfirming traditions.

Jews and Christians may act as covenantal partners with God and creation without having to be in specific covenant with each other. And Jews and Christians have a shared stake and responsibility in such a covenantal ecology. Indeed, Jewish thought, at least as I understand it, attends to this originating framework by referring to a Noahide covenant by which all human beings, Jews and Gentiles, will be held accountable. I would hope, then, that we could speak of *our* responsibilities as covenantal people and even find ways to acknowledge that, while we honor a shared covenantal ecology in discrete ways in separate covenants, we may nonetheless identify this ecology as our covenantal way because it is God's covenantal way with creation that embraces us all. But I do not mean that we share a single covenant in honoring such a partnership with God.

Thus, I must question whether it is as inevitable as David Patterson maintains that Christians must view Jews as "unredeemed." Indeed, it is this kind of logic that I am compelled to reexamine even though it may very well be a central part of my own religious tradition. That is why I have framed the matter within the context of identity formation. As to whether or not Jews should be interested in increased engagement with Christians as Christians or with the other more generally, I cannot answer that question. That is a matter for Patterson to address. I will, however, claim that the problem of the other is an acutely important issue, especially after the Shoah, for anyone whose identity is constructed in a way that displaces others.

Patterson's concern about the Eucharist I referenced may serve to focus the issue of otherness more clearly. He objects to Jews being invited to participate in this sacramental action, explaining that to do so either changes the nature of the sacrament or embodies the supersessionist disdain that the Shoah so tragically enacted. If the Eucharist Patterson criticizes were the Eucharist that occurred, I would concur with his criticisms. But it was not. This Eucharist was celebrated in the presence of Jewish guests, but the invitation to the table acknowledged their presence while recognizing that they would not be participating in its sacramental action. Furthermore, their supportive presence for this act expressed the promise of a different way of dwelling together in a covenantal ecology that could embrace us in our differences. The task was to acknowledge this fact in a way that communicated welcome and respect without compromising the differences that separate us in our distinctive covenants. The Christians in this service were challenged to pray in such fashion that those Jews in attendance could hear themselves being affirmed in their identity as Jews by their Christian friends. The issue turned on the way the other was signified in the telling of the ritual story that grounds Christian identity, as well as in the way the ritual structures were indwelled by the participating parties. In other words, the issue of reconciliation was focused in the reconfiguration of the identity-forming relationship of Christians vis-à-vis Jews that is embodied in this sacramental ritual of Christian identity.

Frede-Wenger concluded her comments asking how the divine-human reconciliation process and the interhuman one are connected. I can think of no more critical way to connect them than to suggest that the way in which the other is configured in one's relationships to self and the world is a reflection of the way in which one relates to the Holy Other who is both host and guest in this sacred meal and in every interaction with the other in one's life.

In response to both Patterson and Frede-Wenger, I would contend that to say one's forgiveness is not complete is not to say that one stands outside the promise or beyond the power of forgiveness. Rather, it is to recognize that forgiveness, like reconciliation, is not static. It is an unfolding reality that may unfold in an apparent, single action; it may equally be occasioned by the steady searching of penitently faithful folks who discover more need for change as layers of remorse and responsibility for hurt are uncovered in successive stages of healing. Consider, for example, a Christian who has struggled with his church's legacy of anti-Judaism in a personally searching way. She or he may be involved in an ongoing process of self/other discovery in which facing anti-Judaic sentiments leads to facing anti-Semitic ones, which in turn leads to grappling with deeply troubling understandings about biblical sources. In each step, forgiveness may be sought and experienced but in a way that leads into further growth in responsibility and a deepened sense of the incompleteness of the healing that has so far taken place. The matters of forgiveness and reconciliation point to a limping pilgrimage that is still under way.

NOTES

1. From our post-Shoah vantage point, the Wesleyan notions of justification, sanctification, and going on to perfection that all United Methodist clergy embrace at their ordination may take on added meaning and offer new ways to approach the significant moments in this process. That reflection must wait for another essay.

2. See my essay "From Shame to Responsibility and Christian Identity," pp. 32–36.

3

Forgiveness after the Holocaust

DIDIER POLLEFEYT

IN HIS *Christian Theology after the Shoah*, James Moore writes, "The question becomes for Christians, can we talk about forgiveness in the same way *even in everyday situations* now that we see how forgiveness can crumble in the face of enormous atrocity? . . . At least, the shadow of Auschwitz looms over this central Christian theological category."[1] Moore's inquiry makes me ask: Isn't evil such a serious thing that every tendency to put the evildoer in another perspective becomes an inhuman act because it does not take human responsibility seriously enough? Even more concretely, isn't it possible that human beings—take the Nazis, for example—have destroyed their own humanity so fundamentally that every restoration through forgiveness (human or divine) becomes impossible? As this essay wrestles with those questions, it focuses not so much on the question of forgiveness *for* Auschwitz as on the possibility that forgiveness has been so compromised that it is no longer authentically conceivable *after* Auschwitz.

THE PROBLEM OF GIVING FORGIVENESS

At the outset, consider Emmanuel Lévinas's warning: "A world where forgiveness is almighty becomes inhuman."[2] Easy and omnipresent forgiveness destroys human responsibility and opens the way for new injustice. Especially for Christians, it is a touchy matter to speak about forgiveness after Auschwitz. As Dietrich Bonhoeffer correctly argued, Christianity has often advanced a discourse of "cheap grace," which especially ignores the victims of atrocity.[3] Cheap grace permits perpetrators to continue their evildoing or to leave the scene of their crimes without moral anguish. Even during the Holocaust, perpetrators could and did participate in rituals of reconciliation (rituals that stressed forgiveness for sexual sins at the expense of attention to political evil). After the Holocaust, the Roman Catholic Church's document "We Remember" (1998) asked forgiveness for the sins of "her sons and daughters" in regard to the Shoah. However, by locating the roots of Nazi anti-Semitism outside of Christianity, the Catholic Church has failed to make an unqualified confession of its particular guilt.

THE PROBLEM OF REFUSING FORGIVENESS

After Auschwitz, not only giving forgiveness but also resisting or rejecting forgiveness has become problematic. Without the possibility of forgiveness, one easily becomes merciless. Persons and communities get locked up in their personal and collective evil; there is no possibility for them to escape that fate or to transcend that identity. Refusing to grant or to receive forgiveness also obscures the potentiality and reality of evil in oneself and one's communities.

An ethical system without forgiveness becomes Manichean. It rigidly separates good and evil in ways that often prove to be heartless. Nazism can be understood along these lines; it was a dualistic worldview in which forgiveness was not needed because supposedly everything was determined by clear categories of good and evil, light and darkness. To be a prostitute or a homosexual, for example, was unforgivable, and the ensuing persecution was ruthless. *Rücksichtslose Härte* (relentless hardness) was a Nazi virtue. By rejecting forgiveness after Auschwitz, one could create a universe with remarkable analogies to the Third Reich's dualistic and pitiless rule. From this perspective, Emil Fackenheim's imperative against granting Hitler "posthumous victories" could also mean to reinterpret the concept of forgiveness as a post-Holocaust category.

MORAL ANGER AND JUSTICE AS APPROPRIATE REACTIONS TO EVIL

No human being is merciful by nature, especially when he or she is a victim of or witness to acts of evil. In confronting extreme forms of evil, such as those embodied by the Holocaust, the first human reactions nearly always involve strong feelings of disgust, anger, rage, and hatred. Rarely are forgiveness and reconciliation the immediate responses. The most common first feelings, such as disgust and anger, reflect not only evil's devastation but also our human desire for goodness. They even open a way to meet God, who, as Lévinas aptly urges, may be revealed in the midst of evil as protest against evil.

Any religion that asks people to overcome their immediate feelings because they are inhuman or un-Christian risks facilitating moral indifference. As the Dutch Jew Etty Hillesum wrote in the diaries she kept in the Nazi camp at Westerbork, moral anger is a necessary "protection against evil. The soul stands up and resists evil with deep indignation. . . . If we had no longer been capable of being angry, we would have become like 'moral cows' in our ponderous easiness. . . . If there is an undertone of moral outrage, but not of personal resentment, in the anger, then this anger is good, valuable, and healthy."[4]

Even a person who forgives may not deny moral anger. In forgiveness the victim is not denying moral anger in confronting the evildoer but at a certain point decides to transcend his or her personal resentment. Hence, forgiveness takes time—sometimes a whole life or even generations. Forgiveness always remains unpredictable, whereas moral anger is expected and logical, for the first and most appropriate response to moral evil is neither forgiveness nor hate but a demand for justice. As the philosopher Albert Camus said at the end of World War II, "Tomorrow, the most difficult victory that we need to gain over our enemies will have to take place in ourselves, in this superior effort to transform hate into a desire for justice."[5]

Justice entails public recognition of the evil done to the victims and their descendants. It requires efforts to restore their dignity and also identification of the perpetrators. Forgiveness presupposes justice.

Therefore, the victim does not abandon punishment even as hate, resentment, and revenge are set aside in forgiveness. At least in some cases, punishment can lead to restitution of damages done to the victims and also, eventually, to the restoration of the perpetrator's self-respect. The problem with justice, however, is that it is intrinsically limited. Even if a perpetrator is caught and punished, the punishment is unlikely to satisfy the victim, who will witness it as disproportionate to his or her irreparable suffering. What punishment, for instance, can provide complete satisfaction to parents whose child has been brutally murdered? Important aspects of a victim's pain and suffering can never be compensated for through justice because the tragic, irreversible nature of moral evil is simply more than the inherent limitations of justice can bear. Victims can ask for ever more severe punishment of the perpetrators, but none will be completely satisfactory. Punished perpetrators may even become convinced that they have become victims, a dangerous outcome, since the perpetrators may find ways to transfer their "victimization" to others.

REMEMBRANCE

At least in part, the administration of criminal justice governs the roles of perpetrator and victim. In this context, the perpetrator will reconstruct his or her (hi)story of evil in such a way that it becomes a form of self-justification. This predictable approach blocks the possibility of forgiveness because forgiveness requires the recognition of guilt. In struggling with the perpetrator and with themselves, victims will also reconstruct history. It is crucial to listen to the accounts of the victims. Hearing a victim's lived story is a public and official event, which is important in doing justice to his or her suffering. Nevertheless, memory is never a pure reproduction of historical facts but always also a reconstruction, one determined not only by *what* is remembered but also by *who* remembers and for what *reason,* in the present or the future. Remembrance usually has a clear goal, namely, that what happened must never happen again. Those who remember always have a history *after* the immediate trauma of evil. This history colors memory.

VICTIMISM

Memory's selectivity means that not only the perpetrator's story but also the victim's story can become egocentric and ideological. What I call *victimism* may result: the victim chooses (mostly unconsciously) to stay in his or her role as victim because that identity sometimes opens an almost inexhaustible "credit line" of sympathy from others.

Even if the reconstruction of history contains few errors, some presuppositions that are not guided by the facts but by the victim's trauma can enter the reconstruction. One result can be what I call *diabolization:* a victim can be so overwhelmed by evil that he or she identifies the evildoer solely by his or her evil acts, disconnecting the perpetrator from his or her psychological and sociohistorical contexts. The space between act and actor disappears.[6] This identification can even take on a collective dimension: for example, every person who shares the perpetrator's nationality may be seen as guilty.

Recognition of the space between an evil act and the person who commits it, and between a perpetrator and his or her descendants or community, is an essential condition for forgiveness. If a person can be completely identified by his or her evil act, which entails that "good" and "evil" persons can be clearly identified, or if the views and deeds of the descendants of perpetrators coincide totally with those of their ancestors, then forgiveness is scarcely possible.

In victimism, the victim receives his or her identity solely through victimhood. Thus, it can happen that the victim is not prepared to accept any form of excuse, reparation, or restitution. He or she may have problems connecting his or her unique suffering with that of others, especially the suffering of others that may be caused by his or her own (actual) position. In this situation, the idea can easily grow that to forgive is the same as to forget, and victims do not want to forgive because they do not want to forget. Victimism gives the perpetrator no exit; he or she is forever and completely identified with evil acts and thus is forced into a defensive position characterized by self-righteousness. But victimism also gives the victim no exit; the victim's life becomes totally determined and ruled by the endured evil. The determination not to grant the perpetrator a "posthumous victory" may even become the victim's primary reason for living. Such victims invest all their energies in the everlasting story of their victimhood instead of working on their traumas. The ironic result is that the perpetrator gains immense and lasting control over the victim. Through forgiveness the victim can make himself or herself independent of the perpetrator.

Most victimism—individual or collective—does not happen consciously. It should not be the object of moral condemnation. In the long run, the victim suffers the most under it. The greatest harm produced by victimism is that it destroys the inner freedom of the victim. The victim links his or her future to that of the perpetrator and becomes dependent on the perpetrator's whim—for example, to repent or to make restitution. Victimism is the impossibility of accepting an interaction between the past event and the future, between the victim's own suffering and the suffering of others, between uniqueness and universality. The present is dominated by the past. Through forgiveness, the victim can be freed from the crushing link with the past and from his or her dependence on the perpetrator. But a key question remains: Does this release mean that forgiveness implies forgetting?

REMEMBERING FOR THE FUTURE

There is a crucial distinction between remembrance and repetition or recital of the past. Remembering is not the same as an endless repetition or recital of the past; instead it is opening the past in the direction of the future. In this way, the universal value of a memory—how particular it is—stands revealed. Remembrance is thus not an eternal emphasizing of victimhood, but a "memory of a promise," a memory for the future.[7] Therefore, a victim needs what Paul Ricoeur calls "labor of remembrance" (forming an identity by storytelling) and "labor of mourning" (establishing distance from the facts without denying them and without blocking the future).[8] At its best, remembering is a creative process in which negative emotional energy is transformed into positive energy that opens up the future. Processes of involvement and detachment interact intensely to produce an interpretation that is not reproductive but productive.

This process can advance when forgiveness is granted. Forgiveness is the opposite of an escape into forgetting. The relationship is not one of forgiving and forgetting. One can only forgive things that cannot be forgotten. "Forgetting," as Lévinas says, "cancels the relations with the past, while forgiving shifts the past into a purified present."[9] Human forgiveness is necessary because some things absolutely cannot be forgotten. Forgiveness, moreover, does not concern evil itself; evil's trace remains even after forgiveness is granted. Forgiveness has to do with the evildoer's *guilt.* Giving or receiving forgiveness releases neither the perpetrator nor the victim from remembrance. The victim is not released from memory but from the weight of resentment and hate. The victim's wound, however, remains as an everlasting scar.

Ricoeur speaks of the healing power of forgiveness, not only for victims but also for perpetrators. The perpetrator is freed neither from remembrance nor from responsibility but from the overwhelming weight of guilt. He or she receives a future because the victim recognizes the space between the evildoer and his or her evil act. In forgiveness the victim says to the perpetrator, You are more than your evil act. In this sense, forgiveness is radically different from amnesty, which seeks to erase not only the burden of guilt but the facts themselves, in an attempt to continue life as though nothing had happened. In forgiveness and through the remembrance it entails, the burden of guilt is transformed into responsibility for the future.

FORGIVENESS AS A FREE ACT

The perpetrator's readiness to submit to a (constructive) punishment should be seen as one of the conditions for forgiveness. However, forgiveness can never be earned, not even by accepting punishment. The perpetrator can never demand forgiveness from the victim; he or she can only ask for it, and the victim can legitimately refuse the request. As Ricoeur puts it, "Pardon demandé n'est pas pardon dû."[10] Like love, forgiveness must be given freely; otherwise it cannot be real. Nobody who is unwilling or unable to forgive can be dismissed, because forgiveness is not a (moral) duty but a transmoral act of love. A situation where forgiveness is not granted cannot be condemned from a moral point of view, even if such a situation can in many cases be seen as detrimental for both perpetrator and victim. The only thing a perpetrator can do is create the preconditions for receiving forgiveness—admission of guilt, repentance, acceptance of punishment, restitution, remembering. But forgiveness itself is a gift; it is given (or not) by the victim. On the other hand, the victim is not allowed to impose his or her arbitrary preconditions on the perpetrator, since forgiveness could then be distorted by feelings of revenge, malicious delight, narcissism, or economic self-interest. Other conditions hold as well: A victim can be willing to forgive a perpetrator, but the perpetrator may be unwilling or unable to receive forgiveness—for example, because he or she has not repented. Or a perpetrator may have grown to confront his or her crime so that a readiness for forgiveness exists, but the victim may be unable or unwilling to grant forgiveness.

THE UNFORGIVABLE

Forgiveness is a relational event that presupposes the perpetrator's movement away from moral self-justification and toward repentance and the victim's movement away from diabolization of the perpetrator. When this process fails, the "unforgivable" results. Here I use the unforgivable as an a posteriori category. After careful analysis, we see the tragic impossibility of forgiveness in some cases—cases in which the evildoer is unwilling or unable to distance himself or herself from the evil done and / or the victim, because of the depth of his or her trauma, is unwilling or unable to see the space between the evildoer and the evil act.

Typically, however, the unforgivable is seen as an a priori category. Some acts—genocide, for example—are considered to be so evil that the space between the evil act and the evildoer disappears forever and completely. I reject the a priori category of the unforgivable because it is based on a diabolizing view that presumes to define a person's identity forever and without any doubt. Furthermore, the a priori category of the unforgivable contains a contradiction. On the one hand, this view condemns the perpetrator because he or she has acted wrongly, but on the other, it refuses forgiveness because it insists on confirming the perpetrator in his or her criminality. But can a person be blamed morally for evildoing if he or she is not capable of also doing good and thus being capable of change that could become at least a precondition for forgiveness?

FORGIVENESS AND RECONCILIATION

Thus far, I have not distinguished forgiveness from reconciliation, but they are not the same. Forgiveness is a healing act centered in the heart of a victim who grants forgiveness to a perpetrator who is ready for it. After forgiveness, victim and perpetrator can go their own ways. Reconciliation, however, goes a step further. It aims at an integral transformation of the relation between victim and perpetrator. Jean Monbourquette argues, correctly I believe, that forgiveness should not automatically imply reconciliation.[11] If reconciliation is presented as the necessary final point of forgiveness, victims can be blocked in their efforts to forgive. There are cases in which forgiveness should not be followed automatically by reconciliation—for example, after sexual abuse between (former) partners. If we do not separate forgiveness and reconciliation clearly enough, even while suggesting that forgiveness also implies readiness to transform the relation, the blurring can be a barrier that prevents the victim's granting of forgiveness. Even if forgiveness is incomplete without reconciliation, forgiveness has value in itself quite apart from reconciliation. Forgiveness is possible without reconciliation. Reconciliation, however, is not possible without forgiveness. A relation that is transformed, but in which the evildoer is not forgiven, cannot be called a relation in the fullest sense of the word.

TO FORGIVE ONESELF

An important starting point for forgiveness is found when perpetrator and victim are able to forgive themselves. If a perpetrator gives up self-justification, confronts his or her evildoing, and acknowledges that evildoing as an aspect of his or her existence, then the perpetrator also needs to learn to accept himself or herself as a person who can be forgiven and loved. In this sense, the perpetrator has to forgive himself or herself. In some ways, the victim also has to forgive himself or herself. The victim has to see not only the good in himself or herself and the evil in the other, but also the potential for and reality of evil in himself or herself and the desire for good in the other. This recognition often includes the painful experience of shame as the victim discovers similarities between himself or herself and the perpetrator and identifies wounds that can only be healed if he or she accepts forgiveness of himself or herself. A victim is sometimes also confronted with feelings of guilt, which may be experienced because he or she failed to avoid violence, or was (in)voluntarily at the origin of violence, or was directly involved in violence. In these cases, for the victim, to forgive oneself means to understand one's own history and to accept one's own emotional injuries and give them a non-destructive place in one's life.

SUBSTITUTIVE FORGIVENESS

Special difficulties arise when the victim is no longer alive and hence unable to grant forgiveness to the perpetrator. Is it possible for there to be substitutive forgiveness—forgiveness given in the name of someone else? In the context of the Holocaust, one often hears that no one can forgive in the name of the victims. In this case, the unforgivable is not the consequence of the unwillingness but of the inability of the victims' descendants to forgive in the name of the victims. Indeed, when the victim is dead, we must speak of a factual (a posteriori) situation regarding the unforgivable. When, for example, a drunk driver kills two young children, no one can forgive in the name of these children. Eventually, their mother could forgive the suffering *she herself* has experienced from the loss of her children, but even she cannot forgive in their name. It is quite evident that in this context forgiveness between victim and perpetrator is no longer possible: the victim is absent. Likewise, the question of forgiveness *for* the Holocaust is absurd. Only the question of forgiveness *after* the Holocaust is relevant now. Forgiveness can only take place between the living. For that reason, the Holocaust itself is factually unforgivable. One cannot reconcile with the dead.

One more point is worth making in this context. Sometimes the descendants of victims say that they cannot forgive in the name of the victims, but their meaning may really be that they *refuse* to forgive in the name of the victims. I believe, however, that it is as illogical to *refuse* forgiveness in the name of the victims as it is to *grant* forgiveness in their name. Refusing to grant forgiveness is also a way of speaking in the name of the victims. Such acts are inappropriate attempts to "manage" history.[12]

INTERGENERATIONAL BONDS AND LOYALTY

What, then, is forgiveness *after* the Holocaust? Forgiveness only pertains to the living. Hence, the question of forgiveness shifts to the relations between those who are touched today by evil: descendants, friends, communities of perpetrators and victims, and, finally, the totality of humanity, since every evil touches and endangers the network of humanity itself.

This shift presupposes a form of intergenerational (collective) guilt. For a long time, I rejected the idea of collective guilt as a dangerous concept, even a Nazi one. When Jews escaped from concentration and death camps, the Nazis often responded to this "crime" by randomly selecting other Jews and murdering them. The "guilt" of one Jew was transferred to all Jews. Nevertheless, I believe today that there is a form of transpersonal and intergenerational guilt, which concerns groups of people and their history even if not every individual *as individual* bears the totality of that guilt. This idea came to me as I reflected on "We Remember," the Roman Catholic Church's post-Holocaust document, in which a distinction is drawn between the Church and the "sons and daughters of the Church," whose "errors and failures" are deeply regretted. I believe that in the document, the (all too) clear distinction between the Church and its members is made in an oversimplified and apologetic way. The relation between an institution or community and its members is much more complex than the document allows. The Church cannot hide behind the acts of some of its members; nor can its members hide behind the Church as an institution.

Sometimes my Jewish friends and partners in Jewish-Christian dialogue say that I am not guilty of the Holocaust because I was born after World War II and I am consciously a post-Shoah Catholic. This assurance is generous of them, but, with due respect, it seems akin to saying, "You are a Jew born after the Shoah, and so you have nothing to do with the Jewish victims of the Holocaust and their suffering." Space does not permit a detailed accounting here, but as a loyal Catholic, I *participate* in a Church community which bears as an institution and a community some degree of guilt for what happened during the Holocaust. It is not abnormal that the victims of this history (and their descendants) see the descendants of the perpetrators as the representatives of that past. In the same way, Christians today participate in the guilt of the Church vis-à-vis the Jewish people.

As a Christian, I always have to remember that my identity has been built on centuries of supersession. Even today, the glass windows in the church where I pray are filled with portrayals of the alleged Jewish desecration of the eucharistic host. The Holy Scripture I read today has anti-Jewish passages such as John 8.[13] The Catholic university where I teach has almost no Jewish professors. I can never disconnect myself from this history, just as I cannot ask a contemporary Jew to disconnect himself or herself from the collective and intergenerational pain of the Holocaust. As he or she suffers when confronted with the catastrophe that struck the Jewish people during the Holocaust, I see my Catholic students suffering when they learn about these dark pages of Christian history. I believe that it is extremely dangerous when Jews neither acknowledge that suffering, even though it is not proportional to Jewish suffering, nor recognize contemporary Christian efforts to confess, repent, and remember.

HOPEFUL STEPS

In the context of the Holocaust and its aftermath, contemporary reflection about forgiveness and reconciliation concerns *actual* Jews and Christians and *actual* "solidarities of love" (to quote Monbourquette), such as Jewish communities and Christian churches. In my view, a unique and hopeful step was taken on the Jewish side with "Dabru Emet: A Jewish Statement on Christians and Christianity," which was signed in 2000 by leaders from all branches of Judaism. This statement recognizes that Christianity's relation to Judaism has changed dramatically in the post-Holocaust decades. Without exonerating Christianity for what has happened in the past, "Dabru Emet" acknowledges the efforts of contemporary Christians and Christian churches to correct their age-old anti-Judaism.

When the document states that Nazism was not "an inevitable outcome of Christianity," it indicates that Christianity is *more* that its anti-Jewish history. In that way, it gives Christians the possibility to be(come) Christian in a post-Shoah way. For me, forgiveness is no more and no less than that—the ability to recognize the space between what someone is and what he or she can be and between persons and their history, and to open for them a space, a future, not *in spite* of their history of evil but *beyond* that history.

As Peter Haas mentions in his essay, Michael Signer, one of the authors of "Dabru Emet," has said that he "would not use the term forgiveness, but reconciliation. In order to reconcile, Christians have to do an accounting of what they have done wrong. . . . Only God can forgive the sins of the past."[14] As I have argued, however, reconciliation is not possible without forgiveness, and relations between Christians and Jews are no exception to this rule. "Dabru Emet" offers a key opportunity to encourage *actual* Jews and Christians to move toward forgiveness and reconciliation as I define those terms in this essay. "Dabru Emet" gives a future to Christianity by transforming Christian guilt for the past into responsibility for the future. I agree with Signer that forgiveness for the "sins [and the sinners] of the past" is something that God and only God can grant. There is a big difference between speaking about forgiveness and reconciliation between contemporary Jews and Christians and between God and the (dead) perpetrators.

From a Christian perspective, it is often asked whether God should forgive the perpetrator if the perpetrator has not been forgiven by the victim. From a human perspective, it is not possible to answer this question, because one cannot put oneself in the divine point of view. The question poses a theological paradox. One can imagine that if perpetrators are confronted by the love of God, they will experience the terrible pain of their guilt. Beyond every form of self-righteousness, they will see how they have betrayed the image of God in the other and in themselves. It is not God who will punish them, but they who will punish themselves when they confront the love of God. But will God ultimately forgive them? If the answer were yes, then we would not be taking human freedom seriously enough, for it entails the human possibility to say no definitively, even to the love of God, and to remain forever unredeemed.

If the answer were no, then we would not be taking the power of God's love seriously enough. Instead we would be affirming that there are people who are so evil that even God's love cannot lure and transform them. Then there would remain forever unredeemed evil, which would coexist eternally with God. Human beings—whether victims or perpetrators—are neither allowed nor able to resolve this dilemma. That task belongs to God.

NOTES

1. James F. Moore, *Christian Theology after the Shoah* (Lanham, Md.: University Press of America, 1993), p. 140. The italics are mine.

2. Emmanuel Lévinas, *Difficile liberté: Essais sur le judaïsme* (Paris: Albin Michel, 1963), p. 37. The translation is mine.

3. See Dietrich Bonhoeffer, *The Cost of Discipleship* (New York: Macmillan, 1995), pp. 43–47.

4. Etty Hillesum, *Etty: De nagelaten geschriften van Etty Hillesum 1941–1943* (Amsterdam: Balans, 1991), p. 417. The translation is mine.

5. Albert Camus, *Combat,* Sept. 1945.

6. See Didier Pollefeyt, "The Kafkaesque World of the Holocaust: Paradigmatic Shifts in the Ethical Interpretation of the Nazi Genocide," in John K. Roth, ed., *Ethics after the Holocaust: Perspectives, Critiques, and Responses* (St. Paul, Minn.: Paragon House, 1999), pp. 210–42.

7. O. Abel, "Tables du pardon," in *Le pardon: Brisser la dette et l'oubli* (Paris: Autremont, 1998), pp. 208–33, especially p. 219.

8. Paul Ricoeur, "Can Forgiveness Heal?" in H. J. Opdebeeck, ed., *The Foundation and Application of Moral Philosophy: Ricoeur's Ethical Order* (Leuven: Peeters, 2000), pp. 31–36.

9. Emmanuel Lévinas, *Totalité et infini: Essai sur l'extéiorité* (The Hague: Nijhoff, 1992), p. 316. The translation is mine.

10. Paul Ricoeur, *La mémoire, l'histoire, l'oubli* (Paris: Editions du Seuil, 2000), p. 626.

11. Jean Monbourquette, *Comment pardonner? Pardonner pour guérir. Guérir pour pardonner* (Ottawa: Novalis, 1992).

12. On this point, see James De Visscher, "Over het vergeven van het nooit

te rechtvaardigen kwaad," *Wijsgerig pespectief op mens en maatschappij* 33 (1992–93): 113–17.

13. R. Bieringer, Didier Pollefeyt, and F. Vandecasteele–Vanneuville, "Wrestling with Johannine Anti-Judaism: A Hermeneutical Framework for the Analysis of the Current Debate," in R. Bieringer, Didier Pollefeyt, and F. Vandecasteele-Vanneuville, eds., *Anti-Judaism and the Fourth Gospel: Papers of the Leuven Colloquium 2000* (Assen: Van Gorcum, 2001), pp. 3–44.

14. Quoted in Victoria Barnett, "Provocative Reconciliation: A Jewish Statement on Christianity," *The Christian Century* (Sept. 27–Oct. 4, 2000).

In Response to Didier Pollefeyt

PETER J. HAAS

DIDIER POLLEFEYT'S ESSAY establishes an important distinction. He tells us, correctly, in my view, that we need to differentiate between forgiveness *for* the Holocaust and forgiveness *after* the Holocaust. He notes, also correctly, in my view, that there can be no forgiveness in the conventional sense *for* the Holocaust. This is not because the Holocaust is in principle unforgivable. In fact, Pollefeyt explicitly rejects this kind of a priori characterization. Rather, there can be no forgiveness *for* the Holocaust largely because so many of the victims, not to mention the perpetrators (and bystanders) are dead. Furthermore, some victims were and are unwilling or unable to offer forgiveness and some perpetrators were and are unwilling to repent and accept forgiveness. But in all events, the essay points out, the status of repentance, forgiveness, and reconciliation among the historical participants can no longer be the focus of our concerns. Instead, as the twenty-first century unfolds, we have to look beyond forgiveness *for* the Holocaust and ask about how we as Christians and Jews are to relate to each other *after* the Holocaust.

At this point in the discussion, it seems to me that the phrase "forgiveness after the Holocaust" can have two meanings, each of which will take our reflections down a different path. One possibility is that forgiveness after the Holocaust has to do with the question of how Jews and Christians should face each other in the wake of the Holocaust. How do I, as a child of survivors, for example, overcome the Holocaust and establish relations with a child of the perpetrators? What role can I or should I play in helping the two of us overcome the past? The other possibility raises a much more theological problem. It asks whether or not the very concepts of forgiveness and reconciliation can have the same meaning after the Holocaust as they did before. That is, *forgiveness* after the Holocaust might bear an entirely different meaning than *forgiveness* did before the Holocaust. Pollefeyt deals in some depth with the first meaning but only hints at possibilities regarding the second.

Pollefeyt's treatment focuses on the psychological impact of repentance, forgiveness, and reconciliation on the individual. He provides considerable insight into what repentance and forgiveness might mean for the person offering it and the person accepting it. He even claims that offering forgiveness reestablishes the humanity of the victim even if the perpetrator does not repent and accept the proffered forgiveness. By the same token, the perpetrators, through repentance, can free themselves of (some of) the burden of guilt and return a measure of human power and dignity to the victims to whom they are now beholden. So repentance, forgiveness, and reconciliation can have important psychological and pastoral ramifications.

One of Pollefeyt's central insights is in his assertion that these mechanisms can continue to have an effect even for those who are born in the post-Shoah world. In a kind of variation on the classical Catholic doctrine of original sin, Pollefeyt seems to argue that members of the Jewish community are in some sense the heirs of the victimhood of the murdered Jews, while Christians are in some sense heirs of the perpetrators. This is so because in each case we as individuals are members of communities that were involved and as such we participate in the relationships the Holocaust has effected between our communities. So repentance, forgiveness, and reconciliation for the Holocaust are not becoming less relevant as the participating generation disappears; on the contrary, such acts are just as important, and perhaps even more so, now. Precisely through such sentiments, Pollefeyt asserts, Christianity can transcend its history, become more than it has been, and move closer to what it wants and needs to become. So acts of contrition and reaching out are still important *after* the Holocaust, even if it is impossible to effect forgiveness *for* the Holocaust.

As I write these words on September 12, 2001, the day after the destruction of the World Trade Center in New York, it seems to me that Pollefeyt's pastoral approach reflects an interesting shift in the meanings of repentance, forgiveness, and reconciliation. For Pollefeyt it appears that the evil introduced by the Holocaust entails that we can no longer think about these theological concepts in the way we did before. The presupposition seems to be that evil no longer concerns only the generation of those directly involved. It captures even succeeding generations in its grip. Repentance, forgiveness, and reconciliation have now revealed themselves to be transgenerational. This sense of inherited guilt and inherited victimhood is brought out explicitly in Pollefeyt's essay.

Pollefeyt's emphasis on the transgenerational nature of repentance, forgiveness, and reconciliation raises the question "Where do we go from here?" Writing as a Catholic theologian, Pollefeyt underscores that Catholic communities must honestly confront their church's involvement in the construction of the Judeophobic background out of which the Holocaust grew. Only in this way can the Roman Catholic Church grow beyond its guilt and complicity and become more like what it is supposed to be. The parallel question, of course, is what the Jewish community is called to do to address its legacy of victimhood. Pollefeyt rightly does not address this question in any systematic way. It is in any case impossible for Judaism to deal with its place in the post-Shoah world in terms and categories drawn from Christianity. But the question of how Judaism could or should respond to such a penitential turn in the Catholic Church remains an intriguing one. From the Jewish side, we might ask whether the whole concept of *teshuvah* needs to change in light of the Shoah, but this response cannot be the place for such a complex project.

Regarding the Roman Catholic Church, however, there is a crucial question that Pollefeyt's essay leaves unanswered. For Pollefeyt, the role of repentance and reconciliation by and within that church is clear. What is not yet clear is what shape that post-Holocaust penitential turn of the

Catholic Church to the Jewish community will take. I do not mean here merely interpersonal relations between members of one community with members of the other. There is the larger problem of whether the Catholic Church, or Christianity more broadly as a religious community with deep historical and cultural roots, can refashion its relation to Judaism at all without fundamentally restructuring its own self-understanding. It seems to me that for a substantive post-Shoah change to occur at this level, there has to be a considerable rethinking of Christianity's conceptual foundations. As I see its implications, this rethinking requires a kind of fundamental transformation analogous to what happens in an individual who undergoes sincere repentance and rebirth. But what such a transformation would mean for Christianity is far from clear. To take the situation as Pollefeyt's essay focuses it, are we to expect Christianity to undergo a radical redefinition of itself analogous to what a repentant Nazi would go through? Such redefinition hardly seems likely for an entire religious community. To be sure, there have been substantive changes in the post-Holocaust Catholic Church, and the publication of "Dabru Emet" acknowledges many of them. Still, it remains unclear what a thoroughly reformed post-Shoah Christianity (as opposed to individual post-Shoah Christians) might be.

There is, then, plenty of room for pessimism. As the Holocaust recedes into history and as papal authority passes to the successors of John Paul II, the chances of a radical repudiation of Christianity's anti-Jewish past might well seem to be less and less likely. In a world where atrocity has become all too routine, the need for reconciliation specifically regarding the Holocaust will seem more and more parochial and so less and less urgent. It is not hard to imagine how Judaism and Christianity could soon revert to business as usual.

On the other hand, there is no doubt that relations between Jews and Christians have changed dramatically since the Holocaust. There is less demonization and more of a sense of joint destiny than there was previously. Whether these developments will produce lasting, substantive change on the communal level, the level of semiotic self-definition, remains to be seen. As Pollefeyt's essay shows, changes at the interpersonal level can lead to significant changes on a broader scale. Basic rethinking is crucial if desirable reconciliation between Judaism and Christianity is to occur in the twenty-first century. Pollefeyt's essay moves boldly in that direction.

In Response to Didier Pollefeyt

JUERGEN MANEMANN

IN MY VIEW, the crucial issue in Didier Pollefeyt's reflections on forgiveness after the Holocaust involves questions about time and justice. Will God forgive the perpetrators? his essay asks, but Pollefeyt is theologically clever enough not to answer this question. At the same time, however, he suggests that, even after a perpetrator's death, God's love might have the power to forgive and transform him or her for the better. Understanding God's love in this way supports the idea of *apokatastasis panton* (the restoration of all things), but that concept is neither biblical nor Catholic from an orthodox point of view. To think of God's love as Pollefeyt seems to we have to suspend the idea of God's justice and, at the same time, combine the concept of God's love with an idea of progress after death.

In the eighteenth and nineteenth centuries, the modern idea of progress was applied even to the concept of heaven. Much earlier, Origen, the third-century Christian leader, had developed his own version of progress in the world to come, which found expression in his concept of *apokatastasis panton.* The present renaissance of the idea of *apokatastasis panton* in Christian theologies, however, depends much more on modern views of progress than on biblical insights or early Christian thought.

What are the characteristics of progress as it is understood today? In Western societies, the modern idea of progress is linked to infinity, but the latter concept is largely secularized. Typically, secularization involves an elimination or at least a reduction of theological language. If theological language is used at all, secularization requires that such language lose its transcendent meanings and dimensions. Strictly speaking, then, nothing in the world can be regarded as truly revealing or embodying what is divine, holy, or sacred. Thus, secularization transforms the religious or theological infinite into the finite, even as it also eliminates the religiously infinite from any participation in what is finite. Secularization, moreover, reduces the theological attribute of omnipotence to power; it treats omniscience as knowledge, providence as planning. But there is another side of secularization as well. It is less reductive because it retains more of the original meaning of theological concepts so as to make sense of secular categories. One example: Secularization did not transform eternity into a long but finite duration. Instead, eternity becomes the infinite. Progress, in turn, gets linked with infinity.

Today's versions of *apokatastasis panton* involve no understanding of eternity that distinguishes it from time. They depend instead on evolution-tinged myths that resist the interruption of our so-called progress. Such understandings of time, unfortunately, are nothing less than a radical proclamation of God's death, for they deny that time is different from eternity and under God's dominion in ways that make time finite. Modern sensibilities imply that time neither begins nor ends. Time, it seems, has supplanted God. Time has no deadlines, a view that biblical conceptions of time decisively reject. Those conceptions underscore that time is limited.

The limitation of time is very important theologically because it is an essential aspect of God's justice. This limitation makes it urgent that repentance and reconciliation be achieved before it is too late—and, the biblical concepts underscore, it can definitely become too late if prompt action is not taken. Yet, even if history is finite, the biblical testimony is that there may still be time enough—but not unlimited time—for repentance and reconciliation to take place. The following passage from the Hebrew Bible's prophecy of Joel (2:12–13, 15–17) is only one of many that underscore these themes:

> Yet even now, says the Lord, return to me with all your heart, with fasting, with weeping, and with mourning; rend your hearts and not your clothing. Return to the Lord, your God, for he is gracious and merciful, slow to anger, and abounding in steadfast love, and relents from punishing. . . . Blow the trumpet in Zion; sanctify a fast; call a solemn assembly;

> gather the people. Sanctify the congregation; assemble the aged; gather the children, even infants at the breast. Let the bridegroom leave his room, and the bride her canopy. Between the vestibule and the altar let the priests, the ministers of the Lord, weep. Let them say, "Spare your people, O Lord."

According to Walter Benjamin, "progress" is the catastrophe. Pollefeyt's progressive theology of forgiveness encourages the problematic teaching of *apokatastasis panton.* The danger of this theology is that it puts a theological gloss on what is essentially a secular way of thinking. In my opinion, Pollefeyt's view would be stronger if it rejected such tendencies and emphasized instead the idea that justice and forgiveness involve interruptions and limited time.

In Response to Peter J. Haas and Juergen Manemann

DIDIER POLLEFEYT

MY ESSAY DISCUSSED forgiveness and reconciliation in two ways: first, as actual human (im)possibilities, and second, as eschatological events. Peter Haas probes the first dimension—forgiveness as an individual and collective human reality today. Juergen Manemann focuses on the second—forgiveness as a final, divine redemption of the world. Their comments include two alternatives to which I want to respond: the passing away or wearing out of evil in the course of history (Haas) and the eternalizing of evil beyond history (Manemann).

Haas finds me saying that forgiveness and reconciliation have meanings after the Holocaust that they did not have before. I do not believe, however, that this shift can be located, as he suggests, in the new, transgenerational meaning of evil and forgiveness after Auschwitz. These collective dimensions of evil are not new to the Holocaust; they belong to the structure of evil itself. Evil always has had and will have an intergenerational dimension, as the traditional theological idea of original sin testifies.[1] From my Christian perspective, what is new after the Holocaust is that Auschwitz forces Christians to accept the factual limitations of forgiveness in the contemporary world.

The Jewish philosopher Emil Fackenheim once asked whether, in Auschwitz, Good Friday had not overwhelmed Easter: "Is the Good News of the Overcoming [of evil in Christ] not itself overcome?"[2] For me, as a post-Shoah Christian, Auschwitz shows that even after Christ came and showed Christians the way to redemption through forgiveness and reconciliation, the world is still unredeemed. Christ's resurrection is not yet the resurrection of this broken world. There is unredeemed suffering, and it will remain unredeemed in this world. The Holocaust means the end of triumphalism in Christian theologies of forgiveness and reconciliation.

Christians live in the tension between the "already" and the "not yet," between redemption and its absence, between forgiveness and the unforgivable. This tension should not lead to paralysis or pessimism. Instead it can and should stimulate Christians to work for redemption and reconciliation—first by converting and forgiving themselves.

Haas is correct: Christianity's self-definition needs radical change. As a post-Shoah Christian theologian who is committed to this work, I understand the impatience and disappointment of my Jewish dialogue partners. The building of a post-Shoah Church is a complex and sometimes painful process. It takes time. Nevertheless, it is as important for Jews to recognize the progress that Christian churches are making as it is for them to criticize (legitimately) the delays and obstacles in that process. So, in particular, I want to highlight Haas's point that Jews and Jewish communities should urgently consider how they could respond adequately—from within their own traditions—to the penitential historical and theological turn that is under way in the Roman Catholic Church. I believe that these processes of conversion and reconciliation can only continue to go well if they take place through dialogue relationships. If there are never replies (including positive ones) to efforts made or progress achieved—even if this Christian progress is often halting and problematic—momentum will be lost, or, even worse, Christian resentment may arise, bringing repetitions of anti-Judaism in its wake.[3]

Again, Haas is correct: As the Holocaust recedes into the past, the chances for a fundamental transformation of Christianity in response to its anti-Jewish tendencies may become less and less likely. Therefore, it is important for Jews and Judaism to keep in close contact—critically and constructively—with Christian efforts to bring about the needed changes. The "Dabru Emet" document is very important in this regard, because it is a unique attempt by post-Holocaust Jewish communities to respond positively to Christian efforts to repudiate and atone for Christianity's anti-Judaic past. However, "Dabru Emet" remains an exception. When and where Christian behavior warrants them, more Jewish responses of that kind are needed to keep Christian communities moving in the right direction.

At the start of the new millennium, too many Christian theologians would like to revert to business as usual. To the extent that this trend dominates, Christian theology that is self-consciously post-Holocaust theology will be marginalized as an outdated twentieth-century scholarly activity. An indifferent, lukewarm, badly informed, or exclusively negative Jewish reaction to the struggle of the Roman Catholic Church with the Shoah will only encourage this marginalization and the return to business as usual that will accompany it. If the work for forgiveness and reconciliation becomes a monologue, it will finally come to an end, because people will start to believe that progress is no longer possible and that energies can be better invested elsewhere. Remembrance's greatest enemy, I believe, is not (actively) forgetting, but (passively) allowing time's passing to carry evil away. Tendencies of the latter kind will relegate the Holocaust to the footnotes of (Christian) history.[4] As my essay argues, reconciliation forms the (only) alternative: it opposes forgetting and indifference by turning the history of Christian evil into remembering for a new future that Jews and Christians can share.

Manemann's response focuses on the eschatological dimension of forgiveness and reconciliation. At the end of time, will God forgive the perpetrator and realize the reconciliation that human beings in this world—even after Easter—cannot achieve? Manemann highlights a classic dilemma that confronts theology: How are God's justice and mercy related? Justice without mercy easily leads to the (hard) concept of a cruel and vengeful God; mercy without justice easily leads to the (soft) concept of a God who becomes an accomplice of evil and injustice. My position is that it is impossible for human beings to resolve the dilemma of which is stronger, God's love or God's justice, because we do not have a divine perspective.

Favoring one side of the dilemma over the other creates more problems than solutions. Manemann's understanding of that point leads him to warn against the heresy of *apokatastasis panton* (universal restoration), a view in which God's love is seen as so perfect and victorious that it will finally win out in every single person's life (see Acts 3:21). Origen thought that "the goodness of God, through the mediation of Christ, will bring all creatures to one and the same end."[5] Correctly opposing Origen on this point, Manemann reminds us that if we take God's love to be too strong, we compromise God's justice and tumble into heresy.

Manemann's position, however, harbors dangers of its own. God's love can never be separated from God's justice, but Manemann runs the risk of divorcing them. If we take God's justice to be too strong, then we compromise God's love. One result is a tendency toward what the Christian tradition calls Manicheanism, a view that recognizes an eternal principle of evil next to God and is likewise condemned by the Church as a heresy. When God's justice prevails over God's love, hell becomes the place where unredeemed people will be intensely and eternally tortured without hope of relief. But how could an all-good God accept or allow such a hell? People would fear, but never love or worship, such a cruel God.

My essay discussed both sides of the eschatological dilemma regarding God's love and God's justice. Therefore, I am surprised that Manemann warns against *apokatastasis* but not Manicheanism. Today especially, it seems to me, the danger of religious Manicheanism is much greater than that of religious *apokatastasis.* In the world's contemporary "holy wars," for example, the conflicting groups all tend to see themselves as "children of light" who can justifiably condemn (eternally) those they allege to be "children of darkness." Nazism was also Manichean. Its ideology had little, if any, place for forgiveness because it divided people definitively in two (ethical) categories: "us" *(Übermenschen)* and "them" *(Untermenschen).* Not mercy but infinite condemnation and extermination were what the Nazis' *Gott mit uns* (God with us) required for the "evil" Jewish "race." After the Holocaust, a merciless God would ensure a "posthumous victory for Hitler"[6] as much as a God who dispenses "cheap grace." After Auschwitz, the theological task is to avoid both *apokatas-*

tasis and Manicheanism; it is to keep God's justice and mercy in tension, to experience and think about them together.

Manemann also criticizes my eschatological ideas about forgiveness because he thinks they apply modern views of progress to life after death. Instead of that outlook, he emphasizes the biblical ideas of limited time and of eternity as "interruption." At least to some degree, however, Manemann's criticism is misplaced. I agree with him that time is limited, and in that way history becomes a unique space for repentance and reconciliation. Nevertheless, for some people, their historical time is too limited, too short, for repentance or forgiveness to be possible within it. From a theological perspective, should what we might call time-trapped perpetrators be condemned eternally? Should time-trapped victims—let alone God—be eternally bereft of the possibility of forgiving? Who would benefit from that?

This line of inquiry can lead to the possibility that God's forgiveness may be extended to perpetrators who repent after death. The traditional image of purgatory is a strong one that can help us envision such a process of conversion beyond the grave. Meanwhile, even after death, repentance is surely not an idea that depends on infinite time. Instead, it is precisely an experience of ultimate "interruption." Repentance and forgiveness—within history or after death—interrupt the logic of this world, where revenge, retaliation, and merciless justice are dominant and even exclusive yearnings. Forgiveness and reconciliation are the interrupting presence of God's dynamic love in the lives of persons and communities and in history itself. By contrast, eternal punishment and condemnation would be the "infinitization" of the merciless and Nazistic logic of this world.

NOTES

1. See my response to Britta Frede-Wenger's essay in this volume.

2. Emil Fackenheim, *To Mend the World: Foundations of Future Jewish Thought* (New York: Schocken Books, 1982), p. 286.

3. On these points, see Ivan Boszormenyi-Nagy and Barbara R. Krasner, *Between Give and Take: Clinical Guide to Contextual Therapy* (New York: Brunner / Mazel, 1986).

4. See Vladimir Jankélévitch, *Le pardon* (Paris: Aubier, 1967).

5. See Paul Koetschau, ed., *Origenes Werke,* vol. 5, *De Principiis* (Leipzig: J. C. Hinrichs'sche Buchhandlung, 1913), p. 79. See specifically *De principiis* I, vi, 2: "In unum sane finem putamus quod bonitas dei per Christum suum universam revocet creaturam, subactis ac subditis etiam inimicis."

6. See Emil L. Fackenheim, *God's Presence in History: Jewish Affirmations and Philosophical Reflections* (Northvale, N.J.: Jason Aronson, 1997), p. 84.

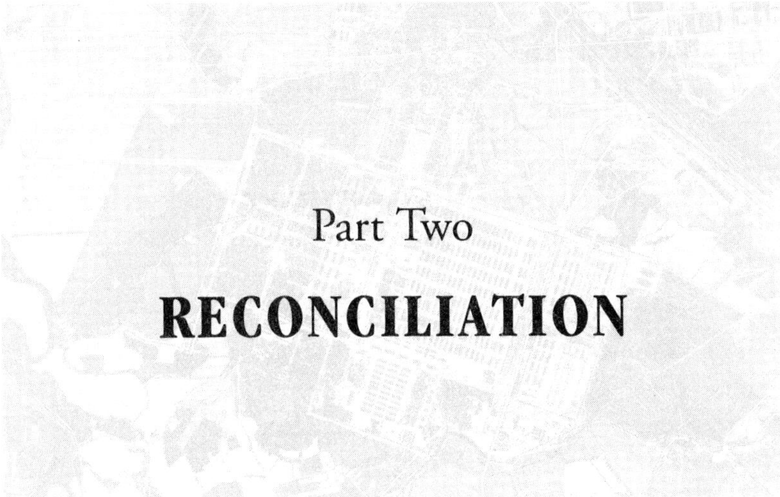

Part Two
RECONCILIATION

Terrible things happen when people do not get along. The Holocaust and September 11 testify to that. Hence, *reconciliation* deserves to be high on the list of important after-words. In fact, John K. Roth's "Useless Experience: Its Significance for Reconciliation after Auschwitz" suggests that *reconciliation* may be the most basic of the three after-words before us, for reconciliation is based on a fundamental humanity shared by all, without which any discussion of forgiveness or justice is vanity. Reconciliation entails repairing action—not action in general but specific, concrete deeds aimed at helping people get along in definite times and places. Roth illustrates this point in the aftermath of the Holocaust by arguing that reconciliation between Jews and Christians, and even among Christians themselves, is linked to the opening of the Vatican's Holocaust-related archives. Of course, as Didier Pollefeyt notes in his response to Roth, there is no guarantee that opening those archives will improve relations between Christians and Jews or between Christians and Christians. What one sees in the dialogue between Roth and his respondents is the double-edged nature of any effort to bring about reconciliation. But do we have the luxury of refraining from trying? Roth says no.

Perhaps this double-edged nature of the effort to reconcile is what leads Britta Frede-Wenger to maintain that after Auschwitz reconciliation is both impossible and necessary. In her essay "Anthropological Remarks on Reconciliation after Auschwitz," Frede-Wenger rejects attempts to reconcile through either amnesty or escape attempts. Focusing on the problem of reconciliation as it confronts a new generation of Germans, she argues that reconciliation requires acts of repentance, a commitment to a democratic society, compensation of survivors, and the hope for a kind of messianic, universal reconciliation at the end of history. Not yet at time's end by any means, we are left, despite our feelings of "unfulfilled justice," to answer continually for who we are in history's contexts. Didier Pollefeyt's response to Frede-Wenger stresses that reconciliation is indeed problematic after Auschwitz, because the evil of history contaminates entire generations; yet reconciliation is not impossible if such evil can be transcended through acts of forgiveness. The questions that remain include the following: Must we wait until the end of history to attain that transcendence? If so, are we to envision the returning Messiah as a returning Jesus Christ? In his reply to Frede-Wenger, Juergen Manemann cautions especially against the latter vision.

Manemann's own essay, "Struggles for Recognition in an Era of Globalization: The Necessity of a Theology of Reconciliation from a Political-Theological Perspective after Auschwitz," is next. For Manemann, theology unavoidably has political dimensions because it must confront suffering and human responsibility for it. Here we see parallels to Roth's insistence on action and Frede-Wenger's concern with identity. Responsibility, says Manemann, is the basis of human identity, and the definition of our identities depends on our actions. If, however, the act of reconciliation entails an act of substitution, as Manemann claims it must, then how can a Christian substitute himself for a Jew without losing his Christianity?—a question that David Patterson raises in his response to Manemann. One danger of reconciliation is what Manemann identifies as the postmodern "unencumbered self," that is, the self free of the responsibilities and commitments imposed by religious tradition. Consequently, Manemann faces another crucial issue: How can we maintain a healthy postmodern critique of authoritarianism without losing the traditional truths that make reconciliation matter? Related to that question is the one couched in Manemann's closing remarks to his respondents, a question that vibrates along the edges of Auschwitz: Where is the God of tradition? As shown by the essays in this book's second part, living *after* puts us in disjointed times and dislocated places. Much needed, reconciliation must be carefully explored as an after-word if it is to be enacted well.

4

Useless Experience

Its Significance for Reconciliation after Auschwitz

JOHN K. ROTH

I am convinced, beyond all personal experiences, that torture
was not an accidental quality of this Third Reich, but its essence.
—Jean Améry, *At the Mind's Limits*

A SUMMER EXAMPLE of what I call *Holocaust politics* erupted in 2001.[1] This flashpoint reignited touchy controversy about a decades-old problem: the Vatican's reluctance, if not refusal, to open fully its archives pertaining to the Holocaust and Pope Pius XII, whose reign (1939–58) included the years of World War II and their immediate aftermath. Scarcely any post-Holocaust rift vexes Catholic-Jewish relationships more than the question of whether Pius XII did all in his power to resist the Holocaust, or even whether complicity pervaded Vatican policies toward Nazi Germany. With the Vatican's plans to confer sainthood on the problematic pontiff already well along, the debate will not go away. So the episode I have in mind provides instructive support for this essay's major claim: namely, that the Holocaust's legacy includes a paradoxical predicament in which reconciliation is problematic but imperative, nearly impossible and yet still necessary.[2]

TWO FEATURES OF RECONCILIATION

Before I describe the incident in greater but incomplete detail, notice that my assertion depends on two of reconciliation's defining features.

First, reconciliation accents a person's or a community's reaching a point of acceptance. The Auschwitz survivor and philosopher Jean Améry illustrated the tension-filled reconciliation I want to identify when he said of the Holocaust, "What happened, happened. But *that* it happened cannot be so easily accepted."[3] Post-Holocaust consciousness must accept that the Holocaust happened—with all the devastation and darkness that admitting the Holocaust includes—but to accept that catastrophe without refusing its acceptability would give undeserved victories to indifference and denial, despair and death. In the first instance, then, relationships between the Holocaust, on the one hand, and the individuals and communities that confront its facticity, on the other, make reconciliation problematic but imperative, nearly impossible and yet still necessary.

Second, reconciliation underscores settling or resolving disputes among people. Here the emphasis falls not simply on the links between an individual or a community and an event but on interpersonal or intercommunal relationships marked by two characteristics: first, those relationships, more or less positive at some time, have been harmed, broken, or shattered, or those relationships have been at odds so destructively and for so long that they have been marked deep down by little else than suspicion, hostility, loathing, or hate; second, those relationships are inextricably bound to destructive historical events—and to the memory and memorialization of these events—in which immense harm has been perpetrated, received, or witnessed without intervention that could and, ethically speaking, should have been forthcoming in response to them.

The Holocaust makes the many variations on these themes far-reaching and persistent. Those realities indicate that reconciliation is imperative because broken and shattered relationships—to say nothing of those that are savaged by suspicion, hostility, loathing, or hate—have already taken an incalculable toll. Unless we invite more of the same and tolerate it repeatedly, reconciliation is necessary because people have to share the earth with one another, and it is better to do so when mutual understanding and respect prevail. Even those considerations, however, do not remove completely the ways in which post-Holocaust reconciliation is problematic and impossible. Again, Améry saw the point when he repudiated "hollow, thoughtless, utterly false conciliatoriness." No way, he said. It would be better to let the Holocaust's "moral chasm . . . remain wide open."[4]

If it is not to be debased by the false conciliatoriness that Améry despised, post-Holocaust reconciliation can only be reached in spite of that chasm. Because the moral chasm cannot be closed—the Holocaust's devastation is too immense for that—the quest for honest and respectful reconciliation becomes more important. Without those efforts, too many wounds will fester in ways that are as undesirable as they are unnecessary.

Some interpreters may say that the priorities for post-Holocaust reconciliation begin or remain with relationships between Germans and Jews, or, as their undeclared war raged in 2001 and beyond, between Israelis and Palestinians. The list, however, will not get very long before relationships between Christians and Jews come to the fore. That recognition leads back to Holocaust politics.

ACRIMONY AND RUPTURE

In October 1999, the Vatican's Commission for Religious Relations with the Jews (CRRJ) and the International Jewish Committee for Interreligious Consultations (IJCIC) announced the creation of what came to be known as the International Catholic-Jewish Historical Commission (ICJHC). Its accomplished six-person team of Roman Catholic and Jewish scholars would analyze *Actes et documents du Saint Siège relatifs à la seconde guerre mondiale (ADSS),* whose extensive contents from the Vatican's Holocaust-related archives fill thousands of pages in eleven hefty volumes.[5] A year later, the ICJHC issued "The Vatican and the Holocaust: A Preliminary Report," a succinct document that underscored forty-seven key questions, which, in the report's words, were "only a selection of those that could be asked." In addition, the ICJHC underscored that *ADSS* alone, however informative, could scarcely answer all the questions that needed to be asked about the Holocaust and the Vatican. Nor could one assume, the scholars continued, that full access to the Vatican's archives would "necessarily lay to rest all of the questions surrounding the role of the Holy See and the Holocaust." Sources outside the Vatican would be required to focus the picture, but the ICJHC's courteous comments made equally clear that "if full access to the archives were granted, . . . this would be a very significant step forward in advancing knowledge of the period and enhancing relations between the Jewish and Catholic communities."[6] This statement implied that post-Holocaust reconciliation between Jews and Christians, Catholics in particular, could be improved by open inquiry and honesty about the historical record, whatever that record might be. That hope's justification—or refutation, which cannot automatically be ruled out—awaits the archives' opening. (In mid-February 2003, the Vatican did open archival holdings from 1922 to 1939, but as of this writing, the wartime archives have not been fully opened to scholars.)

The ICJHC's report created a minor stir, mainly because it raised again—very politely—the old question about the opening of the Vatican's archives. Then the heat of simmering controversy rose toward boiling on June 21, 2001, when Cardinal Walter Kasper, who had succeeded Cardinal Edward I. Cassidy as president of the CRRJ, wrote to the ICJHC. Kasper urged the scholars to "get back to work" so that the ICJHC could make its final report about "what can be said about the history of the Holy See during the Shoah from the material you have reviewed and the answers provided to the forty-seven questions detailed in the Preliminary Report." Kasper's letter, however, contained no answers to the questions raised by the ICJHC. Instead it promised that Peter Gumpel, the German Jesuit *relator* who is preparing Pius XII's case for beatification, a decisive step toward sainthood in the Roman Catholic tradition, would "cooperate in giving answers to the questions." As for the Vatican's archives, Kasper stated that they are "accessible only until 1923. Recently I was informed by the competent authorities that access to the Vatican archives after that date is not possible at present for technical reasons."[7]

Five of the ICJHC's original members—Eva Fleischner had retired—sent their response to Kasper on July 20. The historians said they "had hoped for a more positive response to our appeal for new documentation." It would not be credible for them to do further work "without some positive response to our respectful case for material in the archives that has not been published." Therefore, the scholars concluded, they could not produce the final report that Kasper requested. While remaining open to further discussion about how "we might continue our work together," the historians told the cardinal that they could not "see a way forward at present" and thus "must suspend our work."[8]

Raising more questions than it answered, Kasper's letter did not help Christian-Jewish reconciliation. What were the "technical reasons" to which he alluded? Why could they not be solved in ways that would permit timely examination of the data by qualified historians?[9] Meanwhile, if the communication between Kasper, the ICJHC, and a few other key players was not intended to be a public affair, that condition ended abruptly on July 23, when an IJCIC press release broke the story. Drawing to a close by noting that Pierre Blet and his team had obviously worked extensively in the Vatican's archives as they prepared *ADSS*'s eleven volumes, it ended with a pointed question from IJCIC chairman Seymour Reich, who asked, "Why not also give archival access to the Catholic-Jewish panel and to other respected historians?"[10]

Jewish displeasure extended from "deep disappointment" to allegations about "obfuscation," "deception," and a "cover-up" on the part of the Vatican. Catholic rejoinders ranged from "sadness" and charges that Jewish reactions "misrepresented" the Vatican's position on the archives—Kasper's "at present" qualification, it was argued, did not mean that the archives were irrevocably inaccessible—to allegations that the IJCIC was a problematic dialogue partner. On July 26, the Vatican made public an angry statement by Peter Gumpel—it was not featured in the American press until several days later—which further inflamed hostilities when it accused some of the ICJHC's Jewish historians of "manifestly incorrect behavior" that helped to provoke a "defamatory campaign" against the Roman Catholic Church. The extent of the breach became evident when, on the one hand, Gumpel asserted that Pius XII "made every possible effort to save as many lives as possible, without any distinctions whatsoever," and, on the other, Elan Steinberg, executive director of the World Jewish Congress, was quoted as saying that the Vatican's statement constituted "a disgraceful slap in the face to Jews and Catholics who have worked for reconciliation and understanding," adding that "to defend the silence of Pope Pius XII is to defend the indefensible." Meanwhile, Rabbi Joel Meyers, an IJCIC member and the executive director of Conservative Judaism's Rabbinical Assembly, spoke for many concerned people on various sides when he was quoted as saying that "a war of words" had to be stopped and healed lest it "escalate out of hand."[11]

In mid-August 2001, post-Holocaust reconciliation between Christians and Jews suffered a setback. Recovery from this reversal—it remains to be seen how lasting either will be—still seems to depend on the Vatican's archives. Nevertheless, such a simple conclusion would be misleading. The chief obstacle to post-Holocaust reconciliation between Christians and Jews is far deeper and much more formidable than any archival holdings, open or shut. Indeed, the furor about the Vatican's archives makes sense only if one apprehends that obstacle with undeceived lucidity. One way to identify it is as follows: What I will call *useless experience* permeated the Holocaust to such an extent that unmastered and perhaps unmasterable trauma is the consequence for Jews—and for other people too, albeit in different ways—who honestly and unreservedly face that devastating history.

NAZI "LOGIC"

Adolf Hitler and his Nazi regime intended the annihilation of Jewish life to signify the destruction of the very idea of a common humanity that all people share. Jean Améry, who noted that the Nazis "hated the word 'humanity,'" amplified such points when he stated, "Torture was no invention of National Socialism. But it was its apotheosis."[12] Améry meant that the Third Reich aimed to produce men, women, and children whose hardness would transcend humanity in favor of a racially pure and culturally superior form of life that could still appropriately be called Aryan or German but not merely "human." Insofar as *humanity* referred to universal equality, suggested a shared and even divine source of life, or implied any of the other trappings of weakness and sentimentality that Hitler and his most dedicated followers attributed to such concepts, National Socialism intentionally went beyond humanity. This entailed more than killing so-called inferior forms of life that were thought to threaten German superiority. Moving beyond humanity made it essential to inflict torture—not only to show that "humanity" or "sub-humanity" deserved no respect in and of itself but also to ensure that those who had moved beyond humanity, and thus were recognizing the respect deserved only by Germans or Aryans, had really done so.

Jonathan Glover echoed these strains of Nazi "logic" in his important 1999 study, *Humanity: A Moral History of the Twentieth Century.* Convinced that "the Nazi genocide has a terrible darkness all its own," he locates it in the Nazis' "views about cruelty and hardness, and the appalling new Nazi moral identity." Reflected in pedagogy that would train the young to show cruelty to racial and cultural "inferiors" without dismay, that new moral identity, Glover makes clear, took its goals to include demolishing the idea that Germans, Slavs, and Jews shared the same humanity. Joseph Stalin and Mao Zedong took more lives than Hitler, but Glover thinks that Stalin and Mao defended "hardness and inhumanity," however implausibly, "as the supposed means to a more humane world." By contrast, the Nazis' "twisted deontology" made those qualities desirable in themselves, for they were key characteristics of a National Socialist identity that had moved beyond humanity.[13]

If Améry and Glover are right, and I think they are, then National Socialism entailed that not only Jews but also Judaism and every aspect of Jewish life had to disappear.[14] Hitler and his Nazi followers did not succeed completely in implementing their anti-Semitism, but they went far enough in establishing as a principle what Améry aptly called "the rule of the antiman" that none of our fondest hopes about humanity—including those about reconciliation—can be taken for granted.[15]

USELESS EXPERIENCE

With help from Améry and Glover, I have sketched core features of Nazi "logic." Now I want to suggest how that "logic" still conspires against post-Holocaust reconciliation and, more specifically, why controversy about the Vatican's archives penetrates deeper than the summer episode of 2001 may indicate at first glance. These aims bring *useless experience* to the fore, but first a related point looms large.

Jews inhabit the post-Holocaust world in a distinctive way. To the extent that they confront the Holocaust, their consciousness includes memory that is qualitatively different from any other. Here I want to choose my words carefully, because debates continue about whether the Nazis clearly and distinctly intended that other nationalities or ethnic groups (Sinti and Roma, for example) should also disappear root and branch. So I will make my point as follows: Jewish post-Holocaust consciousness is different from every other because it involves the recognition, beyond doubt or question, that one is part of a people who were targeted for utter elimination—every trace, root and branch—from existence anywhere and everywhere.[16]

Such consciousness means that the full opening of the Vatican's Holocaust-related archives involves more than access to undisclosed documents. A certain civility, perhaps a version of the false conciliatoriness that Améry deplored, may make honesty difficult, but post-Holocaust Jewish consciousness can scarcely be without anger that justifiably borders on rage. I do not presume to speak for Jews on this subject, nor do I assume that there is a single Jewish voice on the matter, but I can speak as an individual post-Holocaust Christian philosopher. That identity leads me to confess the following: Long before and during the Holocaust, we Christians typically and intentionally kept Jews in harm's way. We could and should have done far better. Therefore, just as Jews want to know what the Vatican's Holocaust-related archives contain, we post-Holocaust Christians—Protestants no less than Roman Catholics—must have awareness of those records too.[17] Otherwise, the reconciliation that Christians and Jews might achieve will be jeopardized by dishonesty. The Holocaust will always keep Christians and Jews at some distance, if not at odds. How could it not? But the reconciliation that is needed in spite of the Holocaust will not be possible until those archives are opened fully to the best historical scholarship that human intelligence can muster. Only when that happens will we have the basis for the understanding, however incomplete it must remain, that a post-Holocaust world still badly needs.

The anger and rage to which I have alluded spring from particularities that general references to the Holocaust cannot encompass. What must be faced is not only that Jews were left in harm's way but also how, *in detail,* they were put and left in that condition. Crucial to that perspective is awareness that the Holocaust's details—like the specific torture that Améry experienced at the hands of Gestapo agents in a prison at Fort Breendonk, Belgium, in July 1943—show that Jews were abandoned to *useless experience,* whose particularities are as diverse as its wreckage is vast.

Useless Violence

In *The Drowned and the Saved,* Auschwitz survivor Primo Levi's exploration of useless experience concentrated on the Holocaust's "useless violence," which was characterized by the infliction of pain that was "always redundant, always disproportionate." Levi probes deeply precisely because he does not dwell on the obvious—beatings or hangings, for example. Instead his catalogue of useless violence recalls the cattle cars that shipped Jews to Auschwitz. Their "total bareness" revealed a "gratuitous viciousness" that left people neither privacy nor dignity when they had to relieve themselves. He points out that the loot collected from the arrivals at Auschwitz meant that there were tens of thousands of spoons in that place. None were given to prisoners; they had to fend as best they could, which might mean spending precious food from the camp's starvation diet to buy a spoon on the camp's black market. There were plenty of ways to identify prisoners, but at Auschwitz the Germans implemented "the violence of the tattoo," which Levi describes as "an end in itself, pure offense."[18]

Levi's list continues. Its detail corroborates both Améry's judgment that "torture was not an accidental quality of this Third Reich, but its essence" and Glover's claim that "hardness over compassion was central to the Nazi outlook."[19] In turn, Levi's account resonates with theirs when he concludes by acknowledging that National Socialism's useless violence did have one unredeeming element of utility: "Before dying," Levi observed, "the victim must be degraded, so that the murderer will be less burdened by guilt. This is an explanation not devoid of logic but it shouts to heaven: it is the sole usefulness of useless violence."[20] Levi might have added that the Nazi goal was not simply to lessen guilt's burden but to create practitioners of useless violence who would feel no guilt at all.

Useless Suffering

Useless violence entails useless suffering, a topic that the Jewish philosopher Emmanuel Lévinas explored in an influential essay published in 1982.

As a French prisoner of war, Lévinas did forced labor under the Nazis, and almost all of his Lithuanian family perished in the Holocaust. Calling the twentieth century one of "unutterable suffering," he wrote that "the Holocaust of the Jewish people under the reign of Hitler seems to me the paradigm of gratuitous human suffering, in which evil appears in its diabolical horror." Suffering of the kind that Nazi Germany and its collaborators wreaked on European Jewry is "for nothing." To try to justify it religiously, ethically, politically—as the Nazis did when they made the practice of useless violence essential to the German "superiority" that they envisioned—was what Lévinas called "the source of all immorality."[21]

When Lévinas said that the useless suffering administered during the Holocaust was "for nothing," he was not overlooking Nazi "logic" and what it meant. On the contrary, he saw that National Socialism was ultimately about destruction, its grandiose rhetoric about the creation of a thousand-year Reich notwithstanding. The chief element in National Socialism's destructive arrogance was that regime's resolve to deface the human face—not in some abstract way but by useless suffering visited upon Jewish women, children, and men—and to do so with the remorseless determination that made its anti-Semitic prerogatives dominant until overwhelming force stopped them from doing more of their worst.

Useless Knowledge

At least for those who survive such disasters or contemplate them at second hand, useless violence and useless suffering entail useless knowledge. Hence it is worth noting that Charlotte Delbo was not Jewish, but her arrest for resisting the German occupation of her native France and her deportation to Auschwitz in 1943 made her experience the Holocaust. Witnessing what happened to European Jewry, Delbo survived the Nazi onslaught. In 1946, she began to write the trilogy that came to be called *Auschwitz and After.* Her work's anguished visual descriptions, profound reflections on memory, and diverse writing styles make it an unrivaled Holocaust testimony.

Delbo called the second part of her trilogy *Useless Knowledge.* Normally we think of knowledge as useful, but Delbo showed how the Holocaust produced knowledge about hunger and disease, brutality and suffering, degradation and death that did nothing to unify, edify, or dignify life. "The sound of fifty blows on a man's back is interminable," she recounted. "Fifty strokes of a club on a man's back is an endless number."[22] This is only one example of what Delbo called useless knowledge. Its vast accumulation drove home her point: for the most part, what happened in the Holocaust divided, besieged, and diminished life forever.

THE COURAGE TO TRY

Illustrated by Levi, Lévinas, and Delbo, useless experience particularizes the Holocaust's ongoing devastation. It remains to be seen how far-reaching that devastation will be, and that is where reconciliation in spite of the Holocaust, and the Vatican's archives, come back into play.

Primo Levi concluded *The Drowned and the Saved* by contending that "there are no problems that cannot be solved around a table, provided there is good will and reciprocal trust."[23] Emmanuel Lévinas thought that awareness of the other's useless suffering could evoke responses, intensely meaningful ones, aimed at trying to relieve that suffering. If there is to be post-Holocaust reconciliation between Christians and Jews, it will require a courage that refuses to let skepticism dismiss the hopes of Levi and Lévinas too easily. The Vatican's full and timely opening of its Holocaust-related archives, whatever special effort that might take, remains a decisive step to counter that skepticism.

At the hands of non-Jews, including Christians who stood by or aided and abetted the perpetrators of the Holocaust—if only by uncritical participation in a tradition whose millennia-long hostility toward Jews helped to set them up for the kill—Jewish life was abandoned to, and nearly destroyed by, useless experience that did not have to be. No honesty can or should remove entirely the raw edges of memory that remain, but Charlotte Delbo joins Levi and Lévinas in urging that the post-Holocaust situation not be ignored or closed. "Do something," she wrote, "something to justify your existence / . . . because it would be too senseless / after all / for so many to have died / while you live / doing nothing with your life."[24] No false conciliatoriness could fulfill Delbo's sensibly impassioned imperative, but the courage to keep trying for reconciliation in spite of the Holocaust, which includes doing as much as Christians and Jews can to relieve the useless suffering of others, would help. For Christians, the full opening of the Vatican's Holocaust-related archives will be a step, perhaps as painful as it is necessary, in that direction.

NOTES

1. I use *Holocaust politics* to refer to the ways—often conflicting—in which, on the one hand, the Holocaust informs and affects human belief, organization, and strategy, and, on the other hand, human belief, organization, and strategy inform and affect the status and understanding of the Holocaust. See John K. Roth, *Holocaust Politics* (Louisville, Ky.: Westminster John Knox Press, 2001).

2. Another aspect of this legacy is that the Holocaust grossly scarred the world's moral landscape. In particular, the Holocaust undermined the adequacy and credibility of ideals such as justice and forgiveness. How those ideals might be redeemed after the Holocaust is immensely challenging and important, but on this occasion, I want to reflect primarily on reconciliation. My view is not shared by all the contributors to this book, but I think that reconciliation is the most modest of the three post-Holocaust themes it underscores. Arguments can be made that forgiveness is a prerequisite for reconciliation. My understanding of reconciliation does not entail that relationship. Meanwhile, the idea of reconciliation is also severely strained—almost to the breaking point—by the Holocaust. Nevertheless, in spite of the difficulties, some desirable aspects of post-Holocaust reconciliation can be found. Their importance for re-creating justice and for rethinking forgiveness should not be underestimated.

3. Jean Améry, *At the Mind's Limits: Contemplations by a Survivor on Auschwitz and Its Realities,* trans. Sidney Rosenfeld and Stella P. Rosenfeld (New York: Schocken Books, 1986), p. xi.

4. Ibid., p. ix.

5. The Roman Catholics on the Historical Commission included Eva Fleischner, Gerald Fogarty, and John Morley. The Jewish team consisted of Michael Marrus, Bernard Suchecky, and Robert Wistrich. Edited by Pierre Blet, Robert A. Graham, Angelo Martini, and Burkhart Schneider, *ADSS* was published in French by the Vatican between 1965 and 1981. The third of the *ADSS* volumes contains two books. Thus, some authors mention twelve volumes, but citations to *ADSS* usually refer to eleven. Based on his interpretation of *ADSS,*

Blet's favorable impression of Pope Pius XII's policies and actions during World War II can be found in Pierre Blet, *Pope Pius XII and the Second World War: According to the Archives of the Vatican,* trans. Lawrence J. Johnson (New York: Paulist Press, 1999). Pro and con, much has been written about Pope Pius XII in the past few years. Recent books that praise Pius XII include Robert A. Graham, *The Vatican and Communism in World War II: What Really Happened?* (San Francisco: Ignatius Press, 1996); Margherita Marchione, *Pope Pius XII: Architect for Peace* (New York: Paulist Press, 2000); Ralph McInerny, *The Defamation of Pius XII* (South Bend, Ind.: St. Augustine's Press, 2001); and Ronald J. Rychlak, *Hitler, the War, and the Pope* (Columbus, Miss.: Genesis Press, 2000); and José M. Sánchez, *Pius XII and the Holocaust: Understanding the Controversy* (Washington, D.C.: Catholic University of America Press, 2002). Recent books that criticize Pope Pius XII include James Carroll, *Constantine's Sword: The Church and the Jews, a History* (Boston: Houghton Mifflin, 2001); John Cornwell, *Hitler's Pope: The Secret History of Pius XII* (New York: Viking, 1999); Daniel Jonah Goldhagen, *A Moral Reckoning: The Role of the Catholic Church in the Holocaust and Its Unfulfilled Duty of Repair* (New York: Knopf, 2002); Michael Phayer, *The Catholic Church and the Holocaust, 1930–1965* (Bloomington: Indiana University Press, 2000); Carol Rittner and John K. Roth, eds., *Pope Pius XII and the Holocaust* (New York: Continuum Books, 2002); Garry Wills, *Papal Sin: Structures of Deceit* (New York: Doubleday, 2000); and Susan Zuccotti, *Under His Very Windows: The Vatican and the Holocaust in Italy* (New Haven: Yale University Press, 2000).

6. Quotations from the ICJHC report are from a copy of that document shared with me by Eva Fleischner, who served on the Historical Commission.

7. I quote from a photocopy of Kasper's letter dated June 21, 2001. Earlier on, while the ICJHC worked in Rome, Gumpel met with the Historical Commission, but that meeting put few questions to rest. It should also be noted that the ICJHC did not receive written guarantees that the Vatican's archives would be fully opened for its research, but, according to Eva Fleischner, the ICJHC did have assurance from Vatican authorities that documents going beyond *ADSS* would be available, as needed, for its work. The presumption was not that this material would be filtered through Gumpel.

8. I quote from a photocopy of the ICJHC letter dated July 20, 2001.

9. At the time, according to Peter Gumpel and the chief Vatican archivist, Cardinal Jorge Maria Mejia, the post-1922 documents—more than three mil-

lion pages of them—had not been completely catalogued and therefore were not in suitable condition to be consulted by scholars. Gumpel also stated that it was "resoundingly false" that "the Holy See has no intention to open the archives," adding that "all the material referring to the pontificate of Pius XII will be made available, as soon as possible, not only to them [the ICJHC] but to all scholars." An English translation of Gumpel's statement and the preface to it can be found in "Declaration by Pius XII 'Relator' on Historians' Panel," *L'Osservatore Romano,* Aug. 1, 2001 (weekly edition), pp. 3 and 6. Kasper's "technical reasons" did not specify these cataloguing considerations. If the obstacle to archival access is a cataloguing problem, presumably there are ways to remove it. Blet and the team that published *ADSS* provide evidence in that direction. Of course, it took Blet's team some fifteen years to do its work. Much depends on what Gumpel's phrase "as soon as possible" turns out to mean.

10. I quote from a photocopy of the IJCIC press release dated July 23, 2001.

11. For further detail on the points and quotations in this paragraph, see Gumpel, "Declaration by Pius XII 'Relator' on Historians' Panel," pp. 3 and 6; Eric J. Greenberg, "Bad Faith: In Wake of Collapse of Landmark Catholic-Jewish Project, a Stream of Accusations," *The Jewish Week,* Aug. 2, 2001; Gustav Niebuhr, "After a Vatican-Jewish Project Fails, a Split on Why," *New York Times,* Aug. 4, 2001; Victor L. Simpson, "Vatican Accuses Jewish Historians," *Washington Post,* Aug. 7, 2001; Keith B. Richburg, "Vatican Criticizes Jewish Historians," *Washington Post,* Aug. 7, 2001; Richburg, "Jewish Scholars on Panel Assailed by the Vatican," *Washington Post,* Aug. 8, 2001; "Open the Archives," *Washington Post,* Aug. 14, 2001.

12. Améry, *At the Mind's Limits,* pp. 30–31.

13. The quotations in this paragraph are from Jonathan Glover, *Humanity: A Moral History of the Twentieth Century* (New Haven: Yale University Press, 1999), pp. 327 and 396.

14. Eventually Nazi "logic" would have put Christianity at risk too, but unquestionably the racially anti-Semitic core of National Socialism made the elimination of every trace of Jewish life a "logical," if not political, priority that no other exceeded.

15. Améry, *At the Mind's Limits,* p. 31.

16. This recognition grips me as a Christian who has taught and written about the Holocaust for more than thirty years. Non-Jews can and should do such work, but our consciousness in doing it is fundamentally different from

the Jew's because we are not part of the Jewish people, the ones who were targeted for destruction and death. Especially in post-Holocaust circumstances, this crucial difference between Jew and non-Jew remains, no matter how much we non-Jews may express solidarity with the Jewish people, and that difference deserves respect. We non-Jews carry our own Holocaust legacies—usually related to bystanders or perpetrators—and those responsibilities can be awesome enough, but they are not the same as the trauma that stalks Jews whose families were decimated and who themselves would not be alive today if National Socialism's "logic" had prevailed.

17. The opening of the Vatican's archives must not be regarded as a "Catholic problem" in which Protestants have no interest. Christian identity confers responsibility for the whole Christian tradition. As fellow Christians, Catholics and Protestants must hold each other responsible for doing what is right and good.

18. The quotations in this paragraph are from Primo Levi, *The Drowned and the Saved,* trans. Raymond Rosenthal (New York: Summit Books, 1988), pp. 106, 109, 111, and 119.

19. Améry, *At the Mind's Limits,* p. 24; Glover, *Humanity,* p. 326.

20. Levi, *The Drowned and the Saved,* p. 126.

21. The quotations in this paragraph are from Emmanuel Lévinas, "Useless Suffering," in *Entre Nous: On Thinking-of-the-Other,* trans. Michael B. Smith and Barbara Harshav (New York: Columbia University Press, 1998), pp. 93, 94, 97, and 99.

22. Charlotte Delbo, *Auschwitz and After,* trans. Rosette C. Lamont (New Haven: Yale University Press, 1995), pp. 58–59.

23. Levi, *The Drowned and the Saved,* p. 200.

24. Delbo, *Auschwitz and After,* p. 230.

In Response to John K. Roth

RACHEL N. BAUM

JOHN ROTH CENTERS his thought-provoking essay on an example of what he calls "Holocaust politics"—namely, the controversy surrounding the Vatican's unwillingness to open fully its archives regarding Pope Pius XII. His essay is provocative for its claim—gently but powerfully made—that the Holocaust and its reign of the "antiman" is in some sense not over. Christians, he argues, still do not *see* Jews, do not see their continued suffering and rage. In this context, what is significant is not so much what remains in the archives, but the Vatican's unwillingness to offer even this much, in the face of millions of murdered Jews. Against the Christian narrative of redemptive suffering, Roth insists that Christians must see Jews' *useless* suffering. His essay thoughtfully articulates the complexity of reconciliation after the Holocaust. In response, I want to explore this complexity even further.

Although the example of the Vatican archives is an actual, and significant, example, it is also one rife with symbolism. What does it mean to be "open" after the Holocaust? As Roth understands, at stake is not only the actual information held in the documents, but a larger sense of knowing the other. What do Jews and Christians need to know about each other to participate in reconciliation? What kind of openness is demanded, or even possible, after the Holocaust?

The symbolism of openness is significant, particularly in a church rife with symbolism. This is, after all, the same Catholic Church that opened the Holy Door of Saint Peter's Basilica with a golden hammer at the turn of the millennium. Originally, it was not a Holy Door, but rather a wall that was taken down and rebuilt in each Jubilee year. The ceremony commenced with a golden hammer and concluded with a trowel, themselves suggestive symbols. The work was not without danger; on Christmas Eve in 1974, Pope Paul VI was nearly hit by falling concrete. In 1975, changes were made to the ritual and the wall was built on the inside of the basilica. It is still taken down before the door is opened, but the focus of the ceremony is now on the door itself.

I provide this example as a corollary to Roth's, for it too reveals the difficulty of openness after the Shoah. Pope John Paul II—noted for the advances he has made in Jewish-Christian relations—welcomed the new millennium with an open door, but a door most definitely not open for Jews. Here is how the pope explained the sign of the Holy Door: "[It] evokes the passage from sin to grace, which every Christian is called to accomplish. Jesus said: 'I am the door' (John 10:7), in order to make it clear that no one can come to the Father except through him. This designation, which Jesus applies to himself, testifies to the fact that he alone is the Savior sent by the Father. There is only one way that opens wide the entrance into the life of communion with God: this is Jesus, the one and absolute way to salvation."[1]

Not only is the Holy Door not open to Jews; its very openness denies the Jewish relationship with God. So whether or not the Vatican opens its archives is in some sense beside the point, given that the institution itself is structured on the repudiation of Jewish existence.

That the ceremony evolved from a wall to a door is also quite suggestive. While the ritual probably changed for many reasons, at least one would appear to be the danger in tearing down the wall. How much easier it is to walk through a door than to dismantle a wall. What is at stake in the Vatican documents is, undoubtedly, not only the information therein, but the ability of the Vatican to dismantle its own walls, and to open its doors not only to Christ, but also to Jews and their abiding relationship with God.

And what is at stake for Jews in the opening of the archives? At first glance, the knowledge held in the Vatican documentation is "useful," in contrast to the "useless knowledge" of the Holocaust. But its usefulness is complicated. How do we live together knowing what the other is capable of? We want to know not only of the other's actual culpability, but also of his potential for violence and apathy. While in some sense this is useless knowledge (for why would we want to know how depraved humanity can be?), it is, in another sense, useful. By knowing the depths of the other's misdeeds, we can better judge his efforts to repair them.

There is no issue more crucial for interfaith relations than whether Jews can trust Christians. What is essential to useless experience is that it severs what Jean Améry calls "trust in the world":

> I don't know if the person who is beaten by the police loses human dignity. Yet I am certain that with the very first blow that descends on him he loses something we will perhaps temporarily call "trust in the world." Trust in the world includes all sorts of things . . . [b]ut more important as an element of trust in the world, and in our context what is solely relevant, is the certainty that by reason of written or unwritten social contracts

> the other person will spare me—more precisely stated, that he will respect my physical, and with it also my metaphysical, being.[2]

I take for granted that individual Jews can and do trust individual Christians, but as far as faith communities are concerned, what are the possibilities for trust? This is not only a question for Jewish-Christian dialogue; Christians, I would argue, must confront their own ability to trust Christianity, which failed so profoundly to save the Jews.

Trust and reconciliation require, in part, a belief in a shared humanity, a counter to the principles of the "antiman" that Roth articulates. After the Holocaust, we must take seriously the idea that what is shared among humanity is its capacity for evil. Yet surely this alone is not adequate. What, then, will humanity share after the Holocaust?

Perhaps, ironically, the answer can be found in part in Roth's discussion of Jewish rage. While there is clearly a particularity to the Jewish experience, and subsequently to Jewish rage, we need to take seriously the idea that anger and rage are appropriate responses to the decimation of one's people. If, indeed, we are to see ourselves as a single humanity, then by extension, anger and rage are appropriate responses to the severing of a limb of the body of humanity.

Of course, rage may get people to the table, but there will need to be more to keep them there—hope, for one. But I sense that part of the distrust of some Jews is based on the sense that others do not experience enough rage; that, to paraphrase Roth, they have too much accepted the Holocaust. I am reminded of Czeslaw Borowi, a Pole in Claude Lanzmann's film *Shoah.* When Borowi tells Lanzmann that the Polish farmers were scared of being arrested, Lanzmann asks whether they were afraid for the Jews too. Borowi's interpreter replies: "Well, he says, it's this way: if I cut my finger, it doesn't hurt him."[3] If we take seriously the call to a shared humanity, we must ask how the Jews' suffering in the Holocaust will hurt for non-Jews, too. Thus, the question isn't only why doesn't the Vatican see the suffering of Jews, but why isn't the Vatican suffering? Furthermore, it is not only Jewish suffering that Christians must confront, but also Jewish joy. It is only by appreciating Jewish life that we mourn its murder; it is only by accepting God's love of the Jews that Christians become responsible—morally and theologically—for Jewish survival. To

Roth's concern that Christians must understand the extent to which the Holocaust has wounded Jews, I would add that Christians must understand Judaism as a living religion of joy. Reconciliation depends on the full commitment of Christians to the joyous expression of Judaism, to Jews who are not suffering, to Jews who continue to enjoy a holy relationship with God. Opening the Vatican's archives will be a decisive step in Jewish-Christian relations if it marks an acknowledgment on the part of the Catholic Church that humanity is, in fact, all one people, equally close to God. The door that needs to be open is ultimately, then, neither the door to Christ nor to Jews, but to an all-embracing humanity loved by a single God.

I know that John Roth shares this belief in a single humanity loved by God, as do many other faithful Christians. Perhaps this is the true site of reconciliation—individual acts of good faith. For if the example of the Vatican archives shows anything, it is, unfortunately, that reconciliation on any kind of institutional level remains quite difficult.

NOTES

1. Holy See, "The Opening of the Holy Door of the Great Jubilee of the Year 2000," http://www.vatican.va/news_services/liturgy/documents/ns_lit_doc_14121999_porta-santa_en.html.

2. Améry, *At the Mind's Limits,* p. 28.

3. Claude Lanzmann, *Shoah: An Oral History of the Holocaust* (New York: Pantheon, 1985), p. 25.

In Response to John K. Roth

DIDIER POLLEFEYT

UNLESS JEWS AND Christians seek historical truth, forgiveness and reconciliation are not possible among them. John Roth's analysis of the Vatican's so-called inability ("for technical reasons") to open its archives illustrates very well the difficulties that confront Jewish-Christian reconciliation. A church that protects itself against a search into its own sinfulness is a church that does not believe in its own message of reconciliation and that undermines its spiritual power to witness about this message for others in the world. An important element in Roth's analysis is his argument that not only Jews but also Christians have a strong desire to know historical truth—whatever it may be—so they can come to terms with the history of Christian anti-Judaism. Nevertheless, his analysis contains some presuppositions that I want to question.

The first presupposition is that it seems as though reconciliation is possible only when all of history's details are known. I have the impression that Roth's analysis of the position of the Vatican and its archives implies that reconciliation is almost the same as revealing the historical truth in all its detail. But if reconciliation depends on knowing all the details of evil's history, then reconciliation will be impossible in almost all cases. Most reconciliation happens in spite of a full knowledge of historical details. Moreover, to confess the truth about evil is only a *precondition* for reconciliation, not a guarantee of reconciliation itself. It is uncertain that the opening of the Vatican's archives will bring Jews and Catholics closer to reconciliation. On the contrary, it is possible that critical information about the negative role of the Vatican during World War II will render reconciliation even more difficult, especially if the church deals with this information in an apologetic way, or if Jews use the information as support for their demonization of Christians.

Roth's linking of Jewish-Catholic reconciliation and the opening of the Vatican archives seems to imply another (ecclesiological) presupposition. The Catholic Church is almost exclusively understood here as a hierarchical system in which processes of reconciliation start at the top and work their way down. Reconciliation between Jews and Catholics then becomes (too) dependent on attitudes and policies at the top, including the role of the pope in particular. Catholics, however, live not only in a post-Shoah time but also in a post–Vatican II situation. In the Second Vatican Council's *Dogmatic Constitution on the Church* (*Lumen Gentium,* 1964) we see the development of the concept of the church as "the People of God" (chapter 2). This conciliar document recognizes the supernatural meaning of the faith of the whole people of God *(sensus fidei)* (nos. 12 and 35). For post–Vatican II Catholics, the *sensus fidei* is also an important source of new church life, and the church as hierarchical institution recognizes this reality.

At this point, perhaps a third presupposition can be discovered in Roth's analysis. Often, we understand forgiveness and reconciliation in interreligious dialogue mainly between global communities—for example, *the* Church and *the* Jewish people. Such a view, unfortunately, immediately implies that reconciliation is, to use Roth's words, "nearly impossible." Therefore, I would plead for a fragmentation and moderation of the idea of reconciliation. If we start with the global perspective, reconciliation will never be possible. Forgiveness and reconciliation should start with individual Jews and Christians and with their respective local communities, even if this process could be strongly empowered and stimulated (or blocked) at the global level. These individual efforts at reconciliation, it must be underscored, are not just a preparation for global reconciliation; they represent reconciliation in its fullness, at least for the particular people involved. The global communities will eventually hear the *sensus fidei* of their members, even if the policies of institutional communities could at first hinder the individual voices and the sensitivities that arise from within them. The danger of Roth's position is that by stressing so strongly the role of the opening of the Vatican archives, the possible intractability of that situation can become an excuse for individual Christians and Jews to avoid the tasks of reconciliation in the specific places where they live.

Next, I want to challenge Roth's statement that "[b]ecause the moral chasm [of the Holocaust] cannot be closed . . . the quest for . . . reconciliation becomes more important." Of course, the Holocaust has caused tremendous injuries both to individuals and to civilization. If a wound is open and remains so, then reconciliation is impossible and remains so. In my view, reconciliation is needed precisely because a wound cannot stay open forever, lest it contaminate the body completely. Forgiveness and reconciliation are not cosmetics that hide the injury; they are healing processes that transform a wound into a scar. The Holocaust should become the scar on the twentieth century's face. One can live constructively with a scar, but one can never forget or neglect the injury to which it bears witness.

To return to Roth's image: the chasm can never be filled, but it can be bridged. This point brings me to a central theme in his essay, that of "useless experience," which includes what Emmanuel Lévinas calls *souffrance inutile* (useless suffering). In my reading, *souffrance inutile* is a concept Lévinas developed to recognize that, in principle, (real) evil (including the Holocaust but also other forms of evil) cannot be given meaning.[1] Instead, its evil brings about suffering "for nothing": no (philosophical or religious) reason can justify or legitimate such evil. For Lévinas, therefore, the Holocaust means the end of all theodicy, of all attempts to justify perfectly God's relation to history. Forgiveness and reconciliation, however, do not give "meaning" to evil events. Forgiveness and reconciliation are only possible when evil is recognized unambiguously *as evil.* Useless experience, then, does close off giving meaning to evil and the useless suffering it creates, but useless experience need not close the way to reconciliation. As I argued in my main contribution to this volume, forgiveness starts with the recognition of the space between the evildoer and his or her "senseless" (inexcusable) evil acts. In a less well known text, Lévinas argues that even a Nazi has a "face."[2] Lévinas was able to recognize the humanity even of the Nazi perpetrator. Here a crucial precondition is created for starting a process of reconciliation (not that Lévinas is going that far) even if the suffering of the victim is and will remain useless.

Useless experience sometimes makes it impossible for victims to recognize the face of perpetrators and even of perpetrators' descendants. Roth's perspective is illuminating when he refers to Jean Améry (who committed suicide in 1978), showing how useless experience "conspires" against post-Holocaust reconciliation. In my view, the case of Améry, who was a victim of brutal Nazi torture, is an illustration of how useless experience can become (understandably) not the basis for reconciliation but for its opposite: a legitimation of resentment and even revenge. In *At the Mind's Limits,* Améry calls himself a "self-confessed man of resentments" who "supposedly live[s] in the bloody illusion that I can be compensated for my suffering through the freedom granted me by society to inflict injury in return."[3] He describes the goal of his work as follows: "My personal task is to justify a psychic condition that has been condemned by moralists and psychologists alike. The former regard it as a taint, the latter as a kind of sickness."[4]

I believe that Améry's complex self-appraisal must be taken seriously. It is dangerous to make a philosophy out of resentment and revenge. In my view, Améry's theory of resentment and revenge, understandable though it may be, cannot be the final foundation for moral reflection after Auschwitz, and especially not for thinking about reconciliation after the Holocaust. There are many counterexamples from the Nazi period in which useless experience did not lead to Améry's conclusions. One thinks of the philosophies of Albert Camus, Etty Hillesum, and Simon Wiesenthal in this regard. My point is not that Améry's position has no value in the discussion about reconciliation. "My resentments," he emphasizes, "are there in order that the crime become a moral reality for the criminal, in order that he be swept into the truth of his atrocity."[5] Améry's position is a strong warning against "cheap grace." It also makes us understand that people can be damaged so profoundly that reconciliation becomes impossible.

Nevertheless, Améry remains too close to the Holocaust's reality to give us the help that is most needed for a sound post-Shoah view of reconciliation. Processes of forgiveness and reconciliation require time for reflection, remembrance, and healing action. As the biblical wisdom of Ecclesiastes 3:1–8 reminds us: "For everything there is a season, and a time for every matter under heaven: . . . a time to kill, and a time to heal; a time to break down, and a time to build up; a time to weep, and a time to laugh; a time to mourn, and a time to dance; . . . a time to love, and a time to hate; a time for war, and a time for peace." Even then, after time has created sufficient space for everything human, we have to accept that many fragments of reconciliation will never be possible, at least not through human action.

NOTES

1. Didier Pollefeyt, "The Trauma of the Holocaust as a Central Challenge of Lévinas' Ethical and Theological Thought," in Marcia L. Littell, Eric Geldbach, and G. Jan Colijn, eds., *The Holocaust: Remembering for the Future II on CD-ROM* (Stamford, Conn.: Vista InterMedia, 1996).

2. Emmanuel Lévinas, "La mémoire d'un passé non révolu," *Revue de l'Université de Bruxelles* 1–2 (1987): 11–20, especially 18.

3. Améry, *At the Mind's Limits,* p. 69.
4. Ibid., p. 64.
5. Ibid., p. 70.

In Response to Rachel N. Baum and Didier Pollefeyt

JOHN K. ROTH

DIDIER POLLEFEYT ARGUES, "To confess the truth about evil is only a *precondition* for reconciliation, not a guarantee of reconciliation itself." Rachel Baum asks, "What are the possibilities for trust?" Together they respond to my essay "Useless Experience" by amplifying a key theme that it underscores: namely, that the immense importance of reconciliation between Christians and Jews is matched only by the complexities that attend our steps in that direction. Baum's amplifications emphasize the importance of understanding the full implications of *openness* between Christians and Jews.[1] Pollefeyt's approach criticizes what he takes to be some of my own assumptions, but he makes his criticism in ways that I take to be complementary to my outlook.[2]

As I explored recent episodes in what I call Holocaust politics, my focus on the Vatican's Holocaust-related archives seemed to indicate that reconciliation was primarily about institutional and communal encounters. Both Baum and Pollefeyt are dubious that reconciliation is likely to take place, first or foremost, at that level. I share that view, although I also believe that reconciliation needs to happen at institutional and communal levels if it is even to approach the goals that should be met. At the more personal and individual levels, Baum and Pollefeyt are more hopeful. Pollefeyt urges that reconciliation should start with particular Jews and Christians and their local communities. "[I]ndividual Jews," Baum adds, "can and do trust individual Christians." These notes ring true. They do so to such an extent, I think, that the particularity of the most recent confrontations about the Vatican archives were possible only because relations between individual Jews and Christians included important elements of trust. Otherwise, neither the negotiations nor the heartache and even hostility that followed when the negotiations broke down would be explicable. The key, then, is to keep working on trust-building wherever, whenever, and however the tasks of trust-building can be undertaken.

For the time being, the issue of the Vatican archives remains unresolved and tension filled. One day, I am confident, those Holocaust-related archives will be fully open. When that happens, reconciliation will have gained a step, although it cannot be guaranteed that the findings of such openings will preserve that progress. Time will tell. Meanwhile, the tasks of reconciliation remain, and since we know that they can take place in individual cases and perhaps in small groups, attention must be paid to those relationships, as Baum and Pollefeyt recommend.

Sharing that conviction with them, I want to use the remainder of my response to relate a story of reconciliation. It came to my attention in the summer of 2001, when the issue of the Vatican archives was the subject of much heated debate. The narrative is a parable. It has relevance not only for the Holocaust and its aftermath, but for other situations as well, including perhaps the "useless experience" that resulted on September 11, 2001, when the World Trade Center and the Pentagon were attacked by terrorists using hijacked planes. The story involves men who were strangers twice over. Unacquainted until a book about German Jews and the Holocaust brought them together, Emil Sold and Paul Friedhoff learned that they had once "lived completely opposite lives in what are almost contrary worlds."[3] An odd couple indeed, yet their correspondence on the Shoah produced a friendship that revealed "how similar our fundamental philosophies have become in the end."[4]

The Sold-Friedhoff friendship was neither easily developed nor effortlessly sustained. The two men were aging. Illness periodically stole their time and sapped their energy. Frequently and warmly, the German invited Friedhoff to visit him and his native land. Occasional telephone calls made their voices audible, but no face-to-face meetings enlivened a relationship that depended almost entirely on the written word. Such difficulties made it unlikely that their exchange would last for long, but other threats could have been even more disruptive.

Unless their correspondence was to be superficial, never getting beyond what the Holocaust survivor Jean Améry aptly called "false conciliatoriness," Sold and Friedhoff had to find their way through minefields of emotionally charged Holocaust history.[5] That navigation, at times done by trial and error, had the potential to produce pain, misunderstanding, and hostility more than sufficient to break off the communication between a former Wehrmacht medic and a Jew who fled Nazi Germany in 1934. Nevertheless, as their letters went back and forth across the Atlantic, Sold, the Catholic doctor, and Friedhoff, the Jewish furniture maker who made the United States his home, found constructive ways "to reflect together on a world and a period that we did not intend to create, but in which we must now live."[6]

Their commitment to keep writing to each other validated Friedhoff's judgment that the two of them had "come into a true friendship without ever having seen one another."[7] Written between September 16, 1994, and May 18, 1999, the letters indicate that Sold, the younger by more than a decade, wrote at greater length than Friedhoff. Determined to do what he could to atone for Nazi Germany's genocidal campaign against the European Jews, Sold worked long and hard to preserve the memory of Jewish life in the Rhineland-Palatinate region of Germany where Friedhoff and Sold were born in 1907 and 1920, respectively. His research gave him information, if not answers, to offer in response to many of Friedhoff's questions about Germany past and present.

While Sold spent much of his retirement teaching about the Holocaust and Christian-Jewish relations, Friedhoff observed Germany from a distance, but no less intensely, because Nazism had forced him to abandon his homeland. The Jew's questions about Germany probed deeply. As one question led to another, the lack of closure seemed to haunt Friedhoff more than Sold, who offered his historical and philosophical interpretations in greater detail while Friedhoff characteristically found that "it is difficult to find an answer for what happened."[8] Yet their shared passion for inquiry took them far in following Sold's urging that "there isn't any reason to hold back any questions."[9]

It took time for Sold and Friedhoff to get beyond formality. Almost five years after their correspondence began, Friedhoff told Sold that he still had "the feeling that we're not entirely open with one another."[10] Mindful that they might too easily give offense if their views were completely unmasked, they nevertheless worked to communicate their different experiences with honesty and their divergent beliefs with respect. Sometimes they had to agree to disagree, an outcome illustrated especially by their wrestling with questions concerning how much the German people knew about the destruction of European Jewry. Sold acknowledged that virtually all Germans knew that Jews were persecuted, pressured to emigrate, often sent to concentration camps, and eventually deported from Germany, but he argued that the majority of Germans did not know about the Final Solution, the mass murder of the Jews, until after the war. Friedhoff remained unconvinced, and the partners recognized that this unsettling issue would have to remain unsettled.

The Sold-Friedhoff exchange grew into an ocean-spanning, if not an abyss-bridging, transcultural deliberation whose far-reaching scope was matched by the judicious intelligence and clear expression that two wisely experienced interpreters brought to bear upon it. Embedded in the conversation's unfolding is the philosophy that these men came to share. No summary can do it justice, because that understanding evolved through disciplined effort, study, and reflection honed by their years of interaction. The following themes, however, are as important as they are unmistakable: The Holocaust compels attention. That attention should produce a healthy skepticism about nationalism, religious dogma, and every other certitude that divides humanity in ways that pit "us" against "them." Despite the differences that remain, forthright inquiry about the Holocaust can make people more sensitive and bring them closer together. That inquiry can deepen, as Sold put it, "by listening to the other one in silence, then by thinking, and then by asking additional questions."[11] The point is not that such inquiry will completely heal old wounds, but it can help to define and defend what is most important, namely, profound respect for the preciousness of individual life.

Much of the Sold-Friedhoff philosophy emerged in their discussion of religion, a topic that threads through the letters with regularity. Their traditions and practices diverged, but each took care to become knowledgeable about the other's ways. They respected these particularities keenly, just as they mutually deplored the exclusiveness and hostility that religions so often inflame in spite of their best teachings to the contrary. A practicing Catholic, Sold would not disagree with his more skeptical

Jewish friend when Friedhoff suggested that "the best religion is a good relationship between one human being and another."[12]

Neither man was without pessimistic moments, but both refused indifference and resisted despair. Emphasizing that they could neither change the past nor control the present, their commitment to the future was to use their remaining time and energy for purposes that urge people to care responsibly for each other. Encouraging care that can combat our all-too-human tendencies to isolate one another and to leave people stranded in contrary worlds, Emil Sold and Paul Friedhoff showed how the Holocaust is best remembered.

Emil Sold and Paul Friedhoff kept themselves alert and vigilant at memory's edge. By doing so, they moved their readers to inquire about the past and much more. They put memory in the service of humanity. By helping us consider a time that must not be forgotten, they also summon us to reconsider how to live in the time that is ours. The opening of the Vatican archives and the prospects for post-Holocaust reconciliation hang in that balance.

At some point, if only because death intrudes, people stop writing letters, and a correspondence—even one as long-lived as the Sold-Friedhoff exchange—comes to an end. Such an ending, however, is not the same as a conclusion, for a correspondence like theirs does not conclude, at least not in the sense that there is nothing left to say. One reads their last exchange imagining that these two men, so different and yet so much alike in their caring for each other, want to keep the lines of communication open, on and on.

The last letter was written to Friedhoff by Sold on May 18, 1999. Sold salutes his friend's ninety-second birthday by sending Friedhoff a copy of their complete correspondence.[13] Just above his signature, Sold's closing line—"In old friendship"—conveys a touching affection, as deeply felt as it is simply stated, especially when one recalls Sold's early observation that the two of them had once lived "opposite lives . . . in contrary worlds." Intensified by unexpected Holocaust encounters, theirs was a friendship born in old age and then nurtured to wise maturity that resisted the Shoah's destructive divisions. Through their letters, their friendship lives on. Reaching out to impart its insights to any and all who will receive them, such friendship illustrates what the good prospects for reconciliation—in spite of useless experience—can be.

NOTES

1. Although this response to Baum and Pollefeyt seeks to build on points of agreement between my essay and their critiques, and thus does not intend to concentrate on points of theirs with which I disagree, it is still important to say that in one major way Baum subverts the openness she applauds and seeks to advance. "Whether or not the Vatican opens its archives is in some sense beside the point," she writes, "given that the institution itself is structured on the repudiation of Jewish existence." To use her phrase "in some sense," Baum's claim that the Vatican "is structured on the repudiation of Jewish existence" will not stand scrutiny. Vaguely qualified, Baum's statement is an unfortunate example of pronouncements that are hindrances to the reconciliation badly needed in a post-Holocaust world. That said, I hasten to add that I regard Baum's essay mainly as one that takes my views in directions that are entirely to my liking.

2. I take Pollefeyt's major objections to concentrate on what he thinks are four of my assumptions, each of which he finds wanting: (1) that reconciliation "is almost the same as revealing the historical truth"; (2) that, owing to Roman Catholicism's hierarchical structure, Catholic steps toward reconciliation must come from "the top"; (3) that reconciliation depends mainly on interreligious dialogue between "global communities"; (4) that the Holocaust remains a moral chasm or wound that cannot be closed. Pollefeyt's points really show more agreement than disagreement with mine. First, I neither stated nor implied that historical truth is a sufficient condition for reconciliation, although I do believe that it is a necessary one. Second, I neither stated nor implied that Catholic steps toward reconciliation must only come from "the top," but I do think that the Vatican has a crucial part to play in those steps. Fully opening its Holocaust-related archives is one of them. Third, I neither stated nor implied that global communities are the only players in reconciliation, but I do hold that they have a part to play if reconciliation is to take place. On the fourth point, our disagreement is real, but so is the hope we share. Pollefeyt suggests that the Holocaust can be called "the scar on the twen-

tieth century's face." Unfortunately, I believe, the wounds of the Holocaust's useless experience persist too deeply and openly for only scarring to remain. For that reason, Pollefeyt is exactly right and in agreement with me when he says that "reconciliation is needed precisely because a wound cannot stay open forever, lest it contaminate the body completely."

3. See Emil Georg Sold and Paul Friedhoff, *"That Time Cannot Be Forgotten": A Correspondence on the Shoah,* trans. Ivan Fehrenbach (Bloomington: Indiana University Press, 2002). Sold to Friedhoff, Dec. 16, 1996, p. 82. All subsequent cites of the Sold-Friedhoff correspondence are from *"That Time Cannot Be Forgotten."* My account of the correspondence is adapted from the afterword I provided for the book.

4. Sold to Friedhoff, Apr. 18, 1999, p. 192.

5. Jean Améry uses the concept of "false conciliatoriness" in the 1977 preface to his important book *At the Mind's Limits* (p. ix).

6. Sold to Friedhoff, Dec. 16, 1996, p. 82.

7. Friedhoff to Sold, Apr. 15, 1997, p. 99.

8. Friedhoff to Sold, Oct. 3, 1994, and May 22, 1995, pp. 3 and 37.

9. Sold to Friedhoff, Feb. 14, 1995, p. 20.

10. Friedhoff to Sold, Mar. 9, 1999, p. 183.

11. Sold to Friedhoff, Nov. 27, 1994, p. 8.

12. Friedhoff to Sold, Jan. 2, 1999, p. 176.

13. Sold to Friedhoff, May 18, 1999, p. 194.

5

Anthropological Remarks on Reconciliation after Auschwitz

BRITTA FREDE-WENGER

IN AUGUST 1996, I was traveling in Israel with a group of Canadian teachers working on Holocaust education. I was the only German in the group. One day, after a presentation by a survivor, I asked her whether she would ever go back to Germany. Not knowing I was German she looked at me, smiled, and said very calmly: "No, never! You know, I hate the Germans, even the young ones. I refuse to talk to them, I refuse to buy, eat, or read anything that is German—and I never will." In this essay, I want to approach the question of reconciliation after the Holocaust. And by referring back to the incident in Israel, I want to point out the context of the problem: sixty years after the Holocaust, we are not talking about reconciliation between perpetrators and victims any more, but about reconciliation between the children, grandchildren, and even great-grandchildren of perpetrators / bystanders and their country's past.[1] And we are talking about reconciliation between the young generations of Germans and Jews. This in no way means we can forget or ignore both victims and perpetrators who are still alive. However, I want to point out that the problems of the later generations deserve a consideration of their own. Therefore, writing as a German Christian, I shall focus on the experience of my own generation.

I shall first identify two models of reconciliation, two attempts to come to terms with the German past. The first one is the German reaction to

Daniel Jonah Goldhagen's *Hitler's Willing Executioners* (1996). I shall tentatively deal with this as reconciliation through amnesty. The second model is fictional but it could very well have happened: it is Bernhard Schlink's short story "The Circumcision" (2001), which may help identify a model of reconciliation through escapism. Neither model provides a means of reconciliation that does justice to both past and present. Thus, on the basis of Paul Ricoeur's essay "The Riddle of the Past" (2000), I shall suggest a double reading of the term *reconciliation*. Reconciliation is and remains impossible, and yet, at the same time, must and can be worked on.

I

Reconciliation through Amnesty

Much has been written about Daniel J. Goldhagen's thesis that German men and women were "Hitler's willing executioners." In his book, Goldhagen argues that ordinary Germans actively took part in the destruction of European Jewry due to their "eliminationist mind-set," which was fueled by "a particular *type* of anti-Semitism that led them to conclude that the Jews *ought to die.*"[2] According to Goldhagen, the main reason for the Holocaust lies in this unique characteristic that all Germans shared.

Soon after the book's publication it became clear that the scholarly quality of Goldhagen's thesis was debatable. Nevertheless, when the author traveled to Germany for public lectures and panel discussions, he was branded both "Historians' Nightmare and Popular Hero."[3] Why? Jan Philip Reemtsma posed a crucial question that may explain: "It takes more than quality to make a bestseller. A bestseller is a supply that meets a demand. What demand was that?"[4] Reemtsma was correct when he attributed the book's success to the German public's wish to know about the individual involvement of the everyman. However, if one examines the statements of members of the public,[5] this is only part of the answer. In Germany, the discourse about the Holocaust is part of a discourse about who we are. The basic question of any search for identity—"Who am I?"—carries a time index: "Who am I as the (grand)son or (grand)daughter of someone who may have been a Nazi?" And "What does this have to do with me today?"[6] Obviously, more than historical truth is at stake, and historians are not the only ones who grapple with the issue.

Wolfgang Benz has noted that a historian is successful if he or she meets the public's desire to be freed from the shadow of the past.[7] So the answer to Reemtsma's question is an existential one. Goldhagen managed to meet the public's wish to be reconciled with the past—as paradoxical as this may sound—precisely *through* his thesis of an eliminationist mind-set. For Goldhagen emphasized that Germany today is a different society—even a model society—from which eliminationist thinking has disappeared.[8] This twist of thought allowed people to experience a near-cathartic process of confession and reconciliation. They could confess that Germans had committed the most heinous crimes in the past and then find themselves absolved: "Yes, we are guilty. But the son of a survivor has acquitted us." Several problems arise, however, when one proposes this as a model for reconciling Germans with their own past.

When talking about the Holocaust, nobody will dispute the fact that the crimes of the past are unredeemable and unredeemed. But what kind of a situation does this leave for future generations? They experience a dissonance between a feeling of unfulfilled justice and a feeling of personal innocence: unfulfilled justice because our categories of crime and punishment crumble in the face of genocide; personal innocence because the crime happened before many of today's Germans were born. The members of Goldhagen's audience tried to find a way out of this dilemma by questioning their own innocence. The thesis of the eliminationist mind-set allowed people to identify with the crimes and await punishment. However, by claiming that contemporary Germans are different, Goldhagen in effect absolved them. Paul Ricoeur compares this to a political act of amnesty.[9] But an act of amnesty (when it is not the perpetrators and victims themselves who are involved) cannot bring forth reconciliation for two reasons: First, it actively forgets that the crime did indeed happen. This is a slap in the face not only to the victims who survived but also to those millions who did not. Second, it ignores the consequences of the past in the present, the fact that the past has left a mark on society. As will become clear, however, the past is never "past" in this sense.

Part Two: Reconciliation

Reconciliation through Escapism?

Bernhard Schlink's short story "The Circumcision" is about a young man and woman, Andi and Sarah, who love each other. It is an everyday story but a tragic one, for in the end, Andi leaves Sarah. Andi is a German exchange student in New York. Sarah is Jewish-American. Her aunt and uncle are Auschwitz survivors; other relatives were murdered.

> No difficult questions, no provocative remarks, no embarrassing allusions. Andi had not sensed that anyone expected him to feel any different than if he were Dutch or French or American: welcome, viewed with generous curiosity, and invited to take a curious look of his own at their family.
>
> But it wasn't easy. A wrong word, a false gesture—they might ruin everything. Was their generosity credible? Could he count on it? Might it not be recanted and withdrawn at any time? Didn't Uncle Josef and Aunt Leah have every reason to say their good-byes in a way that would make it clear they didn't want to see him again? Avoiding the wrong words and wrong gestures was stressful.[10]

Andi feels like a suspect: will people hold his being German against him? The conflict reaches a first climax when a former student of Sarah's talks about his year abroad in Germany: "Certain turns of phrase had often bothered him. Germans talked about 'Polish sloppiness' or said 'Jewish haste.' And when they did something to excess, they did it till they were 'gassed'" (p. 213). Andi's reaction is defensive:

> "I have no idea where that expression comes from. I would guess it's older than the Holocaust and either comes from the First World War or from suicide by gas. I haven't heard that in a long time. Nowadays you're more likely to do things 'till you drop,' or 'till you puke,' or 'till you're blue in the face.'". . .
>
> "When they've had enough of something, the Germans say they'll gas it? And what if they've had enough of other people?"
>
> Andi interrupted: "Till you can't do it any more—the phrase is about what you do when you can't go on. Till you vomit, because you can't eat

> anymore. Till you die, gas yourself, because you can't deal with life anymore. It's about yourself, not about what you do to other people." (Pp. 213–14)

When Sarah later asks him why he was so defensive, he cannot explain. What is it that tears Andi apart? Andi loves Germany. When he and Sarah take a trip to his hometown, he cannot stop showing her around. Yet the shadow of the Holocaust paralyzes him. The night before they visit the Buchenwald memorial, the conflict escalates. Andi's uncle claims that after fifty years, we should let the past be. Sarah is desperate when Andi tells her that things are not as simple as she thinks:

> "How complicated is it? The past has to be remembered, so that it's never repeated; it has to be remembered because the respect we owe the victims and their children demands it; both the Holocaust and the war were fifty years ago; whatever guilt the fathers and sons of those generations brought upon themselves, the generation of their grandchildren has nothing to feel guilty about; anyone who has to admit outside of Germany that he's from Oranienburg has it rough; teenagers become neo-Nazis because they've had enough of hearing about coming to terms with the past. And trying to deal with all of that doesn't seem simple to me." (P. 226)

Without noticing, Andi identifies the dilemma described earlier: the feeling of unfulfilled justice and its demand to remember the victims and his feeling of personal innocence. The conflict between the lovers boils down to Andi's remark, "I don't know whether I can handle being liked or loved *even though* I'm German" (p. 240, italics added).

Andi makes a desperate attempt to save their love: conversion. He wants to run away from being associated with Germany's past. So he asks his best friend, a surgeon, to circumcise him. But instead of gaining Sarah (who does not even notice), he loses the ground he stands on:

> He felt stranded, as if he had arrived where he didn't belong, as if the town and its landscape of mountains, rivers, and plain were no longer his home. The streets where he walked were full of memories. . . . He could paint the town with the brush of his memory and in the colours of his

> past happiness, of past hopes and past sadness. But it was different now, he couldn't enter into the picture. When his memories invited him in, when he tried to live in the unity of past and present that mean home, a little movement, an accidental touch of the change purse or key ring in his pants pocket would call up a very different memory—his circumcision and, as part of his circumcision, the question of where he belonged. (Pp. 250–51)

Schlink's story is an illustration of escapism as a model of reconciliation. If amnesty does not work, is escapism an option? The story shows us that it is not. Andi suffers from the dilemma of unfulfilled justice on the one hand and his personal innocence on the other hand, and he fools himself into believing that he can escape it. In the end he loses his home, his identity, and himself. And he gains neither love nor a new home.

II

So far two main points have been made: First, when talking about reconciliation *after* Auschwitz today, we are not talking about reconciliation between perpetrators and victims but between their descendants. Second, neither amnesty nor escapism provides an adequate model for the reconciliation process between persons not directly involved in the original historical events. At this point, after a few preliminary remarks, I shall show that reconciliation is an anthropological issue. My thesis is that reconciliation starts with the realization that reconciliation is impossible.

Paul Ricoeur argues that history poses a fundamental dilemma. On the one hand, the past is past. It is beyond our reach. On the other hand, argues Ricoeur, it is not an abstract idea but something that "has been" (p. 145). Historians may imagine themselves to be back in time; they may re-create the past as the present it once was. "Like us," says Ricoeur, "people in the past were the subjects of the initiative of hindsight and foresight. The epistemological consequences of these reflections are considerable. To know that people in the past had expectations, forebodings, wishes, apprehensions, and plans is to break through historical determinism; once history is viewed from hindsight, it takes on an element of contingency"

(p. 63). Thus the past is discovered as a context that was just as open as the present. As in the present, people in the past acted and through their acts shaped the context they lived in and the future that is now our present. Moreover, the past is discovered as a context in which people could not live up to their own expectations. The past is a "cemetery of broken promises," as Ricoeur states it (p. 65). Here we touch upon the second part of the dilemma: the past is present today.

Traces of the past characterize our present. If the promises of the past had been fulfilled, our present would look different. In thinking about our present, we therefore have to think about the past. We look at it from today's perspective. The past cannot be viewed as something located outside our own minds. It cannot be "owned" once and for all. We continuously re-create the past and its meaning. Thus, while the past is past, it is also present. Therefore the broken promises of the past can call upon us today to watch for the marks of the past in the present and to bear witness to them.

Let us review this concept in anthropological terms. Ricoeur argues that history approaches us even before we act within it, or better: before we react to it. In our very being, we are affected by history. Our being, however, is also constituted by the ability to act, that is, to respond to the situation we live in. These two aspects form the basis for Ricoeur's argument that past, present, and future are connected. We act in the present because we want to shape the way the world looks. But we do this in a context that carries the marks of the past—and against the background of the broken promises of earlier generations. The human being is therefore summoned to remember the past. Why? Because remembering is a condition of the possibility of acting responsibly toward the future. Memory is not identical with archival knowledge of the past. Its relation to the past is not ethically indifferent. Memory attributes meaning to the past in the light of a future that one can shape.

This dialectic and dialogical means of connecting past, present, and future abandons the idea that history is determined. It introduces a hermeneutic of (human) historicity and proposes what I would like to call *diachronic entanglement in history.* Diachronic entanglement refers to the idea that one is a person only within the contexts of living and acting in a concrete historical situation that is shaped by a past. Our acting is directed toward the future, but it cannot be detached from the past. Its relation to the past is not ethically indifferent; that is, although shaping the future takes precedence over looking back in time, looking back is a prerequisite for acting with a view toward the future.

So far I have proposed a precedence of the future over the past; there is also, however, the opposite movement: a precedence of the past over present and future. In this connection Ricoeur introduces the concept of guilt. Historical guilt radicalizes what has so far been said about history: "Guilt is the burden that the past places upon the future. Forgiveness wants to make this burden lighter. For the moment, however, the burdens weighs one down. Indeed, it burdens the future. Guilt obligates. If there is an obligation to remember, it is for the sake of the guilt that, in turning remembrance toward the future, situates it in the future in the truest sense of the word; that is, it sets it in the future tense: Thou shalt remember! Thou shalt not forget!" (p. 56). Guilt is a burden that the past places on the present. Its ethical claim cannot be overlooked. Guilt therefore demands to be remembered *as guilt.*

What does this mean in anthropological terms? We have already seen that human beings are diachronically entangled in history in that they are part of a historical context that is the result of actions in the past. In the case of a crime, however, what remains is not only the trace of the past but also the guilt and its demand to be remembered. Yet guilt is a personal category. It requires a responsible subject. Guilt cannot be shifted from one individual to another, let alone from one generation to another. While individuals can be held responsible for their own actions, nobody can be held responsible for somebody else. What remains is the feeling of unfulfilled justice.

After the Holocaust, the formation of German identity is faced with the problem of integrating a historical context that lays claim to the individual. It results in the dissonance between the feeling of unfulfilled justice and of personal innocence identified earlier in the analyses of Goldhagen and Schlink. The younger generation wants to shape the future, but it cannot and must not let go of a past that it cannot change. A consideration of the biblical story of Lot's flight from Sodom may help clarify the problem. Lot himself was not guilty of anything, yet the people of Sodom were. Lot was given a divine gift that cannot be overestimated:

the gift of being able to escape from an inherited past he could not change. Bernhard Schlink's story, however, teaches us that, unlike Lot, we do not have the option of escaping the dilemma we are faced with. Having to face the Holocaust, we run the risk of ending like Lot's wife, who looked back and turned into a pillar of salt.

III

Can there be reconciliation after Auschwitz? Germans today live in a historical context that carries the marks of the attempted murder of the entire Jewish people. While later generations cannot be held *responsible* for the crime itself, they cannot *escape* their own historical situation without losing their own identity (or not gaining one in the first place). Nothing will bring the dead of the Holocaust back to life. However, the victims look at us today, and they demand to be remembered. In the Holocaust, an entire people was deprived of its most basic human right: the right to live. The trace they left on German society is their absence.[11] Reconciliation is thus rendered impossible because such guilt cannot be atoned for. And mourning for those who affect us by their absence continues to be the only adequate answer.

Can this analysis be the last word on reconciliation? If is it, Germany's situation is tragic in the full sense of the word. For not only is there no way out of history; there is also no way beyond the Holocaust. But if there cannot be reconciliation *for* Auschwitz, can there be reconciliation *after* Auschwitz? I will try to show that while *no* is indeed *a last word* on reconciliation, it does not have to be *the only word.*

The hermeneutic of the historicity of the human condition has shown that while we are already affected by history, we are also free to act in the present. If we look through the eyes of the victims of Auschwitz, we see ourselves caught in the inescapable dilemma of unredeemable guilt and personal innocence. We cannot change the past, but we are responsible for the way we shape our future in and through our own historical situation. In a situation of inherited guilt, however, *is* there in fact a space in which it is possible for young Germans to act freely toward the future *without* escaping the past? In my encounter with the survivor in Israel, no such space was granted to me. In other words: Can we look back and *not* be paralyzed? Can we look back and *not* lose our ability to act?

Here Johann Baptist Metz's key sentence remains crucial: "As Christians today, we can never go back behind Auschwitz; beyond Auschwitz, however, we can go, no longer alone, but only with the victims of Auschwitz."[12] I propose to radicalize this sentence: "As Germans and as Christians today, we can never go back behind Auschwitz; beyond Auschwitz, however, we can go, but only with the (grand)children of the victims of Auschwitz." Why?

I stated above that while no is a last word on reconciliation, it might not be the only word. In terms of reconciliation after Auschwitz, then, there might be two dimensions of reconciliation. If it is possible to open up a new space in which the young generations on both sides can act toward the future in the light of the past, without being paralyzed by its shadow, then this might be characterized as a form of reconciliation. This reading of reconciliation does not mean that two who were set apart have now become one again. It means less and maybe more: the mutual recognition of the other's historical situation. We remain entangled in the same history—but in fundamentally different ways. Reconciliation after Auschwitz starts with the realization that reconciliation for Auschwitz is impossible. However, reconciliation might then lead to a new ability to act in this inescapable historical context.

This reading of reconciliation goes back to its biblical meaning, an inherited memory of both Christians and Jews that long precedes the Holocaust and might therefore function as a reference for both. God's grace offers reconciliation in order to supersede the circle of crime and punishment. Reconciliation is the gift of a new relationship between God and humankind and amongst humans, a new relationship in which covenantal action is possible again. It is also meant to be the model and standard of the social behavior of God's people (see, for example, Deuteronomy 6 and Leviticus 19:18). Reconciliation starts when the crimes of the fathers are not held against the children—and at the same time are not forgotten.

That is why we remain dependent on the (grand)children of the victims of the Holocaust. Reconciliation cannot be "made." Work toward reconciliation must start with the insight that we stand in need of forgiveness and with acts of asking forgiveness—acts that are more than lip service, acts that recognize the risk of being turned down.[13] It is, however, also dependent on an impulse from outside, an act of superseding the logic of crime and punishment. For Ricoeur, a condition of the possibility of reconciliation is a response from the side of the victim. It is a mode of forgiveness as an act of "active forgetting," which is neither amnesia nor escapism; a mode of forgiveness that does not simply balance out the scales. Says Ricoeur:

> Forgiveness is first of all the opposite of a passive forgetting, both in its traumatic form and in the perfidious aspect of escape. Therefore it imposes an additional cost on the "task of remembering." Nevertheless, as already indicated, forgiveness closely resembles a kind of active forgetting; in any case, it would not imply forgetting the events themselves, whose trace, on the contrary, is to be carefully preserved. Rather, forgiveness would imply forgetting the guilt, whose burden paralyzes both remembrance and the ability to draw upon perspectives for one's future in a creative manner. It is not the past event or the criminal act that is forgotten, but rather its significance and its place in the whole of the dialectic of historical consciousness. (P. 145)

Forgiveness as the impulse for reconciliation, however, can only be, in Ricoeur's terms, "difficult forgiveness": "Difficult forgiveness is the kind that takes seriously the tragedy of acting and is aimed at the preconditions of acting, at the sources of the conflict and the offense that needs to be pardoned" (p. 153).

Might this outlook open up the space we have been looking for, the space in which one can reach beyond the terror and act, or, in Richard von Weizsäcker's words, where there is a fresh start but no "zero hour"?[14] Does this perspective not then shed light upon reconciliation even though reconciliation remains impossible? If so, there are several requirements that must be met in order to give ground to reconciliation, both in Christian theology and in the wider German public:

1. Reconciliation requires acts of repentance, acts that recognize the marks of the past in the present. It requires a commitment to a self-

critical hermeneutic of suspicion regarding one's own tradition of thought. We must look for its victimizing elements and develop a hermeneutic of retrieval of a non-triumphalist Christian doctrine, as well as a commitment to a truly democratic society.

2. Reconciliation requires a commitment to redeem guilt that still is redeemable. Survivors must be compensated. Perpetrators must be held responsible. For Christian theology in Germany, it also means examining the role of the churches during the Nazi era and joining attempts to identify the victims of slave labor, denunciation, and collaboration, while at the same time honoring those who resisted.
3. Reconciliation requires a culture of remembrance that does not allow the victims of the past to be forgotten. Solidarity with the victims is solidarity in time and back in time.
4. Reconciliation requires the realization that it will never be achieved—and yet, it is driven by the hope (shared by Jews and Christians) that history is not unending but that the world we know carries the index of "limited time," as J. B. Metz puts it. At the end of time, universal reconciliation is possible only through an act of divine grace. And this hope in turn cannot be a cheap one. The question of theodicy in Christian theology after Auschwitz must play a crucial hermeneutical role.
5. Reconciliation requires ongoing dialogue between the groups that are entangled in the same historical context—in fundamentally different ways. Their diachronic entanglement also binds them together synchronically. Metz said that for theologians there is no way beyond Auschwitz without the victims of Auschwitz. We remain dependent on the support of today's Jewish community to help us reformulate our own beliefs.
6. Finally, reconciliation cannot be conceptualized in terms of before and after. Reconciliation for Auschwitz is impossible for humans. Therefore we have to wait for the "angel of history," to use Walter Benjamin's phrase, to return and rebuild the broken lives. Just as every new generation must find its own way of thinking about the past and acting toward the future, reconciliation is a process that demands continual attention, a process that is part of the construction of identity.

Forgiveness for Auschwitz is not attainable after Auschwitz. However, where (grand)children of perpetrators and (grand)children of victims accept the fact that there is no way out of their own history but that there are ways of acting within the present toward the future on account of the past—individually and collectively—this work will be the beginning of a reconciliation which as universal reconciliation can only be granted at the end of days.[15]

NOTES

1. The categories of victim, perpetrator, and bystander deserve to be discussed. While I find them helpful, they cannot be attributed to the (grand)children of victims or of perpetrators of Nazi crimes.

2. Daniel J. Goldhagen, *Hitler's Willing Executioners* (London: Little, Brown, 1996), p. 14.

3. See Michael Zank, "The Reception of Daniel Goldhagen's *Hitler's Willing Executioners* in Germany," *Religious Studies Review* 24 (1998): 231–40.

4. Jan Philip Reemtsma, "Abkehr vom Wunsch nach Verleugnung?" *Blätter für deutsche und internationale Politik* 42 (1997): 417. All translations are mine.

5. As laid down in a book edited by Goldhagen himself, *Briefe an Goldhagen: Eingeleitet und beantwortet von Daniel Jonah Goldhagen* (Berlin: Siedler, 1998).

6. The letters to Goldhagen show that these questions were indeed on the agenda, and that there were two groups of responses. The first group emphatically denounced the thesis as wrong. The other group thanked Goldhagen for the answer they "had been looking for so long" and that "none of the historians was willing to face."

7. See Wolfgang Benz, introduction to J. Heil and R. Erb, eds., *Geschichtswissenschaft und Öffentlichkeit: Der Streit um Daniel J. Goldhagen* (Frankfurt am Main: Fischer, 1998).

8. See Daniel J. Goldhagen, "Modell Bundesrepublik: National History, Democracy, and Internationalization in Germany," *Blätter für deutsche und internationale Politik* 42 (1997): 424–43.

9. Paul Ricoeur, *Das Rätsel der Vergangenheit: Erinnern—Vergessen—Verzeihen* (Göttingen: Wallstein Verlag, 2000), p. 145. Hereafter cited parenthetically.

10. Bernhard Schlink, "The Circumcision," in *Flights of Love,* trans. John E. Woods (New York: Pantheon, 2001), p. 198. Hereafter cited parenthetically.

11. This is one of the biggest challenges for education in Germany today. How can somebody experience an absence of something he or she has never known?

12. Johann Baptist Metz, *Jenseits bürgerlicher Religion: Reden über die Zukunft des Christentums* (Mainz: Grünewald, 1984), p. 31.

13. See Ricoeur, *Das Rätsel der Vergangenheit,* p. 145.

14. Richard von Weizsäcker, speech given during a commemorative ceremony in the plenary chamber of the German Bundestag, Bonn, May 8, 1985.

15. I want to thank Patricia Plovanich for her critical remarks and support in putting together these thoughts.

In Response to Britta Frede-Wenger

JUERGEN MANEMANN

TO CRITICIZE AN ESSAY is to praise it. In order to take up a critique of Britta Frede-Wenger's reflections, however, I must begin by explaining my understanding of her ideas. Frede-Wenger states her perspective and her intention: she addresses the matter of reconciliation from the perspective of a "German Christian" belonging to the third generation since the Holocaust. Thus she does not intend to talk about reconciliation between perpetrators and victims, but between the descendants of perpetrators and victims. This distinction is very important. But why does Frede-Wenger introduce herself in this context as a "German Christian," a term that the Nazi church movement used to define itself? Instead of adopting the term "German Christian," I would suggest that terms like "German citizen and Catholic" or "German citizen of the Christian faith" would be more appropriate.

At the beginning of her essay Frede-Wenger refers to Paul Ricoeur and makes the following presupposition: reconciliation has to be regarded as a kind of paradoxical phenomenon, which on the one hand "is and remains impossible" and on the other hand "must and can be worked on." After analyzing the Goldhagen debate in Germany from a social-psychological perspective and interpreting Bernhard Schlink's story "The Circumcision," she comes up with her first conclusion: a theology of reconciliation after Auschwitz has to refuse all amnesty and escapism. On the basis of these insights she arrives at reconciliation as an anthropological issue—and exactly at this point I would like to raise some critical questions about her theological remarks. From a philosophical-historical perspective we have to recognize that anthropology has to do with self-knowledge and that this kind of self-knowledge is focused in particular on the question of identity and the longing for it. Anthropology is a discipline that has often provided the individual with a sense of orientation and certainty in situations that are disorienting and uncertain. This has to be kept in mind as one looks at Frede-Wenger's method of developing a basis for a theology of reconciliation.

Frede-Wenger continues her line of thought by pointing out the interrelation between the present, the past, and the future. She says her intention is to look for a "dialectic and dialogical means of connecting past, present, and future." In this context she indicates that the past is established as an essential part of the future and that the present and the future are approached by the past. She then maintains that two things take precedence over the present: the past approaches the present before the present acts toward the past, and the future takes precedence over the look back in time. If this is indeed the case, I do not see why we need speak of a "dialectic and dialogical means of connecting past, present, and future." How can we label this approach "dialogical" if we are influenced by the past before reacting to it, and how can we invite the past into a "dialogue" if the past is itself finished? For if the past is finished, then the persons living in the fading present are no longer co-subjects in the dialogical process. In that case, we must assume a very radical stance toward the monological structure of the hermeneutic process of engaging the past. Through the analysis of this structure we become aware of its violent character, which might lead us to silence the past. Therefore those who have been lost are in need of advocates who make their memories endure, who stand up for the most obscure of all classes: the victims. Hermeneutics has to be worked out as what has been called a "democracy of the dead."

Next Frede-Wenger deals with the precedence of the past in the context of guilt: Guilt, she says, "is a burden that the past places on the present." And she concludes that guilt "demands to be remembered as guilt." However, she emphasizes, since guilt is a personal category, our presence is not characterized by guilt but by the "feeling of unfulfilled justice." But what does this mean for the younger generations? This connection seems to me very important, and I would like to encourage Frede-Wenger to explain this transformation of guilt into the feeling of unfulfilled justice. If this includes the necessity for the descendants to transform the guilt of the grandparents and parents into responsibility, I would agree with her. But what does reconciliation between the descendants mean if it does not have to do with guilt?

From my perspective Frede-Wenger's anthropological understanding of reconciliation focuses too much on questions of identity, so that it runs the danger of repressing an overwhelming cruelty like Auschwitz. Perhaps a theology of reconciliation has to focus more on the nonidentical. As Lévinas states, "nearly every causality is in this sense violent: the fabrication of a thing, the satisfaction of a need, the desire and even the knowledge of an object."[1] He also writes about the necessity of the memory of Auschwitz: "Forgetfulness is the law, happiness and condition of life. But here life is wrong."[2] Frede-Wenger seems to build a wall between the ancestors and the descendants in order to shelter the younger generation from despair—at the expense of the memory of the victims. If this is the case, she runs the risk of creating an attitude of indifference despite her intentions. And then we would be in danger of excluding Auschwitz from history, because as Hegel has stated, "For what is solely negative is in itself dull and insipid and therefore either leaves us empty or repels us."[3] We are consciously connected with the past because it provides us with meaning, but the negative has no meaning; it does not push history forward in a positive sense. Could Auschwitz, then, be defined as a "cemetery of broken promises" (as Frede-Wenger quotes Ricoeur)?

At this point Frede-Wenger explains that reconciliation "starts when the crimes of the fathers are not held against the children—and at the same time are not forgotten." This is true, but does she not undermine the imperative not to forget if she concentrates so much on saving the identity of the descendants? It is understandable and perhaps necessary from a psychological perspective, but a theology of reconciliation should not be satisfied with a merely psychological perspective. Frede-Wenger seems to work out a process of reconciliation based on notions of uninjured intersubjectivity, which in turn is based on the reciprocity of a hermeneutic of free recognition. For me, a process of reconciliation is not only based on such an understanding of intersubjectivity but also on the *memoria passionis,* which resists the reconstruction of life by a discursive rationality and its reciprocity. From my perspective, the theology of reconciliation calls for a new grammar, one that leads to a liberation of the nonidentical. The aim of a reconciled society, then, would be a plurality of differences without anxiety. The memory of suffering implies the demand to focus on an unintentional truth. "What transcends the dominant society," Adorno explains, "are not only the historical laws of motion that have developed from a given potentiality but also what has not genuinely been transformed into such laws of motion."[4] And the "idea" of reconciliation might serve as such a possibility of transcendence.

According to Frede-Wenger, reconciliation cannot be "made." I agree completely, and I think this is one of the most important insights for a theology of reconciliation. But, in a favorable reference to Ricoeur, she writes, "A condition of the possibility of reconciliation is a response from the side of the victim," and here she runs the risk of forcing the victim into the anguished position of being morally compelled to forgive, lest the victim be held responsible for disturbing the future of the descendants. Can there be reconciliation without forgiveness? Yes, I think so, but not universal reconciliation. Here we are challenged by another crucial point of Frede-Wenger's reflections: what does "universal reconciliation" mean in the context of her concept? *Apokatastasis?* Should we regard reconciliation as a process we could continuously work on or do we have to regard it as an interruption of our practice? Universal reconciliation runs the risk of becoming a reconciliation without justice, and such a concept of reconciliation would be a devaluation of human suffering.

Finally, referring to Walter Benjamin, Frede-Wenger transforms the "angel of history" into the Messiah, who returns in order to restore what has been demolished. I would recommend against drawing on a Christian perspective and thus transforming the tragic figure of this angel into a returning Jesus Christ. Reconciliation is a hope, which has to be expressed as a negative theology because, as Benjamin has stated, "[H]ope is given to us for the sake of the hopeless."[5]

NOTES

1. Emmanuel Lévinas, *Difficult Freedom: Essays on Judaism,* trans. Seàn Hand (Baltimore: Johns Hopkins University Press, 1990), p. 6.

2. Ibid., p. 149.

3. G. W. F. Hegel, *Vorlesungen über die Ästhetik,* vol. 1 (Frankfurt am Main: Suhrkamp Verlag, 1975), p. 288.

4. Theodor W. Adorno, "Zu Subjekt und Objekt," in *Gesammelte Schriften,* vol. 10 (Frankfurt am Main: Suhrkamp Verlag, 1977), p. 743.

5. Walter Benjamin, "Goethes Wahlverwandtschaften," in *Gesammelte Schriften,* ed. R. Tiedemann and H. Schweppenhäuser, vol. 1, pt. 2 (Frankfurt am Main: Suhrkamp Verlag, 1980), p. 202.

In Response to Britta Frede-Wenger

DIDIER POLLEFEYT

IN HER ESSAY Britta Frede-Wenger contends that after Auschwitz, reconciliation is a matter between the heirs of perpetrators and victims. This insight is crucial for all thinking on reconciliation after Auschwitz. However, I would like to question the sharp distinction that she, as a young postwar German, draws between perpetrators and their heirs, and especially between the "feeling of personal innocence" and the "feeling of unfulfilled justice" in postwar Germany. I think the depth of this distinction determines the conclusion of her essay, namely that reconciliation remains impossible and at the same time must *and can* be worked on, a conclusion that is in my view a not very operative *contradictio in terminis.*

Frede-Wenger argues that guilt cannot be shifted from one individual to another, let alone from one generation to another. "What remains," she says, "is the feeling of unfulfilled justice" and a personal feeling of innocence. I believe the relation between the individual and the history of his or her community is much more complex. In the opening paragraph, Frede-Wenger relates the story of a survivor who told her that she hates Germans, "even the young ones." Of course, the survivor's statement is understandable due to the immense trauma inflicted upon her, but it is not acceptable from a rational and moral point of view because it risks reproducing the hatred that resulted from the trauma. The statement also reveals that the relation between postwar individuals and their communities is much more complicated than the distinction between (feelings of) individual innocence and unfulfilled justice suggests. I would argue that it is not so illogical and incomprehensible that the heirs of the victims see the descendants of the perpetrators in the light of the crimes of their ancestors. Recognizing and understanding this reality seems to me to be a necessary condition for making reconciliation a real possibility.

Frede-Wenger maintains that the Holocaust has consequences in the present and for the present generation. I would like to make an analogy to reveal the implications of this statement. As a Belgian, I am a citizen of a country that has a history of colonization in Africa. Of course, as an individual, I do not bear the whole guilt for the evil of my colonial ancestors. I cannot be identified with their colonial crimes, but I still participate in some way in the historical guilt for colonization, since I enjoy economic or political benefits, for example, that resulted from the Belgian exploitation of Africa. And even if today I pay for a portion of the exploitation (through my tax bill, for instance, or by developing cooperation with Africa), I can never again totally restore the balance between my country and Africa. It is not abnormal for the victims of this past to see the descendants of the colonial perpetrators as the representatives of this past. And it is not surprising that the descendants of the perpetrators would also like to be forgiven (after repentance) and to be reconciled even after financial restitution has been made.

From my Christian perspective, this situation reflects the theological concept of original sin. Original sin is not just a theoretical idea referring to a mythological past but is the fact that, as an individual, I am immediately and inevitably contaminated by evil—not by evil *in abstracto,* but by very concrete forms of evil, both on an interpersonal level (as in the case of an unfair inheritance in my family) and on a collective level (as in the case of the racist policies of my country). The state of original sin is not due to my intentional faults but to my concrete existence.

Of course, my personal guilt for this evil is rather small. Sometimes it is a "complicity after the fact," as, for instance, in the case of a (Catholic) professor of medicine doing research on the tissue of an aborted human fetus. This professor discovers himself to be placed in a world where even contributing to good can for him no longer be separated from the evil that it presupposes. It is not very pleasant to recognize this contamination by evil. Nevertheless, it is crucial to see that one is involved in the history of evil; the integration of this idea into one's existence is equally crucial for taking responsibility for the future. In this connection, we see how Jewish-Christian dialogue has grown immensely from the moment that Christians recognized their guilt for the Holocaust.

For processes of reconciliation it is important that people (both perpetrators and victims) first recognize this contamination of our personal existence by concrete forms of evil. For me as a Christian, that evil is Auschwitz; as a Belgian, it is colonization, environmental pollution, and so on; as a male, it is discrimination against women; as a white person, it is racism. If we start with just the idea of "personal innocence," then the question of forgiveness and reconciliation between the heirs of perpetrators and victims has no raison d'être.

One could argue that descendants can break with their past. However, in his book *Invisible Loyalties,* the psychotherapist Ivan Boszormenyi-Nagy has demonstrated how difficult it is to break with one's past and how complex ties persist from generation to generation.[1] Focusing on families in which severe forms of abuse have occurred, he shows that we cannot understand the behavior of children in such families if we do not see the "invisible loyalties" that continue to exist between children and their abusive parents, even when the children recognize and condemn the abuse. Children of abusive parents cannot free themselves from the legacy of their parents, and—as sociological research shows—run a greater risk of continuing the abuse than do children who were not abused. In the view of Boszormenyi-Nagy, these invisible loyalties should be recognized so that children can eventually exonerate their parents for the difficult legacy they received from them.[2] In Boszormenyi-Nagy's terms, "legacy" signifies not only the "heritage" children receive from their parents but also the mandate to ameliorate the past and to take responsibility for the future. The German nation, with all its history, belongs to German identity. One can try to escape that identity by converting to Judaism, that is, by identifying with the victims, but then one risks losing one's identity, as happened in the story of Andi.

At this point I would like to challenge Frede-Wenger's claim that Goldhagen's book absolves contemporary Germans of the crimes committed by their parents, grandparents, or even great-grandparents and thus frees them from the shadow of the past. Even if Goldhagen denies it himself, his study is permeated by a generalizing approach to "the Germans" and "German responsibility." Goldhagen "leaves evil in Germany," which explains for me the resistance to the book there, as well as the success of it in countries such as Belgium.[3]

As for "personal innocence," Frede-Wenger argues in favor of it but also thinks that reconciliation is impossible because of "unfulfilled justice." She uses the idea of Paul Ricoeur that the past is past, beyond our reach, even if it influences our present. Of course, the past is irreversible. But if forgiveness and reconciliation would require undoing the past, then they are indeed and forever impossible. Forgiveness and reconciliation are not the same as removing the evil events of the past. On the contrary, their traces should be kept and remembered. Forgiveness and reconciliation have to do with the way perpetrators and victims, as well as their heirs, *relate* to the evil events of the past and to each other. If forgiveness and reconciliation are expected to reverse history, which is impossible, one should not be surprised that people dare not look back, because they are afraid they will turn into pillars of salt.

There are different ways to relate to evil events, even as descendants of perpetrators. Inherited guilt is not the same as innate guilt. Original sin is not a *fatum* but a human condition that must be dealt with creatively and responsibly. Forgiveness and reconciliation are means of dealing with history in a way that does not paralyze us, as happened with Andi. Forgiveness and reconciliation happen when the victims and their heirs give the perpetrators and their heirs the room to deal in a constructive way with their crimes, and when the perpetrators and their heirs have a positive and constructive attitude toward the victim and confess their complicity in the evil. Forgiveness and reconciliation refuse the dilemma created by the irreversibility of evil. They affirm that evil cannot be reversed, but the contamination by evil of relations and attitudes can—not by escaping or forgetting the facts, but by transcending them: beyond Auschwitz, but not without Auschwitz. In this way, forgiveness and reconciliation create a space where it becomes possible for young Germans to move freely toward the future without escaping the past.

An important aspect Frede-Wenger does not deal with is the role of the victim. The victim is absent in her description of the preconditions of reconciliation. If the perpetrators or their heirs give up their innocence and make themselves vulnerable for their evil history, the victims should be willing to take the hands of the perpetrators and their heirs. Are the perpetrators and their heirs prepared to take the risk, or do they choose the safer option of "personal innocence" and "unrealizable justice"? I understand that the story told about the meeting between a young German and a survivor is not very encouraging for taking such a risk. From that perspective, even if reconciliation is an anthropological category, as Frede-Wenger correctly argues, it cannot be understood outside a religious background. When, after terrible events, people extend a hand to each other and thus open a space for the future, this cannot be understood in terms of biological, psychological, or social interaction. It is no more and no less than a miracle.

NOTES

1. See Ivan Boszormenyi-Nagy and Geraldine M. Spark, *Invisible Loyalties: Reciprocity in Intergenerational Family Therapy* (New York: Harper & Row, 1973).

2. See Annemie Dillen, "Vergeving of exoneratie? Kritische kanttekeningen vanuit en bij de theorie van Ivan Boszormenyi-Nagy," *Tijdschrift voor theologie,* no. 1 (2001): 61–84.

3. See Didier Pollefeyt and G. Jan Colijn, "Leaving Evil in Germany: The Questionable Success of Goldhagen in the Low Countries," in Franklin H.

Littell, ed., *Hyping the Holocaust: Scholars Answer Goldhagen* (New York: Cummings & Hathaway, 1997), pp. 1–18.

In Response to Juergen Manemann and Didier Pollefeyt

BRITTA FREDE-WENGER

DIDIER POLLEFEYT AND Juergen Manemann have shown me how much there is to learn when people engage in discussion. They have tested my thoughts and have identified some hidden dangers. But at times I was also misunderstood.

Let me begin by going straight to what needs the most attention. Both Pollefeyt and Manemann look for the role of the victim in my remarks and find it wanting. Manemann writes, "[T]hose who have been lost are in need of advocates who make their memories endure." He sees the lack of advocates in my essay as being grounded in my alleged attempt to "build a wall between the ancestors and the descendants." Pollefeyt argues along the same lines and criticizes my "sharp distinction" between "perpetrators and their heirs." He accuses me of opting for "personal innocence." If this were my intention, he would be absolutely correct in arguing that any "reconciliation between the heirs of perpetrators and victims has no *raison d'être.*" This, however, is not the case.

I believe that any talk of reconciliation requires a close look at who the participants are. It is and should be beyond doubt that the victims are at the center of the attention and that it is necessary, as Manemann writes in his contribution to this volume, to "rub history against the grain." This means, however, that we have to talk *not only* about the victims. The question is, Whom do we see when we try to look through the eyes of the victims? As Christians and as Germans today we see a third and fourth generation of people born after 1945. For this reason, I have opted to focus on the *heirs* of the perpetrators. Does this mean silencing the victims? Does this result in disconnecting the heirs of the perpetrators from the context of a historical guilt? I cannot see that as a necessary outcome. On the contrary, I believe it is necessary to distinguish the heirs from the perpetrators in order to show that the heirs *are* connected to the crimes of their forefathers and are summoned to remember the victims.

This distinction allows me to describe the dilemma in which later generations find themselves. If there were no connection between past and present, there would be no dilemma. The heirs are connected to and affected by a past that they cannot influence. This situation I describe as one of "unfulfilled justice"; perhaps I should clarify it as "consequences of unjustified and unredeemed suffering"—concrete suffering inflicted by my people before I was alive. And I find myself faced with people like the survivor I met in Israel, who are indeed "not so illogical and incomprehensible" if they look at me "in the light of the crimes of [my] ancestors" (Pollefeyt). Both "unfulfilled justice" and "personal innocence" (not "of Germany" but of individual Germans) in my argument should be read as "with regard to the crimes of Nazi Germany."

This is my analytical *starting* point. I do focus on the question of identity, but not in order to "save the identity of the descendant" from despair (Manemann), since there is no identity to *save* yet. The question is how to *gain* an identity that knows despair and transcends it. To me, identity means the ability to actively shape the future of myself and my society. In choosing my examples, I wanted to make clear that opting for "personal innocence," as Andi tried to do, is not an option. On the other hand, identifying with the crime and then calling for amnesty results in amnesia with regard to a crime that must never be forgotten.[1]

How does the past play into the successful formation of identity for the heirs of the perpetrators? According to Ricoeur, past, present, and future approach each other in a dialectical movement. Living in a historical context, we ask ourselves, Why is the world the way it appears to be? Therefore, while I am interested in shaping the future, I turn toward the past and find myself connected to a historical context that "has become." Humankind is affected by and diachronically entangled in history. Looking at the concrete German context, I have to realize that I am "diachronically entangled" in a history of unspeakable crimes. Pollefeyt describes the same situation when he demands that people "recognize this contamination of our personal existence . . . by very concrete forms of evil." Pollefeyt himself concedes that "'personal guilt' for this evil is rather small." The only difference I see between this and my concept of personal innocence with regard to Auschwitz is that Pollefeyt sees the human being as *acting* in his or her historical context, while I concentrate (perhaps wrongly) on identity formation as a cognitive process.

So while personal guilt cannot be shifted—I cannot be held guilty for the crimes of the SS men at their desks, in the camps, and on the streets, or for the church leaders' crimes of silence and omission—as a German and as a Christian I do partake in the historical guilt that my society grew out of. Pollefeyt applies the concept of original sin to this situation. *Original sin* is used here as a cover term for structural and historical sin that *in concreto* differs from society to society. While this is a valuable interpretation, it is not without its traps. *Original sin* is a term that (in both inter-Christian and interreligious discussion) is heavily loaded and prone to being misunderstood. What if one argued against Pollefeyt that the Catholic Church teaches that baptism fully cleanses one of original sin? At this point, further explanation is necessary.

If identity formation requires me to take the historical context seriously in order to be able to move toward the future, then this search must result in an honest attempt to face the crimes of my ancestors and to realize that I am a priori affected by them. Not, however, because I have to take their guilt upon myself, but because I cannot and must not flee from the consequences of this past event for me as a person and as a member of a society or a religion. Of course, this means breaking with invisible loyalties to one's (grand)parents, but I would be careful not to limit the descendants to pathological phenomena. If this were the only option, history would be *determined* to repeat itself. While a total break with the past is not possible, the interruption of the vicious circle of violence is. Here lies the hinge between unfulfilled justice and responsibility.

Where are the advocates for the victims? And isn't my thinking in danger of repressing the overwhelming cruelty of Auschwitz (Manemann)? These are serious questions. However, if one takes the dialectic between past, present, and future seriously, one should be able to avoid this danger. So far I have defended the present subject's look back into history. Such a look back is always guided by a perspective: it *applies* meaning to the past, that is, it *interprets.* "It is not possible to 'write history' without also 'creating a story.'"[2] The past, however, cannot be "had" once and for all.

The ultimate danger lies in forgetting that Auschwitz *continues to resist* any integration. Any meaning we apply to it will be questioned. This is the past's precedence over present and future. Many survivors have related their attempts to describe Auschwitz—and their ultimate silence. Where people claim to have understood the Shoah, Auschwitz is forgotten: "Yesterday, they said, 'Auschwitz? What's that?' Today, they say, 'Auschwitz? I know.'" Auschwitz is and remains beyond comprehension. Therefore, identity after Auschwitz will remain nonidentical. The victims remain at the center. I must listen to the victim *and* to the historian: that is why the dialectic between present, past, and future is also dialogical. I will continue to be disturbed—and yet I must also remember who I am, and what my task is: "to make sure in my thought and actions that Auschwitz not be repeated, that nothing similar happen."[3]

In this context I introduce my anthropological reading of reconciliation. Auschwitz is overwhelming; nothing can undo it. What must be undone is its paralyzing effect on future generations. How can I (from a German and Christian perspective) remember what my people did and not lose the ground I stand on? This is not only a question of Holocaust remembrance, it is a question of identity formation and as such is anthropological. It is indeed a question of how the heirs of both perpetrators and victims "relate to this past and to each other" (Pollefeyt). Where is the space in which we can act according to Adorno's dictum? The opening up of this space is what I call the beginning of reconciliation. It happens when, to quote my main essay, the crimes of the fathers are not held against the children—and at the same time are not forgotten. And it cannot be achieved by one side alone. This is not a functionalization of the victims or their heirs, but a radicalization of the Holocaust's legacy. Reconciliation cannot be "made": in reaching out to the victim, I must run the risk of being turned down, I must make myself vulnerable. And if the miracle occurs and "the victims should be willing to take the hands of the perpetrators and their heirs" (Pollefeyt), this does *not* constitute "uninjured intersubjectivity" (Manemann). For this very reason, Ricoeur calls it "*difficult* forgiveness" and he argues that it will lead to more, rather than less, remembrance.

Manemann accuses me of suggesting *apokatastasis.* It is impossible to speak of universal salvation "in the presence of the burning children," to quote Irving Greenberg (see Henry Knight's essay). Universal reconciliation can *only* be spoken of as a *hope,* not as a claim, not as a belief. If individual reconciliation runs the risk of failing, how much more so does universal reconciliation! And if reconciliation between individuals in this world cannot be based on amnesia, neither is universal reconciliation thinkable without justice. But can we work toward reconciliation in this world *without* hoping for the miracle of reconciliation in the world to come?

Pollefeyt and Manemann have pointed out problems in my essay. Therefore I want to close with a question myself. Manemann has spotted a faux pas: I introduced myself as a "German Christian." This phrase carries associations that I did not intend to convey. It reveals one mark of the past in the present: language has lost its innocence. Does this translate? I have been puzzled many times by Americans speaking about "race," "race relations," "selection," "leaders," and so on, as if they were the most natural things in the world. They are not.

NOTES

1. Like Pollefeyt, I do not see Goldhagen "forgiving" Germans *in his book.* However, his spoken rhetoric allowed his German audience to understand him that way, which made a pseudocathartic process possible. The book (perhaps for this very reason) was an incredible success in Germany. According to figures I received from Goldhagen's publishing house (Siedler Verlag), several hundred thousand German copies have been sold.

2. Ricoeur, *Das Rätsel der Vergangenheit,* p. 67.

3. Theodor W. Adorno, *Negative Dialektik* (Frankfurt am Main: Suhrkamp Verlag, 1966), p. 358.

6

Struggles for Recognition in an Era of Globalization

The Necessity of a Theology of Reconciliation from a Political-Theological Perspective after Auschwitz

JUERGEN MANEMANN

EVERY THEOLOGY IS a political theology because theology is deeply steeped in political meaning, and all religious thought and behavior is subject to political analysis. We can say that theology is "transcendental politics." A Christian theology after Auschwitz needs to be aware of the harm and danger theology has caused in history. Because it is seriously challenged by history and society and vice versa, Christian theology is not a kind of metaphysics. In fact, for Christian theology there is no world history with salvation history after or above it. From a Christian standpoint, the history of salvation *is* world history *(Weltgeschichte)*.[1] Every way of distancing ourselves from this history, from our society, and from the suffering of others produces the danger of creating idols instead of speaking of God.

On the basis of these insights we can conclude that theologians have several primary duties, duties that Cornel West has outlined.[2] First, there has to be a radical transition from system concepts to subject concepts. Second, theology must have the capacity to provide a broad and deep analytical grasp of the present in light of the past. Third, theology must protect narratives, and in order to protect narratives theologians have to "rub against the grain of history," as Walter Benjamin states it.[3] Fourth, we have to criticize every act of distancing ourselves from the suffering of others. In the words of Theodor Adorno, "[T]he need to lend a voice to suffering is the condition of all truth," that is, unless we can hear the voices of those who suffer, we are deaf to the voice of truth.[4] This does not mean that those who suffer have a monopoly on truth, but it does mean that if truth is to emerge, it must be in tune with those who were and who are in misery. Fifth, we have to sustain "hope for the sake of the hopeless."[5] Sixth, we must track hypocrisy, which accentuates the gap between principles and practice. The purpose of this essay is to explore the logic of reconciliation as recognition and the non-logic of forgiveness within this framework.

RECONCILIATION AND FORGIVENESS

A theology of reconciliation and forgiveness has to be worked out as a theology that is unable to distance itself from the suffering of others. This has to be taken into account when one raises the question of how to speak about reconciliation, forgiveness, and justice after Auschwitz.

First of all, it is necessary to diagnose the current situation. Speaking of reconciliation and forgiveness today, we are confronted not only with a first guilt, the deeds of the perpetrators, but also with a "second guilt," as Ralph Giordano describes it: the inability to take responsibility for what has happened.[6] Are we allowed to speak of reconciliation and forgiveness in such a situation? Not only are we allowed to speak of reconciliation and forgiveness; we are obligated to do so if we can show that a theology of reconciliation and forgiveness has the power to rub against the grain of history. Therefore we first have to change our perspective.

A precondition for becoming an individual is a capacity for becoming guilty as a person. Thus it is first of all necessary to recognize that the origin of subjectivity has to do with breaking through the mythical-genealogical relationship between guilt and atonement. Consider the words of the prophet Ezekiel: "Why do you keep repeating this proverb in the land of Israel: 'The parents have eaten unripe grapes; and the children's teeth are set on edge?' As I live—declares the Lord Yahweh—you will have no further cause to repeat this proverb in Israel. Behold: all life belongs to me. . . . The one who has sinned is the one to die" (Ezekiel 18:2–4). Here we face a breakthrough in the collective guilt that gives rise to the individual. Ezekiel continues: "Throw away all your acts of rebellion against me, and you will get yourselves a new heart, a new spirit" (Ezekiel 18:31). To sum up: the human being becomes an individual through the perception of his own sin, and he becomes an I through the power of creating within himself a new heart and a new spirit.[7] Becoming a subject means being responsible. Recognizing sin as my sin is a matter not just of taking on a burden but also of acquiring an ability that forces me to become a subject. This has to be taken into consideration when speaking of reconciliation, forgiveness, and justice. Feeling guilty has to do with recognition because it is at the same time a recognition of oneself as a moral agent.

Both remembrance and forgetting are the secrets of reconciliation. Remembrance is a precondition of reconciliation because it is the counterforce of repression, and reconciliation begins where repression ends. Reconciliation has to do with recognition. We all need recognition, which is why we fight for recognition for the sake of self-confidence, self-respect, and self-esteem. We speak of physical injury as a moral injustice when the afflicted person sees this physical injury as the result of an act that has no regard for his or her self-understanding. Identity is based not on the negation but on the recognition of the other, as well as on being recognized by the other. This struggle for recognition takes part in a symmetrical manner. It is an expression of reciprocity. Reconciliation as recognition is not a kind of appeasement policy that avoids conflict. Such an understanding of reconciliation amounts to a misunderstanding. An ability to reconcile is, in the first instance, an ability to act from within a reciprocal recognition. In such a situation the victim regains his or her sovereignty. Through reconciliation the victim becomes a subject, and the perpetrator becomes an I, in Ezekiel's sense, by admitting his guilt and repenting. Without repentance, reconciliation and forgiveness end up as "cheap grace" and serve as nothing more than an "opiate of the masses." Here reconciliation means *katallage,* a secular term referring to the restoration of harmony in a disturbed relationship between human beings. From a moral point of view, *katallage* is a first step toward recognition: it is a reciprocal recognition between subjects.

Apart from *katallage,* forgiveness has no logic. Here the victim is the only subject of the process. Forgiveness is a giving. Through forgiveness the perpetrator is offered the opportunity to change, to become another. Before continuing these thoughts, however, we must ask, Who raises the question of forgiveness for Auschwitz? Why do we expect the murderers to want forgiveness? Is forgiveness dependent on the response of the one to be forgiven? Is it our duty to forgive others regardless of whether or not they accept their forgiveness or even desire it? Of course, Jesus was willing to forgive those who were crucifying him, even though they did not ask for forgiveness. But did Jesus speak to mass murderers? Jesus never said that every victim has to act in the same manner. His act is not a critique of victims who cannot forgive, but a radical questioning and interruption of the powers that rule the world.

Forgiveness is not a matter of bartering. Such an understanding of forgiveness amounts to viewing it as a financial transaction. Forgiveness should be understood as an expression of a hyperbolic ethics, as an ethics beyond ethics. Forgiveness is the utopia that arises from a process of reconciliation; as such, it is part of an apocalyptic vision of reconciliation, a fragment of a new world within this world. Thus forgiveness does not mean having spiritual investments in the world and history as they are. On the contrary, there is no limit or measure for forgiveness.[8] Because forgiveness simply is, it is not tied to ends; nor should it be regarded as normal or normative or as a return to normalcy. Its role in the process of reconciliation is not merely therapeutic. Rather, inasmuch as it is an attempt at reaching the impossible, forgiveness is an exception.

Does forgiveness, then, exist only where there is something unforgivable? Yes. That is what makes forgiveness something impossible to achieve. This impossibility can come into existence only if one does the impossible. Reconciliation initially follows a certain logic, whereas forgiveness has no "logic"—it is interruption and incalculability. Forgiveness is independent of justice. Although a perpetrator has to be judged, the victim nevertheless might forgive him. So forgiveness is not necessarily connected with amnesty. With reconciliation the victim gains back his or her sovereignty, but with forgiveness we are challenged by an unconditional act that renounces sovereignty. In addition to being a form of giving, forgiveness has to do with a certain kind of forgetting. It is what Paul Ricoeur refers to as "active forgetting," which does not mean that history is forgotten but that its meaning for the present and future is remembered.[9] Forgiveness, as David Blumenthal has noted, indicates that the crime remains, that it cannot be forgotten, but that the debt is forgotten.[10] The atrocious past will be overtaken and at the same time it will become the immemorial, which makes it the unforgettable.[11]

The highest expression of reconciliation is substitution. Lévinas wrote, "No one, not even God, can substitute himself for the victim."[12] Here we realize that the content of Christology is irrevocably challenged. Substitution in this context is a category reserved for the victim—not for others. But at this point we have to emphasize that substitution is not to be understood as an imperative. What does substitution mean? According to Lévinas, it is "an expression of the most active activity in the most passive passivity."[13] Substitution means that one takes more responsibility upon oneself: "Father, forgive them for they know not what they do" (Luke 23:34). Facing this outcry of Jesus, we have to remember that this begging for forgiveness was absent in important Christian manuscripts. Did Christians regard it as disturbing, especially during the later attacks against the Jews? To invoke forgiveness from a Christological point of view is to face the subversive content of this cry. At the same time, this cry has to be heard together with another cry of Jesus: "My God! My God! Why have you forsaken me?" (Matthew 27:46). Both belong together: the cry for justice and forgiveness.[14]

At this point one comes up against the limits of a Christian affirmation. Could such a theory of substitution and forgiveness be applied to Auschwitz? Would this not have to be formulated as "Father, forgive them not, for they do know what they are doing!"? A victim praying in this way, who will never reach the level of reconciliation as forgiveness, does not act in a way that is morally wrong. As Blumenthal has argued, a victim is not obliged, nor is it morally necessary, for him or her to forgive.[15]

Forgiveness is not a principle subject to calculation.[16] Forgiveness is grace, and grace is something we receive without justification. Christians, says Eugene Fisher, "can, as established by evidence of changed teachings and changed behavior, repent and work toward mutual reconciliation with Jews. But [they] have no right to put Jewish survivors in the impossible moral position of offering forgiveness, implicitly, in the name of the six million. . . .

Placing a Jew in this anguished position further victimizes him or her."[17] Hubert Locke's statement should also be mentioned: "If God was silent, dare any of us to speak?"[18] Why should we answer this question of forgiveness when not even God knows the answer (see the book of Jonah)? Only a theology that resists forgiving the unforgivable can become a theology of reconciliation in the future. But such a reconciliation might lead dialectically to another understanding of forgiveness.

THE UNENCUMBERED SELF IN A POST-TRADITIONAL SOCIETY

Inasmuch as it is concentrated on this world and on the actions of people, any theology of reconciliation is deeply political. Its political interest lies in building up a community of people who live together. Because it would force society to transform itself into a more just society, there is a certain subversive element in the non-ontological dimensions of a theology of reconciliation.

Addressing the meaning of reconciliation in our context, we first have to face the fact that our society has changed significantly. Some intellectuals claim that we are entering a new stage of modernity, which they refer to as a *second modernity.* This second modernity is characterized by globalization, individualization, and societies without employment crises and ecological crises. Ulrich Beck, a sociologist from the University of Munich, is the head of a group that works on the so-called second modernity project. Beck and his colleagues do not merely diagnose the risks and crises of the second modernity in a negative way; their intention is to open our eyes to the potential for new freedom.

According to Beck, two occurrences have signaled a second modernity: the nuclear crisis at Chernobyl and the collapse of the Berlin Wall. Both call our rationality into question. Both undermine the foundation of our thinking. Both confront us in a radical way with an incalculability that introduces uncertainty and ambivalence into the heart of contemporary institutions, practices, and discourses. Beck states that the centrality of incalculability, uncertainty, and ambivalence heralds the emergence of a new stage of society, which he calls *reflexive modernity.* Because of this radical uncertainty nothing can go unchallenged. In the context of his analysis of the second modernity, Beck points out the end of traditions and proclaims his vision of an unencumbered self.[19]

A society that emerges in the era of the second modernity is a society ridden with an uncertainty that fundamentally defines a post-traditional society. A post-traditional society, as Beck points out, is a society that is no longer based on traditions but on the knowledge of experts. Today Beck celebrates the shift from a traditional to a so-called post-traditional society as progress, because tradition is labeled with negative words like *authority, obedience,* and *circularity;* the liberation from tradition in general, on the other hand, is described with words like *freedom, emancipation, dialogue,* and so on. Indeed, the post-traditional stage of society appears to be the endpoint of the bourgeois emancipation. Of course, the theorists who promote such an understanding of the second modernity are aware of the fact that our situation is double-edged. Due to the rise of uncertainty, fundamentalism, racism, and other resentments might also arise.

The apologists of the second modernity take such negative developments to be the outcome of religion, as well as tradition in general. Instead of speaking in a differentiated way about religions and traditions, Beck and others extol the unencumbered self that acts on its own. This self, they maintain, should become the foundation of society and an end unto itself. From this perspective, religions based on traditions, institutions, and community are regarded as something that we have either already or will soon overcome in order to create a better democratic society. If this is really the case, then true reconciliation might become impossible, since it is deeply grounded in an identity characterized by anamnesis. How, indeed, can an unencumbered self feel guilty? According to Ezekiel, such a self would not be a subject. If this is the case, then we have to question the thesis that a democratic society without tradition and religion is much more democratic and liberating than a society influenced by traditions and religions.

As a risk-oriented society, ours bears many liberating possibilities. But it also harbors the danger of constructing identities by way of dualistic distinctions, such as the distinction between friend and enemy. Speaking of reconciliation in such a situation is a challenge, both to the post-traditional society that avoids the past and to concepts of identity based on the negation of the other. Why?

THE DANGER OF RECONCILIATION: THE APOCALYPTICAL DIMENSION OF A NEW WORLD ORDER

Reconciliation is based on a symmetrical foundation as well as an asymmetrical one. The subjectivity that expresses itself in this process is not the traditional identification of the subject with the *cogito;* rather, its epistemological foundation is the *communicatio.* The communicative process of reconciliation is deeply connected to an "otherwise than being" or a "beyond being," to use Lévinas's term. In its struggle for recognition such an identity aspires toward a world beyond victims and perpetrators. It is universal in a temporal sense: it is an anamnestic solidarity with the dead. But this reconciliation does not mean *apokatastasis,* since, as Lévinas has stated, "a world in which pardon is all-powerful becomes inhuman."[20] Of course, *apokatastasis* is a biblical term found in The Acts of the Apostles (3:21); here the term signifies a restoration "of which God spoke in ancient times by the lips of his holy prophets," a restoration that is combined with judgment. Whoever speaks of *apokatastasis* without judgment indulges in idle chat. That is why the church deemed *apokatastasis* to be heretical.

No one claims that the alternative to *apokatastasis* is the damnation of others and / or an eternal dualism. To come to the point: if I were to go to heaven someday and meet Adolf Hitler there, would this be a case of *apokatastasis? Apokatastasis* does not lead to a more just society. On the contrary, speaking of *apokatastasis* amounts to a cover-up of injustice and an attempt to escape the political impact of theology. But we also must ask ourselves whether there might be another grammar that is able to combine both justice and forgiveness in a non-ontological manner, which brings us to the "God of reconciliation."

Believing in reconciliation means suffering unto an unredeemed world. Here we confront an apocalyptical understanding of reconciliation; this understanding, however, is not based on Origen's concept of *apokatastasis,* where God is the subject of a reconciliation that is focused on the utopia of a new earth and a new heaven. From an apocalyptical standpoint, to speak of reconciliation and to reconcile are to behold the fragments of a new world; it is apocalyptical because it is an expression of protest. To undertake a theology of reconciliation is to resist any spiritual investments in the world as it is. And here we see that reconciliation has to do with mercy *and* judgment. The problem is that theologians are in danger of dividing mercy and justice, but this is a problem of perspective, for God's judgment is mercy, salvation, and liberation. Further, in an apocalyptical context, both reconciliation and mercy must be viewed from the perspective of the victim. As Krister Stendahl has pointed out, the aim of mercy is to bring justice.[21] Mercy is a manifestation of God's sovereignty. Reconciliation based upon justice and mercy brings a new world order: the first will be last and the last will be first—this is the mercy the Bible is speaking about. So the question is: for whom are judgment and mercy negative terms?

"Mercy and forgiveness," writes Stendahl, "are not merely motifs of gentleness, not a counterforce that softens the blow of God's judgment, a protection, or a kind of asbestos against the heat of judgment." Rather, mercy means that there is time for repentance, for metanoia. But, Stendahl adds, "[T]here is little mercy except the chance of repentance for us who sit in judgment, but when judgment comes upon us, there is much mercy for the oppressed."[22] Reconciliation is not justification but an expression of protest. A theology of reconciliation as an apocalyptic category has to be a negative *(apophatical)* and not a positive *(kataphatical)* theology. Reconciliation *after* Auschwitz makes us sensitive, as Didier Pollefeyt emphasizes, to the danger of a gnostic dualism, which divides the world into holy and unholy, light and darkness.[23] Reconciliation is a necessary category particularly for religious people; without it we are in danger of creating a religious segregation that might run deeper than a racist one, because it is guided by the highest motivations.

Until the end of the nineteenth century, peace treaties were based on a general pardon and a forgetting of all injustices. Article II of the Treaty of Westphalia, for example, states, "Sit utrinque perpetua oblivio et amnestia omnium eorum" (a perpetual forgetting and amnesty for all transgressions are hereby declared). Today we know that a *perpetua memoria,* or perpetual remembering, is the *conditio sine qua non* of a just society, but this *perpetua memoria* is not necessarily connected with a *perpetua memoria culpae,* that is, a perpetual remembering of guilt. Through the *perpetua memoria* the *memoria culpae* has to be transformed into a *perpetua responsum,* and the word *responsum* is the root for the word *responsibility.* Such a transformation is necessary to society. But is a post-traditional society capable of such a transformation? I doubt it. The theorists of a post-traditional society underestimate the struggle for recognition in an era of globalization, in which universalism is defined by economic activities and dependencies. In such an era the struggle for recognition might be resolved on the basis of gnostically structured identities.

At this point the political theology of Carl Schmitt might be one of the most dangerous temptations, at least within the German context. "Carl Schmitt, Theorist of the Reich," as Joseph Bendersky calls him,[24] has been described both as "the Hobbes of our age" and as "the philosophical and juridical godfather of Nazism." For Schmitt, the political pertains to the ability to distinguish between friend and enemy. Schmitt's concept of the political is rooted in a negative anthropology based on the dogma of original sin. After World War II, Schmitt regarded himself as a Catholic, not only by confession but also by race. If fascism could be described as a resistance against theoretical and practical transcendence, Schmitt's theory has to be characterized as a fascist theory. Furthermore, Schmitt was very sensitive toward the anti-apocalyptical foundation of the Catholic Church. This anti-apocalyptical orientation motivated a closer relationship to gnostic ideas, and gnosticism continues to be a temptation in Catholicism and in Christianity in general.

As early as 1923, Schmitt wrote, "Every actual democracy rests on the principle that not only are equals equal but unequals will not be treated equally. Democracy requires, therefore, first homogeneity and second—if the need arises—elimination or eradication of heterogeneity. . . . A democracy demonstrates its political power by knowing how to refuse or keep at bay something foreign and unequal that threatens its homogeneity. The question of equality is precisely not one of abstract, logical-arithmetical games. It is about the substance of equality."[25] And in 1927 he declared, "Whoever says humanity will betray."[26] From Schmitt's perspective we are not living in a universe but in a "Pluriverse," in which a government acquires its sovereignty by making decisions on its own and being able to abolish any law for the sake of self-preservation.

Under the current circumstances, theology can oppose Schmitt's violent homogeneity only if it is rooted in an asymmetry in which speaking of God, morality, and meaning arises not from a homogeneity that excludes the non-homogeneous or from an unencumbered self but from the demand, the appeal, and the call of the other for the other. This asymmetry is the foundation for a non-totalitarian "reiterative universalism" (to quote Michael Walzer). The counterconcept of Schmitt's political theology, then, would be a utopia resulting from an unconditional act that renounces all sovereignty.

Here we see the importance of reconciliation—not to give up hope for reconciliation but to work out this hope as a rubbing against the grain of history and as a "hope for the sake of the hopeless."[27] Reconciliation implies hope, but to hope is to grow furious against the powers that would justify history. This growing furious is neither a gnostic negation of the world nor a dualism; nor is it a retreat to the victim / perpetrator relation. Its focus, rather, lies "beyond being." This hope is an expression of a love for life—and to love life is to love God. Such a theology is grounded in a dialectical relationship between a theoretical pessimism and a practical optimism under the priority of praxis. The epistemological principle of reconciliation is not the *cogito,* not the "I think," but the "I grow furious." As Albert Camus has stated, "I grow furious, therefore we are."[28] This principle shows us that the human being is not an unencumbered self but one who is emotionally tied to others, and that makes the human being a *zoon politikon.*

If reconciliation is deeply connected with this solidarity, it is obvious that a theology of reconciliation that does not lead to liberation or fight oppression is sheer hypocrisy. From this perspective a fight against oppression is always a fight for the oppressed—as well as for the oppressors, since it includes the hope that such a liberation would offer the opportunity to liberate the oppressors from their idolatry and help them become human again.

NOTES

1. See Johann Baptist Metz, "Unterwegs zu einer nachidealistischen Theologie," in J. B. Bauer, ed., *Entwürfe der Theologie* (Graz, Vienna, and Cologne: Verlag Styria, 1985), p. 215.

2. See Cornel West, *Prophetic Thought in Postmodern Times: Beyond Eurocentrism and Multiculturalism,* vol. 1 (Monroe, Maine: Common Courage Press, 1993), pp. 2–6.

3. Walter Benjamin, "Über den Begriff der Geschichte," in *Gesammelte Schriften,* ed. R. Tiedemann and H. Schweppenhäuser, vol. 1, pt. 2 (Frankfurt am Main: Suhrkamp Verlag, 1980), p. 697.

4. Theodor Adorno, *Negative Dialektik* (Frankfurt am Main: Suhrkamp Verlag, 1982), p. 29.

5. Walter Benjamin, "Goethes Wahlverwandtschaften," in *Gesammelte Schriften,* ed. R. Tiedemann and H. Schweppenhäuser, vol. 1, pt. 2 (Frankfurt am Main: Suhrkamp Verlag, 1980), p. 202.

6. Ralph Giordano, *Die zweite Schuld oder Von der Last Deutscher zu sein* (Munich: Knaur, 1990).

7. See Jacob Taubes, *Vom Kult zur Kultur: Bausteine zu einer Kritik der historischen Vernunft: Gesammelte Aufsätze zur Religions- und Geistesgeschichte* (Munich: Wilhelm Fink Verlag, 1996), pp. 343–45.

8. See Jacques Derrida, "Jacques Derrida im Gespräch mit Michel Wieviorka: Jahrhundert der Vergebung. Verzeihen ohne Macht—unbedingt und jenseits der Souveränität," *Lettre international* 48 (2000): 10–18.

9. Paul Ricoeur, *Das Rätsel der Vergangenheit: Erinnern—Vergessen—Verzeihen* (Göttingen: Wallstein Verlag, 2000), p. 155.

10. David Blumenthal, "Repentance and Forgiveness," *Cross Currents* 48 (Spring 1998): 79.

11. Ricoeur, *Das Rätsel der Vergangenheit,* p. 155.

12. Emmanuel Lévinas, *Difficult Freedom: Essays on Judaism,* trans. Seàn Hand (Baltimore: Johns Hopkins University Press, 1990), p. 20.

13. Emmanuel Lévinas, *Die Spur des Anderen: Untersuchungen zur Phänomenologie und Sozialphilosophie* (Freiburg: Verlag Karl Alber, 1983), p. 323.

14. See Tiemo Rainer Peters, *Mystik—Mythos—Metaphysik: Die Spur des vermissten Gottes* (Mainz: Grünewald, 1992), pp. 112–13.

15. Blumenthal, "Repentance and Forgiveness," p. 80.

16. See Peters, *Mystik—Mythos—Metaphysik,* pp. 121–25.

17. Eugene J. Fisher in Simon Wiesenthal, *The Sunflower: On the Possibilities and Limits of Forgiveness,* ed. Harry James Cargas and Bonny V. Fetterman (New York: Schocken Books, 1997), pp. 132–33.

18. Hubert Locke in Wiesenthal, *The Sunflower,* p. 193.

19. See Ulrich Beck, *Die Erfindung des Politischen* (Frankfurt am Main: Suhrkamp Verlag, 1993).

20. Lévinas, *Difficult Freedom,* p. 20.

21. See Krister Stendahl, *Paul among Jews and Gentiles* (Philadelphia: Fortress Press, 1976), pp. 99–100.

22. Ibid., p. 103.

23. Didier Pollefeyt, "The Kafkaesque World of the Holocaust: Paradigmatic Shifts in the Ethical Interpretation of the Nazi Genocide," in John K. Roth, ed., *Ethics after the Holocaust: Perspectives, Critiques, and Responses* (St. Paul, Minn.: Paragon House, 1999), pp. 228–39.

24. Joseph W. Bendersky, *Carl Schmitt: Theorist of the Reich* (Princeton, N.J.: Princeton University Press, 1983).

25. Carl Schmitt, *The Crisis of Parliamentary Democracy,* trans. Ellen Kennedy (Cambridge, Mass.: MIT Press, 1986), p. 9.

26. Carl Schmitt, *Der Begriff des Politischen: Text von 1932 mit einem Vorwort und drei Corollarien* (Berlin: Dunker & Humbolt, 1963), p. 55.

27. Benjamin, "Goethes Wahlverwandtschaften," p. 202.

28. Albert Camus, *Der Mensch in der Revolte,* trans. Justus Streller (Reinbek: Rowohlt, 1964), p. 27.

In Response to Juergen Manemann

PETER J. HAAS

JUERGEN MANEMANN HAS given us a carefully thought out discussion of what the basis of a Catholic theology of reconciliation should be in the post-Shoah world. It places great stress on the need for moving beyond the past without forgetting the past, and for stressing individual responsibility and relations with the other in a world rapidly moving toward globalization. It is also a call for a reaffirmation of the role of tradition, religion, and historical memory in the emerging postmodern world.

Granted that this short essay is but a part of a larger reconsideration of Catholic theology, there are nonetheless a number of troubling features in its overall strategy. I want to focus in particular on one of the most troubling of these features for me, namely the theology's focus on the perpetrators and the concomitant theological marginalization of the victims. To some degree this emphasis is perfectly understandable. After all, it was the oppressors who in the name of Christianity perpetrated the most heinous genocide on record. So the need to deal with the role of Christians and Christianity among the perpetrators is quite naturally a primary concern of Christian theologians. But in the process, I want to argue, the victims are in a sense being pushed to the side and so victimized again. I do not mean to imply that this is Manemann's intent. On the contrary, he goes out of his way to stress the need for sensitivity to the victim, in fact to restore the victim's humanity. But the very structure of the theology as he lays it out appears to me to undermine his own intentions.

Manemann's basic presuppositions are set forth early in his essay. Just after his introductory paragraphs, he notes that "[a] theology of reconciliation and forgiveness has to be worked out as a theology that is unable to distance itself from the suffering of others." In other words, reconciliation must revolve around the suffering of the victims and the perpetrator's relation to that suffering. It is the perpetrators who must recognize their guilt for the suffering they have inflicted and thereby initiate the mechanism of reconciliation. On some level, of course, this makes perfect sense. If the perpetrator feels no guilt or remorse, how is reconciliation even possible? But there is a deeper implication that is more troubling. A few paragraphs later Manemann notes that "[a] precondition for becoming an individual is a capacity for becoming guilty as a person." On a general level this means that one becomes a mature adult only insofar as one takes responsibility for one's choices and actions. This is a sort of trivial truism that does not really address the radical evil of the Holocaust. It is in fact clear from what follows that this is not the meaning that Manemann wants us to come away with.

The more theological interpretation, which is what I think Manemann really has in mind, is that one must, to be an individual, accept the general sinfulness of being human. That is, the perpetrator's confrontation with his or her own evil as a perpetrator must include also a confrontation with his or her evil as a human. Such a set of confrontations is part of becoming more fully human. This is fine as far as it goes, but it leaves no room for explaining how the victim achieves greater personhood. In fact, to my mind at least, this sounds like a version of the classic Catholic doctrine of original sin. The implication is that one has to participate in this characterization of the human condition in order fully to enter into human personhood. If this interpretation is in fact the case, then there is a real problem regarding how Jews, victims of the Shoah or not, can become fully human. Are they expected to act upon this doctrine of Christian theology as well in order to become human? If so, then the Jewishness of the Jewish victims is denied. If not, then how can they still be regarded by this theology as fully human?

Let me turn to another aspect of the situation of the victim in this theology. Consider the statement that "[t]hrough reconciliation the victim becomes a subject, and the perpetrator becomes an I, in Ezekiel's sense, by admitting his guilt and repenting." There is certainly a deep psychological truth here. The perpetrator must transcend his evil deeds, recognize the evil that has been done, and take responsibility for that evil. At the same time, this taking of responsibility does restore a measure of humanity to the victim. But the theological implications of this transaction are troubling. Turning away from their evil and offering reconciliation, the perpetrators become reborn as new subjects, and, in Christian theology, this rebirth is of course the essence of becoming human. But what about the victims? What opportunity do they have to undergo the same kind of rebirth into humanity that is available to the perpetrators? Manemann surely does not mean to ascribe positive redemptive power to the status of being a victim. It thus must be the case that this theology implicitly assigns redemptive power to the oppressor, since it is after all the oppressor's reconciliation that has the capacity to effect the rehumanization of the victim. The problem, of course, is that in this situation, the victim once again is in the position of being reliant on the will of the perpetrator.

One last example of how this theology puts the victim in an awkward position emerges from Manemann's treatment of forgiveness. As the essay lays it out, this is a two-step process. The first step is reconciliation, which flows out of the perpetrator's ownership of human sinfulness, as discussed above, and his or her subsequent move toward reconciliation. This leads, in turn, to "the restoration of harmony in a disturbed relationship between human beings." It is "a first step toward recognition: it is a reciprocal recognition between subjects." The second step, forgiveness, comes from the victim. But here again, the logic of the theology dehumanizes to a degree the victim. After all, the beneficiary of the act of forgiveness, as Manemann lays matters out, is once again the perpetrator, who now has a second opportunity to change and become another. There is no corresponding redemption flowing to the victim. But this is not all. For the perpetrator, as we have seen, the first act of reconciliation is rationally and theologically warranted. But the second move, the part of the victim, is not logical at all, but is in fact illogical. It is a pure act of giving for no reason. Or, in Manemann's own words, "Reconciliation initially follows a certain logic, whereas forgiveness has no 'logic'—it is interruption and incalculability." In fact, Manemann talks about such forgiveness as impossible. So where, again, does this leave the victims? One reading is to conclude that the victims are without logic, without the power to rehumanize the perpetrator, without the ability to transform themselves and become another. In short, the victim emerges as nothing more than the passive, non-logical foil, against which the perpetrator can achieve rebirth. On this reading, it would seem, the victim has become dehumanized again.

To be sure, Manemann does not take this reasoning to the logical possibility I just spelled out. But he does, curiously, get very close to going in the exact opposite, and just as dangerous, direction. The one model for this kind of illogical act of forgiveness in the face of evil is, of course, as Manemann notes, Jesus on the cross. So this kind of forgiveness, resting in the hands of the Jewish victims, is to become "Christ-like," as it were. The force of this logic appears a few paragraphs later, when Manemann tells us that "[f]orgiveness is grace, and grace is something we receive without justification." So the victims find themselves maneuvered into becoming what only God can be. To be sure, Manemann tells us that the victims can never be morally or otherwise obligated to offer forgiveness. But by juxtaposing the victim's expected response to the "perfect" response of Christ, Manemann has ipso facto put the Jewish victims in a no-win situation vis-à-vis their Christian counterparts. What does it say of the Jewish victims if they do not come across with Christ-like forgiveness?

Manemann has done important work in thinking through the theological implications of the Shoah for the perpetrators. He has not, however, made room for the humanity of the victims. They are still playing the role of passive theological ciphers for the postmodern Christian. If it hopes to truly humanize and enter into communion with the other, a Christian theology of reconciliation may have to transcend not only the categories of victim and perpetrator but also the very categories of traditional Christian theology.

In Response to Juergen Manemann

DAVID PATTERSON

IN HIS ESSAY on a theology of reconciliation after Auschwitz, Juergen Manemann makes many points that are deeply insightful. One good example is his demonstration of the need for a theology that "is unable to distance itself from the suffering of others." Manemann understands that this proximity to others is not a matter of empathy; it is a matter of *responsibility for* their suffering. Such a theology, he goes on to explain, includes a theology of personal identity, since human subjectivity is constituted by this responsibility: to determine who I am is to determine that I am the one responsible. "Becoming a subject," says Manemann, "means being responsible. Recognizing sin as my sin is a matter not just of taking on a burden but also of acquiring an ability that forces me to become a subject." Which means: I draw nigh unto the other as a penitent whose very existence comes at the expense of the other.

Here lies a key to Manemann's astute point concerning a "second guilt" that haunts the post-Holocaust era. The first guilt belongs to the perpetrators; the second guilt lies in the inability to take responsibility for what has happened. Until we come to terms with that second guilt, we have no identity; instead, we choose an indifferent anonymity in the face of both the living and the dead. Looking out for Number One, we become a zero, an emptiness that can be filled only by emptying ourselves of our self. That emptying out comes with the transformation of difference into non-indifference. In my complacency I hide in the indifferent neutrality of being. Thus camouflaged in mute silence, I incur the second guilt through my failure to answer, "Here I am." This "Here I am" is who I am, and it is the first utterance of the penitent. "Without repentance, reconciliation and forgiveness end up as 'cheap grace,'" Manemann asserts, and it *is* a matter of grace: the movement of repentance is a drawing nigh unto G-d by drawing nigh unto the human being. If it is simply a matter of making up, then reconciliation does not involve repentance because it does not entail the transformation of difference into non-indifference to become someone other than who I had been.

Here we can take to a deeper level Manemann's point that reconciliation lies both in remembrance and in forgetting. Remembrance is the remembrance of who we are *in truth* that arises in the realization that we are responsible. What must be forgotten is not the transgression but the nothingness into which the soul has tumbled in its drifting off into indifference. The *slipping* into nothingness, however, becomes *unforgettable.* The forgiveness and reconciliation that accompany the movement of repentance, therefore, do not entail a return to normalcy, as Manemann correctly notes. If the debt is forgotten, the crime is memorialized, so that "[t]he atrocious past," as Manemann states it, "will become the immemorial, which makes it the unforgettable." Once the transgression belongs to the immemorial, it becomes part of the eternal, so that, once again, the relation to the human being in time opens up the relation to the Eternal One. Thus reconciliation always harbors a theological dimension.

Because "[t]he highest expression of reconciliation is substitution," Manemann observes, reconciliation poses a specific challenge to Christians and Christianity, inasmuch as Christianity is founded on the most radical of substitutions, the substitution of G-d for humanity on the cross. And if the Christian is to find reconciliation after Auschwitz, he must undertake the same substitution. Indeed, it is only *after* Auschwitz that the Christian *can* undertake the same substitution, for, unlike the Christian perpetrators of the Holocaust, the post-Holocaust Christian is innocent of the crimes committed at Auschwitz. The problem for the Christian, however—both then and now—is that he cannot substitute himself for the Jew without renouncing his Christianity. And yet, if he is to be a Christian, then he must make that very movement of substitution in order to attain reconciliation and forgiveness.

And so we have the conundrum that Manemann opens up but does not articulate: in order to be a Christian, the Christian must renounce his Christianity and take his place on the cross, where the Jew was crucified in the heart of Christendom. Although the Christian can no longer enter the murder camp, after Auschwitz there is no shortage of opportunities for the Christian to take his place alongside the Jew and endure the hatred aimed at the Jew. And yet if the Christian is hated, it is not because he is a Jew but because he has *done* something to aid the Jew. If substitution is the highest expression of reconciliation, as Manemann maintains, then perhaps nothing short of conversion to Judaism can win for the Christian the forgiveness and reconciliation—the grace—that he seeks. Only then can he take on a new, non-indifferent identity that would make possible a substitution for the victim, for only then could he become a victim in the same sense that the Jew has been a victim. Christianity, of course, cannot be expected to get rid of itself in this way any more than Germany can be expected to become a Jewish nation. There is one political-theological response, however, that approaches the substitution necessary to reconciliation: German churches could urge Germany to move its embassy to Jerusalem, and the Vatican could undertake a similar move, in a recognition of the Holy City as the eternal capital of the Jewish state. Thus becoming part of a Jewish future, these Christians might approach a post-Holocaust reconciliation with the Jews and Judaism.

But there lies the problem: the Jews *and* Judaism. It is a problem because, as Manemann rightly sees, the postmodern political self is "the unencumbered self," for whom there is no reality apart from power and no responsibility apart from attending to one's own interests. The Jews and the Judaism they signify, on the other hand, are precisely what encumbers the self, proclaiming a *divine* commandment, imposed from beyond being, to attend not to one's own needs but to the needs of the widow, the orphan, and the stranger. Manemann's insights into the dangers of "the unencumbered self in a post-traditional society" enable us to realize that anti-Semitism is not racism but is essentially the radical opposition to the teaching that comes to the world through the Jews, namely that there is an absolute law and judgment that transcend being, before which we must justify our being. Vehemently opposed to such a position, the postmodern, post-traditional society is an anti-Semitic society. If the Christian is to find grace in the eyes of the G-d who is otherwise than being, then he too must incur postmodern society's contempt for the Jew.

Recognizing a certain dualism that may arise in such an opposition to the post-traditional society, Manemann warns against the dangers of dividing the world into the holy and the unholy or light and darkness. He points out that the meaning sought in a higher truth—a truth that sanctifies the project of forgiveness, reconciliation, and justice—can never arise "from a homogeneity that excludes the non-homogeneous." True enough. But the dualism that Manemann invokes does not pose the danger he thinks it does. It is quite possible, for example, to declare that the Holocaust and its perpetrators are radically evil without falling into the "gnostic dualism" that Manemann fears. Judaism, for example, declares the absolute evil of Amalek (as in Deuteronomy 25:17–19, for instance) and at the same time maintains that there are seventy different paths toward an understanding of Torah (see the *Or Hachayim* on Leviticus 26:3). To be sure, the Talmud teaches that each of the seventy languages of the seventy Gentile nations harbors a spark of the Holy One, which in turn harbors a trace of Torah (see *Shabbat* 88b). Hence in Judaism we have the notion of the Righteous Gentiles, a concept utterly alien to Christianity, which divides the world into the saved, according to their embrace of Christ, and the damned, according to their rejection of Christ: there are no saved, hence no righteous, non-Christians. This Christian dualism resembles the gnostic dualism that Manemann warns against.

Just as Manemann threatens a foundational teaching of Christianity by implying the elimination of such a dualism, he threatens a foundational teaching of Judaism when he asserts that necessary to reconciliation is a hope that grows "furious against the powers that would justify history." For the Jewish affirmation of G-d's presence in history is a justification of history. And only if G-d is at work *in* history can we argue with G-d *about* history—another Jewish notion that is alien to Christian tradition. Without that divine presence and the wrestling with G-d that goes with it, all we can do is rail against the rock, as Albert Camus advises in his essay on Sisyphus. It turns out that, especially in the post-Holocaust era, we have to either argue with G-d or get rid of him. With his invocation of Camus's "I grow furious, therefore we are" at the end of his essay, Manemann—quite unintentionally, I am certain—leads us to get rid of G-d and replace him with our own defiant fury. How does such an excellent thinker as Manemann come to this unintentional turn? It is precisely because he is a *Christian* thinker who has the insight and the courage to think against his own Christianity. While he has opened a fearsome door, he has not quite thought his way through it.

In Response to Peter J. Haas and David Patterson

JUERGEN MANEMANN

I AM GRATEFUL to Peter Haas for his critical remarks, because he challenges me to clarify my thoughts. Haas begins by characterizing my reflections as a "strategy." A strategy implies hidden intentions, and Haas tries to investigate them. By consciously making the victims into ones who are "Christ-like," says Haas, I am unconsciously dehumanizing them. Haas's critique is very radical, since being wrong or inconsistent is not as problematic as consciously thinking in ideological terms. And using an argument as a strategy amounts to consciously thinking in ideological terms. (A few lines later, however, Haas refers to "what Manemann really has in mind" and suggests that I did not intend what he criticizes). Of course, on the unconscious level I am influenced by ideologies that emerge out of my Catholic background and the German environment I live in. Therefore it is absolutely necessary for me to be criticized and thus become aware of the dangerous aspects of my way of doing theology.

After these preliminary remarks I would like to examine Haas's critique point by point. First, Haas begins with a historical mistake: the Nazis did not perpetrate the annihilation of the Jews "in the name of Christianity." Of course, without Christianity the Holocaust would not have been possible, but it is historically false to conclude in a general way that the Holocaust was perpetrated "in the name of Christianity."

Second, according to Haas, my reflection on the relationship between guilt and responsibility is "a sort of trivial truism that does not really address the radical evil of the Holocaust." Haas is right, but I did not intend to apply this reflection on the relationship between guilt and responsibility to Auschwitz. While my thoughts on the matter may express a very simple truth, the simple truths are often the most important. To say something is simple or naive is not an argument against it.

In his critique, moreover, Haas fails to recognize that I am working within a framework of a theology of reconciliation *after* Auschwitz and that the presumption of such a theology is to resist a theology of forgiveness *for* Auschwitz. With regard to my reflections on guilt and responsibility after Auschwitz, what I "really have in mind," Haas supposes, is that "one must, to be an individual, accept the general sinfulness of being human." Taking this statement to be a reference to the doctrine of original sin, Haas appears to be reading a Catholic theology into my reflections; at times his comments strike me as pejorative. My remarks on becoming an individual, however, concern a moral guilt and have nothing to do with "the classic Catholic doctrine of original sin," which does not pertain to a moral sin. So what do I really have in mind?

Further, in my subsequent thoughts on reconciliation Haas sees a "deep psychological truth," but he says that he does not agree with the "theological implications" of the argument. What Haas fails to see is that I draw a distinction between different steps of reconciliation. Thus he is unaware of the fact that an understanding of reconciliation as *katallage* bears no theological implications.

Similarly, in his comments on my remarks about forgiveness, Haas does not take into consideration the fact that my argument is not based on a binary logic. That is to say, he does not acknowledge that the term *logic* is set into quotation marks in order to posit a different sort of logic, which is neither irrational nor counterrational; rather, from a totalitarian perspective, it is nonrational. To speak of forgiveness as an act performed by the victim, therefore, is to characterize the act not as "illogical" but as an act that "has no 'logic.'" In my reference to the forgiveness Jesus offered, Haas overlooks my emphasis on the point that it is not possible to apply this forgiveness to Auschwitz. Furthermore, I do not see why "a pure act of giving for no reason" is a strictly Christian category, as Haas seems to suggest. It is a biblical category, and one can find it in Jewish thought as well.

Haas demands that "the very categories of traditional Christian theology" be transcended in order to "truly humanize and enter into communion with the other." But here we must ask: What are the "very categories of traditional Christian theology"? The apocalyptical dimensions of reconciliation in my reflections culminate in a strong critique of the Catholic Church as a form of power.

Terms have acquired more than one meaning. Thus no thought is immune to miscommunication.

With regard to David Patterson's response, he calls my theological perspective into question in a very radical manner, so radical that I must confess he is right in saying that I have opened "a fearsome door" and that I "have not quite thought [my] way through it." Before responding to this challenge, I would like to discuss his commentary on my reflections on substitution. Patterson interprets substitution as a model of reconciliation for the Christians, but I speak of substitution neither from a Christian nor from an explicitly christological perspective. On the contrary, I refer to Lévinas in order to grasp substitution as a category which is reserved for the victims. The Christian task is to become a responsible I in the sense Patterson mentioned at the beginning of his critique. To switch the places of perpetrators and victims—to get rid of Christianity—would be to flee the burden of history and cover up what has happened.

Patterson's remarks concerning the relationship between Jews and Judaism on the one hand and postmodern society on the other are too one-dimensional. In my reflections on postmodern society I do not criticize this society in general, but only specific concepts used to understand it, concepts intended to get rid of religions grounded in tradition. Our relationship to postmodern society should be a dialectical one, so that opportunities may open up for such a society. Of course, the postmodern society is in danger of rendering us religiously naked, but it also gives way to the irreducibility of individuality within participatory communities; therefore it could be regarded as a means of resisting rapacious individualism and authoritarian communitarianism. Thus I do not criticize postmodern society per se, but only certain interpretations of it. If we are told that God's commandments aim at rescuing the human being in his or her uniqueness, sanctity, and dignity, then we should participate in building up a just society that includes this sensibility toward the other in his or her otherness.

Next Patterson states that perceiving the Nazis as radically evil does not necessarily mean falling into a "gnostic dualism," and he is absolutely right. He is also correct in pointing out that Christianity inherits a gnostic dualism in its division of the world into the damned and the saved. In his critique of Christianity, German philosopher Hans Blumenberg makes this point very forcefully.[1] Christian tradition has yet to succeed in getting rid of the gnostic temptation.

In his last critical argument Patterson discusses my reference to Camus's statement, "I grow furious, therefore we are," which he sees as a threat to a foundational teaching of Judaism concerning God's presence in history, since, according to my interpretation, this is a growing rage against the powers that justify history. For Patterson, the Jewish affirmation of God's presence in history amounts to a justification of history. I do not think this contradicts what I intend, since it depends on how one understands the term *history.* I use the word in a Hegelian sense, taking *Weltgeschichte* or "world history" to be a *Weltgericht* or a "last judgment" of the world.[2] But God's presence in history is not identical with the process of *Weltgeschichte.* On the contrary, it challenges such an understanding.

So let me come to the last remark: Do my reflections lead to a replacing of God with our own defiant fury? I do not think so, but I must confess I do not know where God is. In my theological thinking I am trying to work out the absence of God.

Part Two: Reconciliation

NOTES

1. See Hans Blumenberg, *Legitimität der Neuzeit* (Frankfurt am Main: Suhrkamp Verlag, 1996).

2. G. W. F. Hegel, *Vorlesungen über die Philosophie der Geschichte* (Frankfurt am Main: Suhrkamp Verlag, 1970), p. 559.

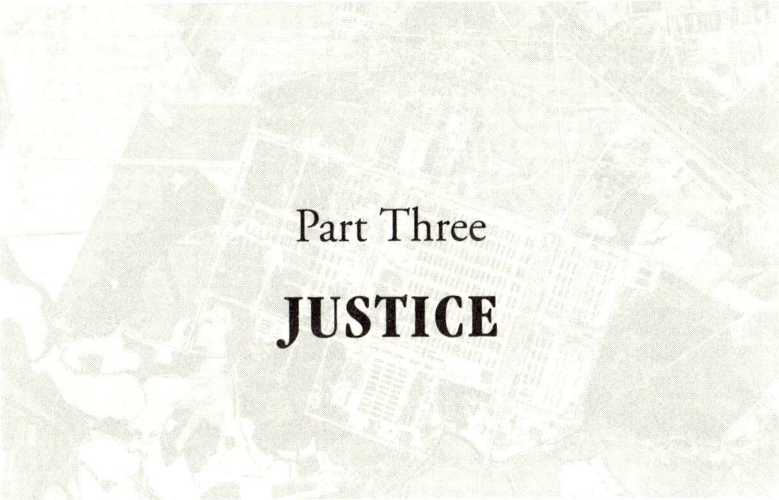

Part Three
JUSTICE

"Let justice roll down like waters," proclaimed Amos, "and righteousness like an ever-flowing stream" (Amos 5:24). Almost always, as that Jewish prophet knew, *justice* is an after-word because cries for it and appeals to it are usually pronounced when something has gone badly wrong. If life were fair, unscarred by greed, terror, war, or genocide, to name but a few of the follies and disasters that infect it, there would be little need to give justice a second thought. Justice, however, deserves and requires much more than that. It does so because *justice* also remains an after-word in the sense that it is something we so frequently profess to pursue and yet so rarely achieve. If reconciliation reached farther and forgiveness went deeper, justice might roll down like waters. Yet, as revealed by the dialogues in this third part of *After-Words,* matters are not that simple. We need more reconciliation and greater forgiveness if justice is to be found, but the lack of justice in the world is also what makes forgiveness and reconciliation so immensely difficult to achieve. Inseparable, forgiveness, reconciliation, and justice can scarcely be realized one at a time or enacted one without the others. Hence, *forgiveness, reconciliation,* and *justice* are closer to being one word than three. In their varied ways, the inquiries that follow bear witness to these relational realities.

David Patterson sees that the Holocaust demolished the old idea that justice is a balancing of scales. There is no recompense for Auschwitz or Treblinka. Well-intentioned and helpful though they may be, efforts to provide restitution to Holocaust survivors can never set things right. For the dead, nothing can be done except to remember them, which brings scant comfort. Nevertheless, standing in the tradition of Amos, Patterson yearns for justice to roll down like waters, and he thinks that it can do so if our understanding becomes more Jewish. Movement in that direction would entail hearing God's commandments, which emphasize responsibility to act in loving kindness toward one's neighbors. As Britta Frede-Wenger and John Roth point out, however, Patterson's position is not without problems: Is it too particularistic? In arguing for his perspective, is Patterson unfair in his critique of Christianity? Is it credible to speak about God's commandments after Auschwitz? As the dialogue unfolds, it becomes clear that justice depends on a multifaceted restoration in which reconciliation and forgiveness have key parts to play.

Leonard Grob engages the Israeli-Palestinian conflict in a post-Holocaust context. He senses that the phrase *just peace,* which is often used in and about that struggle, can never be convincing unless Jews and Palestinians retell their histories in ways that make room for each other. Only then is it likely that these unreconciled people can make safe space for each other in a land that they seem destined, one way or another, to share. When Henry Knight and John Roth respond to Grob, they wonder whether his idealism is too high and his estimate of Israeli-Palestinian intractability too low. But Grob rightly comes back to insist that there will be no just peace until people do a better job of encouraging dialogue about their memories and their hopes, their fears and their dreams, doing so in ways that enable careful listening. If progress can be made for getting along—reconciliation—like that, then a just peace among Israelis and Palestinians, and elsewhere too, may still be some time off but not delayed forever.

When things go wrong, Rachel Baum underscores, the hurt, loss, and grief that victims feel does not go away quickly. The Holocaust and September 11 bear witness to that. One of her points is that, as with forgiveness and reconciliation, justice has much to do with memory and with the ways in which human hearts as well as minds are moved by remembrance. Memory can intensify hostility; it can fuel hate and inflame revenge. Driven by injustice, memory can produce more of the same. But memory can also do much more and much better than that. Keeping her focus on the Jewish heart, but in ways that make her outlook accessible to people of diverse traditions, Baum argues that "[t]he challenge is to keep the memory of the Shoah alive while creating a Jewish community of compassion, love, and openness." When Leonard Grob and Henry Knight respond, they are supportive critics who urge Baum to amplify further the constructive themes about human relationships that her emphasis on Jewish heart and soul suggests to them.

"Who will we *be,* after . . . ?" That question, Baum suggests, may be the most important one that remains as her reflections end but do not close. Where forgiveness, reconciliation, and now the after-word *justice* are concerned, that question is one that ought to keep dialogue alive.

7

G-d, World, Humanity

Jewish Reflections on Justice after Auschwitz

DAVID PATTERSON

WHILE THE PROBLEMATIC nature of attaining justice *for* Auschwitz is clear enough, the status of justice *after* Auschwitz is not so evident. With regard to justice for Auschwitz, the apparent silence of G-d, world, and humanity lies at the root of the problem; for where there is silence—the silence of indifference—there can be no justice. This silence, however, is not confined to the era of Auschwitz. It persists. It is evident in the growing despair over the very possibility of justice in a world where the mass slaughter of human beings is increasingly commonplace. The hope that the horror of Auschwitz would deter such atrocities has not been realized. In fact, Auschwitz has all but normalized mass murder and subsequently has all but rendered meaningless the notion of justice. When tens or hundreds of thousands are slaughtered, there can be no balancing of the scales, either through world courts or through truth and reconciliation commissions. The purpose of this essay, then, is not to offer a solution to balancing the scales. Its aim, rather, is to rethink the notion of justice: that is, to think otherwise than in terms of balancing the scales.

One reason for the bankruptcy of our thinking about justice is that the philosophical and religious worldviews that contributed to the creation of Auschwitz continue to dominate our thinking after Auschwitz. Auschwitz was *in part* the product of a totalizing ontological mode of thinking that characterizes the Cartesian "I think, therefore I am." Emphasizing the self's autonomy, authenticity, and resolve, this thinking follows a line of development in German philosophy from Immanuel Kant to Martin Heidegger. It deduces everything from the ego and thus, as Franz Rosenzweig astutely pointed out, " 'reduces the world' to the perceiving self."[1] Here Being is precisely thinking, thought is the comprehension of Being, and knowledge is the self's appropriation of everything outside itself. With this thinking, all values, moral and otherwise, are a product of either natural accident or human will, and nothing outside the self has any inherent or absolute value.

Continuing along the same ontological lines, philosophy perceives little connection between itself and the Holocaust. Few see the connection between a thinking that rids the world of G-d by equating G-d, at best, with some supreme form of Being and an ideology that sets up the Führer as G-d in his embodiment of the Volk. Few see the connection between a thinking that reduces the world to a mute material object of contemplation and world conquest in the name of *Lebensraum.* Few see the connection between thinking that drains humanity of its divine image and the Nazis' degradation of the human being. Nevertheless, this speculative tradition that contributed to the creation of Auschwitz continues to influence our understanding of the world afterward. Power is now taken to be the only reality and justice a matter of getting even. That is why justice after Auschwitz is a problem for philosophy.

Justice is also a problem for elements of Christian tradition that contributed to the Holocaust and that, like philosophy, persist in maintaining a business-as-usual stance. Christianity's contribution to the Holocaust lies not only in its anti-Semitic, supersessionist teachings; it is also rooted in fundamental elements of Christian doctrine, specifically the doctrine of inherited sin and the teaching that faith (not deeds) is the key to redemption from that sin. According to this view, the human being's very existence is a state of sin, a condition that can be overcome only by the content of belief, namely that Christ paid the ransom not only for what we have *done* but also for what we *are.* The blood of Christ redeems the believing Christian from judgment for the crime of being; those who, like the Jews, explicitly reject Christ as their redeemer are subject to that judgment. Justice in this instance is a matter of paying a death penalty for being alive, as the Jews of Nazi-occupied Christendom did. This "justice" must be avoided by believing in the Christ, who has paid the penalty on the cross; thus we may defeat death.

To the extent that this Christian doctrine persists after Auschwitz, the view persists that the nonbeliever's being is unredeemed and is therefore sinful. From the standpoint of a justice understood as paying a debt, the nonbeliever deserves either death or damnation. Belief in Christ Jesus, however, opens up an alternative to this balancing of the scales: forgiveness. Thus the Christian invokes forgiveness, and not justice, as the path to reconciliation. Faith brings forgiveness, but it cannot bring justice. What is needed after Auschwitz, however, is not forgiveness for transgression but a justice that affirms moral action. What is needed is not belief in a redeemer but deeds of loving kindness toward the neighbor. What is needed, in short, is the Jewish thought that was slated for annihilation in the extermination of the Jews.

In his Warsaw ghetto diary Chaim Kaplan declares, "Either humanity would be Judaic, or it would be idolatrous-German."[2] To be "Judaic" is to seek salvation in deeds commanded from beyond the world. Jewish thought arises not in the wonder of speculative philosophy but in the realization of a responsibility. It rests not upon the autonomous ruminations of reason but on a commandment to seek justice. This commandment is imposed upon us from on high: "Justice, justice [*Tsedek, tsedek*] shall you seek" (Deuteronomy 16:20). *Tsedek* is the *justice* that is also *righteousness:* for Jewish thought, justice demands entering into a higher relation. It demands joining the horizontal human-to-human relation with the vertical human-to-divine relation through deeds of loving kindness. As Abraham's argument with G-d over the fate of Sodom and Gomorrah implies (Genesis 18:22–33), justice is more a matter of sparing the innocent than of punishing the guilty.

Justice, moreover, is *tsedakah,* which is charity or giving without expectation of reciprocation. It is not getting even *with* the other but an offering *to* the other, as when care is shown toward the widow, the orphan, and the stranger. For Jewish thought, G-d, world, and humanity are not reducible to manifestations of Being that we simply experience or appropriate through knowledge; rather, each of these terms denotes a discrete but interconnected realm of relation.[3] Because the Nazis were more successful than we realize, after Auschwitz we are faced with the project of seeking justice in the distinct contexts of G-d, world, and humanity. Which means: we must come to hear once more the commandment that arises from G-d, world, and humanity. Jewish thought is about that hearing, and that hearing is where justice begins; for what is heard is the commandment of the Holy One, who summons from us the justice that is also righteousness.

Let us consider, then, the Jewish notion of justice within the realms of G-d, world, and humanity.

JUSTICE WITH REGARD TO G-D

For Jewish thought, G-d is neither "in me" nor is G-d some "higher self." He is neither essence nor being nor even Supreme Being. Rather, G-d is the One who commands from beyond Being—and who inserts Himself into Being through His commandment: through His commandment His transcendence is transformed into immanence. Justice—*tsedek*—begins not with the faith that G-d is love but with the response of *Hinehni,* "Here I am for you," to the commandment to love the neighbor. This response is an offering of the self to and for the Holy One who commands, and not a contemplation of the essence and attributes of G-d or an effort to bring the "good news" to another soul. Even as we ask whether justice is possible, justice, as commanded by G-d, is already asking us: Where are you? Whereas justice appears to be impossible to the speculative thought that seeks a balance, to Jewish thought the possibility of justice is not a question. For justice summons us before we can raise the question.

After Auschwitz, the difficulty with regard to G-d is not to forgive Him for His silence; the problem, rather, is to *hear* Him as He commands us to seek justice and righteousness. Hence the Jews raise their voices in prayer twice a day, as a voice from on high vibrates on their lips, crying, "Shema, Yisrael"—Hear, O Israel! Rather than an urging to think or to believe, the injunction is to *hear* and to *heed,* for both are meanings of *shema.* Philosophy's speculation on the call of Being renders us deaf to the call of the Holy One, as does Christianity's emphasis on belief over action. One key to hearing G-d lies in regaining a capacity for prayer, the very thing that Kant held in contempt.[4] While Christians do not hold prayer in contempt, the Christian view of prayer is rather different from the Jewish view.

As the words *deomai* in Greek and *precari* in Latin suggest, prayer, in the Christian view, is generally associated with supplication, entreaty, and pleading; Christian prayer is prayer *for,* an asking for something, either for oneself or for another. Jewish thinking about prayer is quite different, as the Hebrew word for "prayer," *tefilah,* and its cognates suggest. While the root *pilel* may imply supplication, it also has meanings associated with decision, analysis, and judgment; its cognate *naftulim* means "struggles" or "wrestlings," so that here prayer is not a request but an encounter—at times adversarial—between G-d and the soul, as when Jacob wrestled with the angel at Peniel. Like the commandment to seek justice, prayer comes from beyond the one who prays. It takes hold of us and sets a task before us: to pray is to be commanded to act. Through prayer, therefore, we do not speak to G-d—G-d speaks to us, just as He speaks to us and commands us through our study of Torah. That is why in the Jewish tradition Torah study is a form of prayer; and yet, the Talmud teaches, the *deed* born of Torah study is greater than the study itself (see *Berakhot* 7b). To be sure, there is no prayer without the deed: a capacity to pray is a capacity to act justly. And the just action—the *mitzvah*—is a prayer in the form of a deed.[5]

Justice in our relation to G-d, then, requires prayer.

In the words of Elie Wiesel, prayer is "the substance of language and the language of silence."[6] Where there is prayer, word is tied to meaning, and silence assumes an eloquence that surpasses utterance. So it is with justice: justice is the return—the *teshuvah*—of word to meaning. The bridge between word and meaning is the bridge Rosenzweig described when he affirmed that language is the bridge between G-d and world.[7] If judgment transpires on a bridge, as the Talmud affirms (*Shabbat* 32a), this is the bridge where it unfolds. Where there is justice, there is an undoing of the assault on the word undertaken by the Nazis and perpetuated by a postmodernist philosophy that would understand meaning in terms of power, and not as a bridge between G-d and world. The judgment that occurs on this bridge is a judgment on the

Nazis' undoing of the bridge. It is also a judgment of our response to that undoing.

If G-d is *HaShem*—the Name—it is because His is the Name that imparts meaning to all the names (to all the words) that form the landscape of the world, beginning with the word *tsedek.* To assert that word is tied to meaning is to affirm that G-d is linked to world. And that link is justice: justice joins word to meaning by bridging G-d to a world that is otherwise a wasteland.

JUSTICE WITH REGARD TO WORLD

While Christianity would affirm the bridge between G-d and world through the Incarnation, at the same time the Incarnation erases the bridge through Jesus' assertion that "my kingdom is not of this world" (John 18:36). Thus Christianity plays into the hands of ontological philosophy by situating G-d in an elsewhere to which we have no access except via the Christ—through whom salvation comes not by justice but by grace. Here justice in the world may be desirable, but it is not essential, since the relation to the Christ rests on faith, not on justice.

Departing from the Christian teaching, ontological philosophy removes the hope of grace from this vale of tears. From the standpoint of ontological philosophy, Christ's elsewhere is nowhere, since there can be nothing more than all there is: the world is a realm without exit. Intellectual, cultural, technological, sensual, and above all egocentric, this philosophy makes the world into an arena in which nothing is true and everything is permitted. With such a philosophy there can be none but a socially or politically acceptable "justice," a justice that rests strictly on horizontal relations among people, without the vertical relation to the Most High implied by *tsedek.* Once again, justice is desirable, but it is not essential, since an "authentic" presence in the world rests on the *resolve* of the thinker, not on his or her righteousness.

Conceived not only as justice but also as righteousness, however, *tsedek* is a matter neither of faith nor of resolve but of ethical action, as exemplified by the Righteous among the Nations. *Tsedek* introduces a vertical dimension to the horizontal relation and thus makes justice essential as an absolute condition for salvation. And unless we understand justice to be essential, it will never be more than superficial—a justice, be it noted once more, whose significance lies more in protecting the innocent than in prosecuting the guilty. Only where justice is essential does *dwelling* become possible in a world that is otherwise no more than a wilderness in which only the fit survive. Defined by the dimension of height or of the holy, dwelling is characterized by giving, as when we invite others to our table and offer them bread. Here justice is not only *tsedek* but also *tsedakah,* a giving of time, energy, and talent, without any vested interest in reciprocity or in balancing the scales. It is a justice conceived as gratitude, as a gratitude for gratitude itself, a gratitude not for receiving but for giving. Giving lies at the heart of community, and community lies at the core of world.

The *I think* of philosophy does not give—it thinks. The *I believe* of Christianity does not give—it believes. Each operates within the individual's solitary being—philosophy in its thought, Christianity in its faith. Therefore each easily grows deaf to the cry of the other. From a Jewish standpoint, by contrast, justice or *tsedakah* requires neither thought nor belief but an *act* of giving to another, without which there is no dwelling in the world. Dwelling, moreover, takes place within community, within *edah,* to use the Hebrew word, which also means "testimony." Testimony to what? Not to a philosophical system or to a theological doctrine but to justice as defined by the *mitzvot,* that is, by divine commandments. Focusing on the individual, the death that concerns both philosophy and Christianity is *my* death; focusing on community, the death that concerns Jewish thought is the death of the other. Jewish thought, therefore, opens up a place for justice in the world by opening up a responsibility for the death of the other. This is not the death that must be avenged or even forgiven; it is the death that must be prevented—that is the demand of *tsedek.*

Because only others are among the dead—and the murdered—the responsibility that characterizes Jewish thought opens up the dimension of time in such a way that time is defined by the responsibility that I have *yet* to meet. This *yet* is what constitutes a *path* into the world. G-d commands. I answer, "Here I am." No sooner do I answer, however, than I realize that I am too late. Although I may have given much, I realize through my very utterance that there is infinitely more that I might have given. The world, then, is the place where justice has *yet* to be fulfilled.

This point may provide some insight into the fact that *olam,* or "world" in Hebrew, also means "eternity." When the world takes on meaning, we encounter the eternal in time as the eternally meaningful. To have a meaning and mission in life is to be summoned from beyond the world to add what is *better* than the world *to* the world, that is, to add to the world *more* than all there is. That *more,* that trace of the eternal, is justice. A world drained of justice, then, is a world drained of the eternal and therefore of time, so that the future collapses into a present without presence, and the past fades into the forgiven and forgotten. Looking at ontological philosophy, we realize that if being in the world lies in the comprehension of Being, then there is no time and therefore no justice *yet to be* attained. The problem Christianity faces, by contrast, is its very solution to the problem: it is a redemption *already* attained through the crucifixion and resurrection of the Christ. Time and eternity—and therefore justice—in this realm thus become superfluous. All that is left to do is to wait and believe.

With regard to the world, then, justice is the fabric of time. Inasmuch as justice is an issue after Auschwitz, justice is the *after* in "after Auschwitz." The future opened up through a seeking after justice is neither the opposite of the past nor the outcome of the past—it is the outcry of the past. That outcry is not an abstraction but is as concrete as the flesh and blood of the human being. This brings us to a third context for our rethinking of the notion of justice.

JUSTICE WITH REGARD TO HUMANITY

If justice with regard to humanity is to be more than an abstraction, then our concern with humanity must be a concern with *this* human being who now stands before us. As all of humanity was gathered into Adam, so is all humanity gathered into each human being. That is why the Talmud compares saving a single life to saving the world (*Sanhedrin* 37a). That is also why *panim,* the Hebrew word for "face," is plural: each person bears his own face as well as the face of Adam, the face of humanity. The other human being, then, has no essence—she has a name that situates her not within the categories of essence but within a relationship to a family, community, world, and G-d. The realization of justice in the world, then, begins with acting justly toward *this* person, who is entrusted to our care. Those who would rob the person of such an absolute by viewing him as an animal or a specimen play into the hands of those who would destroy the divine image within the human being, as the Nazis did in their creation of the definitive denizen of Auschwitz: the *Muselmann.*

If justice is to be a possibility after Auschwitz, our thinking about justice requires an overcoming not only of the Nazi view but also of the Christian view of the human being. Ontological thought sees the human being as an accident of nature; Christian thought sees the human being as one entrenched in a sinful nature. Both positions are blind to the face of the other human being. The face commands us to attend to the need of the other human being *absolutely,* apart from excuses, contingencies, and contexts. Because, as Emmanuel Lévinas has argued, we encounter the commandment of the holy through the face of the human, the face situates the other in a position that is higher than my own.[8] Better than Being, the face of the other person is a breach in Being: it summons me to give and thus opens up the exigency of justice as *tsedakah.* Whereas ontology sets out to enlighten the mind and Christianity to save the soul of the other, *tsedakah* attends to the body, as when we snatch the bread from our own mouths and offer it to the hungry. With regard to humanity, justice is a matter that concerns the *body:* only one who eats can be just. For only one who eats can understand himself to be *already* indebted to the other, a realization that neither ontology nor Christianity can attain.

To the extent that they take the other to be *inherently* in error, neither philosophy nor Christianity can arrive at an understanding of justice as *tsedakah.* Here we see an important link between justice in the world and justice in human relations. We also perceive a difference between *tsedek* in the world, with its emphasis on protecting the innocent, and *tsedakah* between person and person, with its emphasis on a giving that is beyond any determination of guilt or innocence. The difference here lies in the distinction between the communal concern and the personal demand. Just as seeking justice in the world is not about balancing scales, being just toward the other is not about being fair. It is about being responsive to the divine commandment that summons us from the depths of the human face. It is about being responsible beyond the contingencies of "fairness."

The one who has a name calls me by name and thereby implicates me by asking, "Where are you?" Suddenly I realize that the question of justice after Auschwitz is not whether G-d, world, or humanity will be just but whether *I* shall be just. And that is determined according to a response to two other questions, the questions G-d put to Cain: "Where is your brother?" and "What have you done?" Indeed, Primo Levi feared that in a post-Auschwitz world each of us has become a Cain to the other,[9] usurping the place of the other in a struggle for power, possessions, pleasure, and prestige. Where human relation is characterized by such a struggle, the question of justice is the question posed by Lévinas: do we live by killing?[10]

If justice—*tsedakah*—is to be possible in the human-to-human relation, then it must be understood as a being for the other that manifests itself in a doing for the other. With regard to humanity, then, justice is an event that transpires between two; it is the event of the unfolding of meaning as one becomes, through the act of giving, a sign of the infinite dearness of the other. Without justice there is no meaning. And without meaning there is no word. As justice is a link between G-d and world, so is it the link between word and meaning.

Where does justice form a link between word and meaning? Not in negotiation or manipulation, not in conversion or instruction, but in a bearing witness that is akin to bearing wounds—for the sake of the other. Understood as *tsedakah,* justice requires this radical vulnerability, precisely in the way that identity requires vulnerability. Answering "Here *I* am" before the other, I expose myself to and for the other. In the realm of humanity, then, justice is not something I enact; rather, it is something I act upon as a response to a summons. Like the Good that chooses me prior to my choosing between good and evil, justice lays claim to me before I act. That is why justice *matters.* That is why we feel so empty without it. Thus, we come full circle: the reflection on justice with regard to humanity echoes a prior reflection on justice with regard to G-d. Add to these connections the emphasis on giving and testimony, and you have a link to justice with regard to world. This outcome, of course, is no accident. The relation to each requires the relation to the other. And justice after Auschwitz requires all three.

CONCLUSION

If we are to change not only *what* we think but *how* we think about justice, then we ourselves must change—not into something else but into who we are: children of the Holy One who are chosen to act ethically toward one another, declaring where our brother is according to what we have done. Only in this way can we free ourselves of the mark of Cain. Such a change requires *teshuvah*—a return to who we are *in truth,* through an act of repentance. We are taught that repentance is among the six things whose existence preceded creation (*Bereshit Rabbah* 1:4), for repentance requires opening a portal *in* creation so that what is *beyond* creation may enter. Wherever such repentance takes place, justice enters.

Repentance for what? Not just for Auschwitz, but for the ontological thinking and the Christian theology that persist *after* Auschwitz. Without this repentance we are in no position to seek justice in the form of *tsedek* and *tsedakah,* for without such repentance we remain paralyzed. Speculative philosophy would have the world and humanity without G-d; Christian doctrine would have G-d and humanity without world. Inasmuch as each eliminates a third term in this triad, both lose any possibility of justice after Auschwitz.

What, then, must be done? If justice is to be possible after Auschwitz, then a repentant philosophy must make ethics its first philosophy, and a repentant Christianity must seek atonement through deeds of loving kindness, not through the blood of a loving Christ. Philosophy must cease in its efforts to enlighten minds and Christianity in its efforts to save souls. After all, Jesus, as a Jew, enjoins his followers to feed the hungry and to comfort the sick—not to save the sinners (see Matthew 25). As for the Jews, the movement of return entails repentance for imitating the ways of those who have murdered the Jews. There also *teshuvah* is a return to who we are *in truth.* The task is one that confronts us all, Christian, philosopher, and Jew. It is as difficult as it is needful. And yet it is very nigh unto us.

NOTES

1. See Nahum Glatzer's introduction to Franz Rosenzweig, *Understanding the Sick and the Healthy,* trans. Nahum Glatzer (Cambridge, Mass.: Harvard University Press, 1999), p. 24.

2. Chaim A. Kaplan, *Scroll of Agony,* ed. and trans. Abraham I. Katsh (Bloomington: Indiana University Press, 1999), p. 130.

3. Rosenzweig's *Understanding the Sick and the Healthy* is a concise statement of the distinctions that belong to these three separate realms of relation; he examines the three realms to provide an antidote for the paralyzing nature of the philosophical tradition of German idealism.

4. See Ernst Cassirer, *Kant's Life and Thought,* trans. James Haden (New Haven: Yale University Press, 1981), p. 377.

5. See Abraham Joshua Heschel, *Man's Quest for God* (New York: Charles Scribner's Sons, 1954), p. 69.

6. Elie Wiesel, *Paroles d'étranger* (Paris: Éditions du Seuil, 1982), p. 172.

7. See Rosenzweig, *Understanding the Sick and the Healthy,* p. 71.

8. See Emmanuel Lévinas, *Ethics and Infinity,* trans. Richard Cohen (Pittsburgh: Duquesne University Press, 1985), pp. 105–6.

9. See Primo Levi, *The Drowned and the Saved,* trans. Raymond Rosenthal (New York: Summit Books, 1988), pp. 81–82.

10. See Lévinas, *Ethics and Infinity,* p. 120.

In Response to David Patterson

BRITTA FREDE-WENGER

INTERRELIGIOUS DIALOGUE is challenging. Among other things, it can involve explaining what and how—in our view—the other person believes. It is as if I held a picture or an image in front of the other and asked him or her, "Is this what you look like? Do you recognize yourself in this? If not, why?" These questions are on my mind as I think about David Patterson's essay. To reply to him means to try to translate from one system of thought to another. My remarks, therefore, are not so much a critique as they are an attempt to grasp Patterson's outlook and to correct his sometimes oversimplified view of Christianity's ideas about justice.

Underscoring that the world is one in which "mass slaughter of human beings is increasingly commonplace," Patterson recognizes key dilemmas that confront thinking about justice *after* Auschwitz. Ordinary understanding suggests that justice means a balancing of scales and giving to each "what they deserve." Patterson argues that such understanding does not grasp what justice ought to mean. He is right that there is no balancing of the scales in or after genocide, a judgment that is ironically confirmed by the fact that the words *Jedem das Seine* (to each what he deserves) were the ones that the Nazis put on the gates at their infamous Buchenwald concentration camp.

Patterson offers the Jewish understanding of *tsedek* (justice) as a way to "think otherwise than in terms of balancing the scales." In Jewish thought, he shows, justice is a doing rather than a state in which somebody or something is just. The ethical impulse that is aroused by hearing a divine commandment (Deuteronomy 16:20) constitutes and drives the dynamic between God, the world, and humanity in history. *Tsedek,* Patterson adds, is an "absolute condition for salvation." This thinking is presented as an alternative to both ontological philosophy and Christian doctrine. Those two, he contends, have severed one link in the triadic relationship. Putting the autonomous self in place of the divine, ontological philosophy contributed to the creation of Auschwitz by making it possible for Führer and Volk to become absolutes. Overemphasizing the soteriological (salvational) relationship between God and the individual, Christianity has become blind to the suffering of others.

Let me take a closer look at Patterson's argument. In Christianity, the teaching of original sin and of the salvation of the individual through faith has resulted in a concentration on the relation between God and the individual. Patterson finds Christian views of justice to be rooted here. If human beings are inherently and essentially sinful, then—thinking in terms of balancing the scales—God's justice cannot mean anything but death and damnation for them. Yet God has provided a way out: through faith in Christ, but only in this way, divine forgiveness can be obtained and salvation achieved. The Christian alternative seems to be either faith and forgiveness or death and justice. No room is left for responsibility for the other; no room is left for the non-Christian believer. According to Patterson, "The blood of Christ redeems the believing Christian from judgment for the crime of being; those who, like the Jews, explicitly reject Christ as their redeemer are subject to that judgment. Justice in this instance is a matter of paying a death penalty for being alive, as the Jews of Nazi-occupied Christendom did."

Patterson sets Nazi ideology and Christian thought next to each other—the problematic difference being that in Christianity, conversion makes it possible to avoid a "justified" death. If this logic applies, its consequence can only be an "effort to bring the 'good news' to another soul." Obviously, Patterson rejects what he takes this version of Christianity to say and imply: "If justice is to be a possibility after Auschwitz, our thinking about justice requires an overcoming not only of the Nazi view but also of the Christian view of the human being."

Does Christian theology have a way out of the dilemma that Patterson poses for it? In his view, Christian thought has to reformulate itself so that it "seek[s] atonement through deeds of loving kindness, not through the blood of a loving Christ." Although his diagnosis of Christian doctrine is devastating, Patterson offers a reminder that may be as hopeful as it is sobering: as a Jew, Jesus himself was rooted in the doing of justice *(tsedakah).*

Patterson's line of argument about Christian doctrine is well taken when he emphasizes that the alternative of conversion or death has led to incredible suffering. This alternative was based on a triumphalist security of a fulfilled *overcoming* of human sinfulness through the death of Christ in which *believing Christians alone* could partake. As a result, the relation of many Christians to non-Christians was characterized not by righteousness but by self-righteousness that condemned others. Now, going beyond Patterson and in some ways correcting his oversimplifications, it is important to stress that these results took place, at least in part, because the Christian outlook identified by Patterson is one that has rested on three false assumptions: first, original sin is necessarily an ontological category; second, divine justice leads to damnation; third, there is no theologically grounded notion of human justice as distinct from divine justice.

Consider these points in more detail by noting, first, that Patterson is correct when he diagnoses a seeming paradox in Christian thought. Franz Schupp put the point in the following way: "Christian theology's understanding of creation is stoic, and its view of salvation involves a gnostic understanding of humanity and the world."[1] In other words, while humankind is created in God's image and is inherently good, human beings are at the same time in need of salvation. The concept of original sin is the link between these two claims. As created by God, humanity is good, but, as Augustine stated, in Adam all humankind sinned and in its very ontological essence was changed. In sin, humankind is totally dependent on God's grace and cannot achieve salvation by itself. God's saving grace, however, can cleanse the human essence from Adam's sin. Thus, Christian tradition often held that baptism "reorganizes" a person *ontologically.*

Scripturally, this entire perspective rested on a problematic Latin translation of Romans 5:12, which in the Vulgate read that "*in* Adam" all had sinned. A more accurate reading of the text, however, makes clear simply that all have sinned, not owing to Adam's fallen nature being ontologically passed on to every other human being but because each person, without exception, has fallen short of what he or she ought to be. That condition, moreover, remains unchanged. Hence, theologians today try to reformulate original sin in a way that frees it from ontology. Instead, original sin focuses on sin's being a universal and yet personal reality. Since Adam, but not *in* Adam, every human being has sinned. Human power is not sufficient for any of us to escape this universal entanglement. Men and women stand in need of salvation, which only God can grant. Patterson goes too far when he claims that "the blood of Christ redeems the Christian from judgment *for the crime of being*" (my italics). The right to live is not taken away. But everybody stands in need of salvation from being *a sinner.* Faith and baptism do not reorganize human beings ontologically, but in Christian thought they are the human answer to God's justifying grace.

Now two further questions arise: Is "divine justice" nothing more than the damnation of all non-Christians? Is the human part in the salvation process nothing more than to wait and believe? Patterson's argument rests on the assumption that Christianity takes God's justice to entail condemnation of humankind because of sin. In this view, justice means death. The only way out is to invoke God's mercy through belief in Christ. What Patterson overlooks is the Christian teaching that God's justice and grace do not form an either / or alternative, but instead are a pair. This pairing means that all persons will be held responsible for their actions, for God is not indifferent to the lives that people lead, and yet that God's doing of justice is not something that condemns but rather saves and "justifies." In Christ, God approaches humankind as God's opposite and offers "justification." God alone is the "justifying" subject, but that reality does not make men and women merely passive recipients, because God's justifying and saving power requires a human answer, an affirmation of the human will to enter the dynamic of divine salvation.

As spelled out by Patterson, a fundamental difference seems to exist between Christian thinking about justice and the Jewish idea of *tsedek.* Whereas in Christian thought, God is the subject of justice, the subject of *tsedek* is man: "Justice—*tsedek*—begins not with the faith that G-d is love but with the response of *Hinehni,* 'Here I am for you,' to the commandment to love the neighbor." Through acts of loving kindness, God, world, and humanity are connected. God commands men and women to strive for justice in the world, and the *mitzvot* are the "absolute condition for salvation." In the Jewish notion of *tsedek,* God calls upon human persons to become active. Solidarity with the suffering is a prerequisite for human salvation. In the Christian notion of justice, God himself is the primary subject who offers salvation. A person's response is to agree and to receive God's transforming grace—not to save oneself.

Does this Christian teaching mean that the connection between people is severed? Does this perspective legitimate one person's distancing himself or herself from the suffering of another? Where justice means that God acts toward the salvation of humankind and world, human affirmation of this action cannot be passive. It must be a distinctly human answer, neither independent of nor unaffected by God's justice. Men and women are called to enter God's universal work; the Christian is called to love God but equally important is the love of the neighbor, regardless of his or her faith (Matthew 22:37–39). This love is asymmetrical and grounded in God's justifying love for humankind. Even if a person joins God's work, human actions differ from God's. Human beings must not judge, at least in the sense that when human justice partakes of God's love, it can never claim to rule ultimately about salvation or damnation.

Patterson oversimplifies when he claims that "Christianity does not give—it believes." History, however, *has* shown that Christianity has too easily "grown deaf to the cry of the other."

In Jewish thought, acts of loving kindness contribute to salvation, whereas Christianity teaches that no human effort can earn salvation, which is always a divine gift. Yet no Christian can justly distance himself or herself from suffering in history. On the contrary, acts of kindness are a necessary expression and outcome of the human affirmation that God intends to redeem the world that God created.

My intention has been to reply to David Patterson, not to criticize him. He is correct: Perhaps because in Christianity human deeds seem to have a different soteriological status than the *mitzvot* in Judaism, Christians have too often and too long forgotten to care for those who suffer, regardless of their faith. Patterson rightly calls for "a repentant Christianity [to] seek atonement through deeds of loving kindness, not through the blood of a loving Christ." The issue, however, is not a matter of *either* the one *or* the other. Both go together.

NOTE

1. Franz Schupp, *Schöpfung und Sünde* (Düsseldorf: Patmos, 1990), p. 553. The translation is mine.

In Response to David Patterson

JOHN K. ROTH

ON FRIDAY, SEPTEMBER 14, 2001, President George W. Bush spoke at a service of remembrance and mourning at the National Cathedral in Washington, D.C. Responding to the terrorist attacks on September 11, which damaged the Pentagon and devastated the World Trade Center in New York City, leaving thousands dead, Bush said that America's "responsibility to history" had become nothing less than "to answer these attacks and rid the world of evil." Several days later, it was announced that the American response to the attack launched with hijacked aircraft would be called Infinite Justice, a code name with expectations so grandiose that it was soon replaced by the more modest Enduring Freedom.

Insofar as "justice rhetoric" assumes a balancing of the scales so that a fair equilibrium is restored by setting right the wrong that has been done, David Patterson's essay is a reminder that talk about Infinite Justice, let alone ridding the world of evil, is scarcely credible in a post-Holocaust world. Even Enduring Freedom is not guaranteed in circumstances that continue to be rife with threats of terrorism. Auschwitz, Patterson rightly contends, "all but normalized mass murder." If so, bombings like those that killed innocent civilians in New York and Washington cannot be completely surprising, American shock notwithstanding, nor are they likely to be eliminated altogether.

During the Holocaust, human life was disrespected to such an extent that no forms of violence are unthinkable any more. The unprecedented has become a precedent. Even if nothing equivalent to the Holocaust has taken place, violence that defaces human life has become so massively commonplace that the scales of justice cannot be balanced by world courts, truth and reconciliation commissions, or any other campaigns aimed at setting things right and returning the world to a state of "normalcy," to use the term that has so often been bandied about in the United States in the aftermath of the September bombings. Indeed, Patterson suggests, the immense harm that people continue to do to one another leaves the scales of justice shattered beyond repair. In the midst of these ruined scales, however, Patterson refuses to relinquish the concept of justice. Instead, he urges, we must rethink what it means.

I have no quarrel with Patterson's view that destruction's power renders incredible any balancing-of-the-scales interpretation of what justice means. On the other hand, I am not convinced by his rethinking of justice. Believing that sin is so great that human deeds cannot bring a messianic age and redeem the world, I find parts of his perspective overly optimistic. More importantly on this occasion, I think he comes dangerously close to a Judeocentric perspective that is exclusive and even—paradoxically and ironically—supersessionist in reverse. I hasten to add that my knowledge of Patterson as a scholar and a friend makes me wonder whether I have misread his intentions, if not the words he has written. Nevertheless, my impression to the contrary persists. If Patterson's rethinking about justice is to be sound, he needs to clarify, and perhaps to disavow, some points that seem central to his Jewish reflections on justice after Auschwitz.

To document and amplify why Patterson's essay troubles me, I need to identify myself as a philosopher and a Christian. For Holocaust-related reasons that are understandable, Patterson comes down hard on both of those traditions. Opposing it to the Jewish thought he favors, Patterson tends to equate philosophy with "a totalizing ontological mode of thinking" that drained "humanity of its divine image" and thus "contributed to the creation of Auschwitz." According to Patterson, the outcome is that philosophy cannot escape the implication that power is "the only reality" and that justice is about "getting even." Unfortunately, for a thinker who loathes "totalizing" as much as Patterson professes to, this monolithic description of philosophy—derived from his adherence to Emmanuel Lévinas's brand of postmodern philosophy—is such a sweeping indictment that it seems out of character. If rethinking justice involves getting rid of "totalizing" thinking, as Patterson urges, then one wonders if he has done justice to philosophy.

A similar situation exists with Patterson's interpretation of Christianity. When it comes to Christianity's "contribution to the Holocaust," he contends that its supersessionist, anti-Semitic tradition is only part of the problem. Still more fundamental elements of Christian doctrine, he insists, must be taken to task. Specifically, Patterson finds Christian teachings about sin, forgiveness, and redemption especially culpable. He implies that they amount to a cosmic balancing act in a scenario where sin so infests the human condition that redemption can be found only through divine forgiveness that is obtained through confession and belief in Christ Jesus. But, Patterson suggests, this unfortunate balancing of the scales excludes those who do not confess Christ as savior, and in that way, it sets Jews up for the kill.

Patterson's account correctly holds Christians accountable for the Christocentric exclusivism that bedevils my tradition, but as his account continues, it strays from the mark in crucial ways. "[T]he Christian," writes Patterson, "invokes forgiveness, and not justice, as the path to reconciliation." Again, Patterson's totalizing tendency comes to the fore. As a Christian, I have difficulty recognizing his description of Christianity, which, I believe, does not drive the wedge of either / or between forgiveness and justice. "Faith," Patterson continues to inveigh, "brings forgiveness, but it cannot bring justice." Not one to nuance his generalizations, Patterson overgeneralizes once more. Failing to see that faith, partly because it involves forgiveness, might very well put one on paths that bring justice, he also overlooks the fact that Christianity, like every religious tradition, is far more pluralistic than his sweeping assertions acknowledge.

Largely dismissing Christian teachings about sin, redemption, and forgiveness as misguided or worse, Patterson ramps up his generalizations by adducing further either / or dichotomies of dubious distinction. The need is not for "belief in a redeemer," he tells us rather simplistically, but for "deeds of loving kindness toward the neighbor." In sum, he says, the need is for "the Jewish thought that was slated for annihilation in the extermination of the Jews." At this point, I ask, has Patterson, however inadvertently, revealed himself to be a supersessionist in reverse? Having trashed so much of philosophy and Christianity, which in their ways claimed precedence over allegedly benighted Jewish ways, does he now play a trumping Judeocentric card, which holds, in effect, that Jewish thought contains the truth as nothing else can properly claim?

With approval, Patterson cites Chaim Kaplan's Warsaw ghetto diary: "Either humanity would be Judaic, or it would be idolatrous-German." Apparently accepting this unshaded dualism, Patterson glosses Kaplan by saying that "[t]o be 'Judaic' is to seek salvation in deeds commanded from beyond the world." Commanded by God "from beyond Being," the deeds required are those of charity, which is "giving without expectation of reciprocation." This understanding of justice does not stress balancing or even fairness. Before we can ask whether justice is possible, God commands that we respond to a summons that requires protection of the innocent, caring for the other, and "a giving of time, energy, and talent, without any vested interest in reciprocity or in balancing the scales."

Patterson seems to think that the Jewish tradition has a monopoly on an ethics of this kind, a point that becomes apparent as he develops his outlook in contrast to the deficiencies that he continues to find in "ontological thought" and "Christian thought." Both, he claims, are "blind to the face of the other human being"—an indictment as problematic as it is huge—and thus they remain closed to the truth of Jewish thought as Patterson invokes it. Patterson actually has much to say about being and beyond, which makes me wonder whether he avoids some version of the "ontological thought" he deplores. Meanwhile, he says that prayer is a key way to hear God and to discern God's commands, but even if Christianity is better than philosophy because "Christians do not hold prayer in contempt, the Christian view of prayer is rather different from the Jewish view." At least in this case, unless his words do not say what they imply, "different" means "not as good as," because "prayer is not a request but an encounter," and "Christian prayer is prayer *for,* an asking for something." Comparisons and contrasts of this sort, which are so pronounced as to be unhelpful and even harmful, are what give me the impression that Patterson comes dangerously close to supersessionism in reverse. He trumps philosophy and Christianity with Jewish thought in ways akin to those that would offend him if the tables were turned.

Even if human effort can neither rid the world of evil nor bring about infinite justice, a point that Christian realism has long emphasized, Patterson gives good value when he encourages rethinking of justice that emphasizes loving kindness instead of scale balancing, giving instead of getting even, caring for the other instead of reciprocity. But his inclination toward Judeocentric exclusivism, which approaches crediting Jewish thought alone for advancing these ethical views, is as shortsighted as it is one-sided. Here's why.

In a post-Holocaust world of terrorism and wanton violence, two things are clear. First, Jewish thought is not going to be universally embraced. Like all religious traditions, it is too particularistic for that. For example, relatively few people (and not even all Jews) are going to accept Patterson's conviction, if they even discern what it means, that justice is commanded by "the One who commands from beyond Being." Second, if Patterson is serious not only about rethinking justice but also about encouraging people to be more just, then he should be seeking allies, but not necessarily converts, wherever he can find them. Both philosophy and

Christianity may contain them, but less so to the extent that acceptance of Patterson's polemics becomes a necessary condition for cooperation.

Patterson's essay concludes with a plea for repentance, but it is scarcely irenic. Polemical and dualistic to the end, at least on this occasion, Patterson claims that philosophy should stop trying to "enlighten minds" and put ethics first. As for Christianity, it "must seek atonement through deeds of loving kindness, not through the blood of a loving Christ." By contrast, as Patterson identifies the Jewish task, its repentance requires no comparably fundamental revisions, but instead Jews should just stop "imitating the ways of those who have murdered the Jews." Time runs out before Patterson can elaborate whom "those" includes and what "imitating" them involves. Meanwhile, he leaves me puzzled about much more than that.

In sum, as I write these words in the season of Yom Kippur, the Day of Atonement, Patterson makes me ponder: Does his rethinking of justice require rethinking, if not repentance? Am I the one who needs to repent for having misunderstood his intentions, his words, and their implications? Or is the need for our dialogue to continue until greater reconciliation is achieved? The last question is crucial. It will surprise me if Patterson's reply does not take steps in that direction.

In Response to Britta Frede-Wenger and John K. Roth

DAVID PATTERSON

SØREN KIERKEGAARD ONCE said that the greatest service that a friend can do for a friend is to oppose him. With this in mind, I want to begin by thanking Britta Frede-Wenger and John Roth for their careful and critical reading of my essay. Their sound insights demonstrate that thinking is a dialogical affair that transpires between people.

One reason for my beginning with Kierkegaard is to put to rest Roth's concern about my equating philosophy in general with a totalizing, ontological mode of thinking. For, like many thinkers, Kierkegaard is a philosopher who stands outside the philosophy that I am taking to task. My intention was not to indict all philosophy but to oppose a line of philosophical development that begins with the Cartesian equation of thought with Being and culminates in the Heideggerian notion that man is justified by resolve alone. In between I see figures such as Immanuel Kant, G. W. F. Hegel, and Friedrich Nietzsche, who, despite the important differences among them, understand freedom in terms of a self-legislating autonomy. In contrast to thinkers such as these, I see Kierkegaard, Blaise Pascal, Leo Tolstoy, Franz Rosenzweig, Martin Buber, Emmanuel Lévinas, and others, who, also despite significant differences, understand freedom in terms of adherence to a divine commandment. Therefore I do not think my complaint about a certain line of philosophical development amounts to a sweeping indictment of philosophy.

Other points raised in the critiques offered by Roth and Frede-Wenger, however, are more problematic for all three of us. Frede-Wenger identifies some of these problematic issues, one of which has to do with original sin as an ontological category. She argues that I go too far in my claim that Christianity requires redemption from the crime of being, since "the right to live is not taken away." Yet she concedes that *everyone* is in need of salvation for being a sinner. That is precisely my complaint: from a Christian standpoint, being means being a sinner, from the instant we emerge from the womb. True, one has a right to live and to repent, where repentance means embracing the redemption from sin attained through the Cross: the blood of Christ *alone* can alter the ontological status of the human being as sinner. Therefore, I do not think it is heresy to assert that, according to the Christian doctrine of inherited sin, a human being, in his or her very being, is in a state of sin *from birth,* so that Christ is not superfluous but is *necessary* for the redemption of all. Those who consciously and explicitly reject Christ may have a right to live, but they live outside the circle of grace, entrenched in their sinful being. My claim is that this result poses a problem for our thinking about justice and our relation to non-Christian human beings, who in their essence remain in a state of sin.

Related to the matter of our inherently sinful being is another of Frede-Wenger's concerns: the question of whether divine justice leads to damnation. If "he who commits sin is of the devil" (1 John 3:8) and if the blood of Christ alone cleanses us from sin, then it would seem that those who reject Christ merit the fate of the devil. After all, one might be led to think—indeed, Christians in the past have been led to think—only someone who is evil, like the devil, would reject the salvation offered by the Christ. What, then, is the just desert to be meted out to such a person? Is such a person not damned, according to Christian teaching? As far as I can tell, it is not heresy to associate divine justice with damnation in such instances. This too, I think, renders the pursuit of justice problematic.

This deliberate rejection of salvation on the part of those who have "spurned the Son of G-d" (Hebrews 10:29) is the deliberate sin that the New Testament refers to when it asserts, "If we sin deliberately after receiving the knowledge of the truth [that Christ alone brings salvation from sin], there no longer remains a sacrifice for sins, but a fearful prospect of judgment, and a fury of fire which will consume the adversaries" (Hebrews 10:26–27). Is this text not invoking a divine justice that amounts to damnation for those who refuse Christ? Or is it a divine judgment that withholds justice, since justice may lie in salvation, not in damnation? As Frede-Wenger points out, under a Christian notion of justice, G-d is "the primary subject who offers salvation" from our sinful nature, and, due to that sinful nature, the human being cannot bring about his or her own salvation. To be sure, it seems that, from a Christian standpoint, receiving forgiveness and salvation *is* divine justice (see, for example, 1 John 1:9). But if that is the case, then my critics must explain the distinction between divine judgment and divine justice. Perhaps one point of my own confusion lies in supposing that divine judgment and divine justice are not opposed.

Adding to my confusion is a point that Frede-Wenger makes regarding a human being's ability to atone for his or her sins through deeds. She rightly points out that, from a Christian perspective, no human doing can earn atonement, yet she insists that seeking atonement through deeds is part of seeking atonement through faith in Christ. Her point seems to be that while deeds of loving kindness are indeed necessary, they are not enough for salvation—a view that Roth shares in his assertion that human deeds cannot bring a messianic age and redeem the world. But can Christian faith accomplish what human deeds cannot? The traditional Christian answer is yes: "By grace you have been saved through faith, and this is not your doing, it is a gift of G-d, not because of works" (Ephesians 2:8–9). Roth suggests that I am overly optimistic about the efficacy of human works and that relatively few people will accept my conviction, which may well be the case. But Roth knows very well that truth is not determined by taking a vote, and the prospects for success do not determine the value of the endeavor. The fact that we cannot merit the Messianic Age is not a reason to refrain from the aspiration. And one thing is certain: deeds of loving kindness may not be enough to save us, but without them we are lost.

The point that I do need to clarify is connected to this matter, and it is perhaps a point on which Christians and Jews can agree, despite the tension between faith and deeds. What I propose is a laboring for justice not through deeds that we *choose* to do but through deeds we are *commanded* to perform under the Law. Yes, as Frede-Wenger says, salvation comes from G-d—not, however, because the blood of Christ comes from G-d but because the *commandment* comes from G-d. According to the Torah, which both Christians and Jews embrace, G-d places in our hands the means of our salvation: the commandments of Torah (see Deuteronomy 30:19). And G-d does not command the impossible. Or rather, He is involved in what He commands: the attempt to bring justice to the world may look as impossible as crossing the Sea of Reeds, yet Nachshon descended into the waters. And *that* is where faith comes in.

If my emphasis on the commandment and not on the faith that comes from G-d is Judeocentric, then I accept that charge. Should the Jewish reflections of a Jew not be Judeocentric? I understand that Roth's objection to my Judeocentrism concerns a potentially dangerous reverse supersessionism, where Judaism might supersede Christianity. Putting aside the question of whether what precedes Christianity can supersede it, let me say this: *something* needs to supersede the traditional forms and teachings of Christianity, so that the age-old teaching of contempt for the Jews, the view that those who reject Christ are lost in a state of sin, and the assertion that we are justified by faith *alone* may be deemed heretical. As a Jew, I see in Judaism an alternative to such teachings, but it is not the only alternative. Indeed, in Judaism it *is* heretical to maintain that one must be an adherent of Judaism in order to have a place with

G-d. After all, the notion of the Righteous among the Nations—that is, the idea that there are righteous non-adherents of Judaism—belongs to a distinctly Jewish tradition. Therefore I take Roth's phrase "Judeocentric exclusivism" to be a contradiction of terms.

Regarding Roth's complaint that I present the Jewish tradition as if it had "a monopoly on an ethics of this kind" and that I credit "Jewish thought alone for advancing these ethical views," I do need to make some clarifications. First, I do not maintain that the Jewish tradition enjoys any monopoly on these ethical injunctions, but I do maintain, as Christians do, that these injunctions come from G-d and into the world through the Jewish people. From the standpoint both of Judaism and of Christianity, neither Jewish thought nor any other purely human thinking can be credited with advancing these ethical views. According to both religious traditions, these views are not concepts derived from thought—they are commandments revealed by G-d to the Jews, who, through their adherence to the commandments, bring the light of the ethical teaching to the world. The aim is not to make all the world Jewish but to make all the world just. As the calculated effort to exterminate the Jews and Judaism from the world, the Holocaust was characterized by the Nazis' endeavor to extinguish from the world that light, and with it the commandment to seek justice.

My thesis is that after Auschwitz the pursuit of justice entails the restoration of that light. And since that light is the light of Torah—that is, of Jewish teaching—the restoration of that light requires an engagement with Jewish teachings on justice. I see this as neither supersessionist nor exclusivist but as necessary to a response to the Nazis' attempt to obliterate the Jews and the teachings that originally came into the world through them. *After* Auschwitz, it seems to me to be not only legitimate but also needful to examine what was slated for destruction *in* Auschwitz.

8

The Israeli-Palestinian Conflict

Just Reconciliation in the Shadows of the Holocaust

LEONARD GROB

AUSCHWITZ CONTINUES to cast its long shadow over all that is human. Like the other contributions to this volume, this chapter strives to further the process of reexamining fundamental ethical concerns in the post-Holocaust world. I will focus here on the notion of genuine reconciliation—reconciliation within a commitment to justice—between conflicting parties in the post-Auschwitz world. My choice of parties to a conflict is not arbitrary. In our time, there are few conflicts that appear to be more intractable, more impervious to notions of reconciliation and justice, than the Israeli-Palestinian conflict. Indeed, we have before us nothing short of what has been termed a new Hundred Years' War. Furthermore, the specter of the Holocaust haunts, unrelentingly, the turmoil in the Middle East. The adversaries in this conflict do not hesitate to make references to the Holocaust in the course of creating their rhetoric of war. And even when no explicit references are made, the events of 1933–1945 never cease to cloud that war-torn landscape. If we are to reflect on reconciliation of a conflict fought in no small measure against the backdrop of the Holocaust, it is to this century-old conflict that we must turn.

That Israeli Jews perceive themselves to be fighting battles in the shadows of the Holocaust is certainly not surprising. Although the Zionist dream has roots in the millennia-old aspirations of the Jewish people,

Israel itself was born, in some substantial sense, out of the ashes of the destruction of two-thirds of European Jewry. Holocaust allusions abound in the Israeli press, the majority bringing to mind the claim that a people newly empowered with statehood must not allow themselves to become, or to be perceived as becoming, weak in their struggle with the Palestinians, their current "Amalek" or inveterate foe. Explicit contrasts are drawn between the powerlessness of Jews in Europe during the Holocaust and the military might of the Israel of today. Those who would wish to retain land on the West Bank for Israel make reference to the pre-1967 boundary lines as "Auschwitz borders." Indeed, the oft-quoted phrase "Never again" is most often applied, in its literal rendering, to the Palestinian-Israeli conflict. Threats—perceived or real—to Israel's continued existence keep the "ghost of the Holocaust" alive and well.[1]

Palestinians, too, allude with increasing frequency to the Holocaust. The allusions are multifaceted. Israeli treatment of Palestinians is sometimes compared in the Palestinian press to Nazi treatment of Jews at Auschwitz. Israelis have been accused of a racism which rivals or runs deeper than that exhibited by the Nazis. Some Palestinian spokespersons sound a theme that can be roughly characterized as "My Holocaust is as traumatic an event for my people as yours is for your people." Finally, elements of denial of the Holocaust have also found their way into Palestinian rhetoric. Familiar terms, such as "forged claims" regarding "alleged acts of slaughter," have appeared in the officially sanctioned Palestinian press, upping the ante in a battleground of words which has so often become a battleground of rocks, bullets, and mortars.[2]

That the Palestinian-Israeli conflict stands in the shadows of the Holocaust, and that it is a conflict in desperate need of just reconciliation, needs little further comment. I wish, however, to add another note regarding my choice of these parties to a conflict. As a Holocaust scholar, as a Jew, and as a human being vitally concerned with *tikkun olam*—the healing of the world—I see in a morally sound resolution of these hundred years of enmity in the Middle East an opportunity to cast light on a vital aspect of the human condition as such.

It is unquestionably the case that Jews have suffered appallingly from anti-Semitic acts over the course of two millennia. It is also the case that these acts came to a head in the murder of European Jewry during the

Holocaust—whatever other factors contributed to the creation of the Nazi genocidal mind. As a stateless people, Jews had no access to those instruments of power by means of which they could contend with those who would eliminate them from the earth. A people formerly unable to defend itself with the force of arms has now, however, become a potent military force, not only in the Middle East, but in the world at large. An oppressed people has become empowered with arms and the technical knowledge needed to use them. To employ an analogy: the abused child has grown up, assuming the reins of power.

Just how are these reins to be assumed? Is the oft-told tale of the oppressed become oppressor to be repeated yet one more time? Or will the use of power be subject to the ongoing and sustained critique of justice—itself a concept vital to the Jewish prophetic tradition? Where, on the continuum created between these two poles, will Israel, newly empowered with the force of arms, fall with regard to its less powerful Palestinian neighbors? How will mainstream Israeli leaders address occasional references, from some on the far right of the political spectrum, to the "transfer" and "resettlement" of Palestinians?[3] Responses to these queries, I believe, have important ramifications not just for the story to be played out in the Middle East, but, even more significantly, for the possibility of an expanded human story. Such a story would speak to the potential of the powerless become powerful to lead an ethical existence, an existence infused with awareness of the sacredness of the other.

The issue of the oppressed becoming the oppressor having been raised, two clarifications are immediately in order. First, it is to walk the minefields of ethico-political discourse to suggest terms in which the oppression of Palestinians could be thought to be equated with the genocide of European Jews. Even after considering critiques of any "hierarchy of suffering," I wish to make clear that I am not making any facile equation of the (manifestly) acute oppression of Palestinians with the systematic murder of European Jewry. The endeavor here is not to perpetuate a contest in which the moral high ground is claimed by that party to a conflict which has allegedly suffered more than its adversary. Rather I wish to honor the vital concern of each group to make its claim to the distinctiveness of its own history of oppression and to attempt to learn lessons from that history. The rhetoric of "my Holocaust is greater than yours" must be eliminated without giving rise to a homogenizing of the sufferings of all peoples.

Raising the question of the abused becoming the abuser calls for a second clarification. Having implied in this discussion of the military empowerment of Israeli Jews that the major burden of responsibility for just reconciliation in the Middle East lies with Israel—a contention on which I will elaborate below—a note of caution must be sounded. I do not seek to remove from the Palestinians their own responsibility for creating just reconciliation in the Middle East; nor do I wish to relieve Palestinians of responsibility for contributing to the creation of many of the impasses that have dominated the history of the conflict to date. During a century of Middle East conflict, there have not been, nor are there at present, any innocent parties. Reconciliation, if it is to be just, will not come about by the acts of one party alone; reconciliation is dialogical at its core.

This is not to say that reconciliation is to be identified in some facile manner with compromise. Just reconciliation is not fully achieved when two parties, driven solely by considerations of expediency, consent to halt hostilities. (This is not to minimize the benefits of any agreement that leads to the cessation of bloodletting, however temporary or for whatever motive.) Genuine reconciliation aims for ontological or structural change in the relationship of conflicting parties. Such change demands that each side call into question the nature of a self-interested seeing which has led it to posit its own set of claims—what I term its story—as an unquestioned absolute. For reconciliation to occur, each side must radically call into question the dominant story or narrative that has guided its adoption of positions during the course of conflict.[4] Self-critique lies at the heart of all genuine reconciliation.

In this regard we have much to learn from the events of 1933–1945 in Europe. The Holocaust has demonstrated all too clearly the need for the "brokenness" of all claims to absolute truth.[5] If, as I have suggested, we view these claims as stories, then all stories become suspect. With regard to our concerns, it becomes especially important to call into question the mythico-poetic tales in which nationalisms inevitably root themselves. In the shadows of Auschwitz—itself made possible largely by ideology run wild—both sides to a conflict must learn to question their dominant narratives. The Nazi reification of the idea presents us with the danger, writ large, of an uncritical, totalizing vision: All peoples were judged according to those fixed racial doctrines of the Third Reich, doctrines to which masses turned in idolatrous worship. In the wake of the rule of unchecked absolutes in the 1930s and 1940s, the conditions for genocide ripened. Idolatry—adherence to the idea as absolute—contributed directly to the murder of millions.

Nor was racial doctrine the sole absolute which came to serve as the object of Nazi idolatry. Totalizing claims are not only to be found in the static pronouncements of ideologues; they can also be detected in the unquestioned ways in which meaning is constructed all across a given society. Obedience to authority and conformity to peer groups served as uncritical categories of meaning-making for millions during the Nazi regime. Knee-jerk compliance with the petty rules of entrenched bureaucracy constituted yet another fixed or "unbroken" absolute. Seemingly remote from the triumphalism of Nazi racial doctrines, the structures of instrumental reasoning, so vital to the functioning of bureaucracies, led just as certainly to mass murder. Utilitarian thought processes, devoid of any moral critique of the end to be sought, allowed the dominant Nazi narrative to be realized. The compliant functionary in the Nazi system shares responsibility for genocide along with the raving anti-Semite.

What we can learn from the Holocaust, then, is that each party to a conflict must transcend its absolutist or master narrative, the story within which it uncritically justifies its own existence, while at the same time assigning its partner in conflict the status of "other." Such narratives, I have argued, must be broken. "Brokenness," rather than being understood as merely an absence of wholeness, is the key to the creation of an entirely new kind of wholeness. In the spirit of self-critique and in hope of genuine reconciliation, I accept my limitations, my finitude, as I accept yours. Each party to a conflict accepts its wounded state; each shows its wounds to the other in the dialogical endeavor to heal them. In jointly confronting the brokenness of both narratives, conflicting parties escape the seeming inevitability of violent action and reaction; they create a "third way" or "creative middle": the authentic "whole" of dialogue.

This new whole is thus not just a larger set of static pronouncements. Dialogical reconciliation is more verb than noun, more process than product. Within the encounter of each party with the other, both master narratives are replaced by a meta-narrative, a super-story existing on a plane radically different from that of the story each side has been telling itself—or even of their amalgamation. Rather than being posited as a set of ideas in some arsenal of ideological claims, this tale is something enacted, something witnessed-to. The meta-narrative is not merely told, but fundamentally told-to. In the course of creating a meta-narrative, each truly listens to the other's story, to the point of returning to it at the very juncture when one is most excited about the central points of one's own story.[6] Reconciliation requires nothing less than each group's becoming fully present to the other.[7]

Within this meta-narrative, the other, far from being seen as an object occupying a fixed (and subordinate) place within my narrative, now becomes my co-subject. In genuine engagement with the other, I strip away those layers of meaning within which I have constructed his / her persona. Each party to conflict is seen to transcend the series of characterizations, which had been seen to constitute the totality of his / her being. The other whom I engage in genuine dialogue is infinitely more than what I had formerly deemed him / her to be.

Being present to the other in a super-narrative as process does not mean that narrative in the ordinary sense—history as it has been told—is entirely forgotten. To engage in reconciliation as a dialogical process is not to embrace any ecstatic moment that would free us from the concreteness of history. We all bring with us the baggage of finite, temporal beings. In order to reconcile, we need not forget this baggage; indeed, we cannot do so. Rather, the meta-narrative is constructed by authentic meeting. Thus, what was once a fully self-justifying narrative, accompanied by the well-rehearsed recitation of the evils perpetrated by the other, now becomes the mutual recognition of the partial validity of each side's claims. Each party goes over to the other side, meeting in a space the German Jewish philosopher Martin Buber named "the Between": the very point at which broken visions meet.

How are we to apply this understanding of just reconciliation to the very flesh-and-blood strife in the Middle East? In the case of the Middle East conflict, each party must rethink its dominant narrative without losing sight of the uniqueness of the history in which, in part, it is grounded. If Palestinian and Israeli narratives are to be understood within the brokenness of the post-Holocaust world, each side must attempt to demythologize its narrative in the course of dialogical engagement with the other. Each side must be seen as transcending the totalizing set of images employed by the other to capture his / her personhood within fixed categories of thought.

Palestinians might be asked, for example, if the story of an indigenous people robbed of their land by foreign invaders could be rendered more complex by the fact that Jews were fleeing oppression—later, almost certain death—in Europe, and had set out for a land with which they had their own history of intimate connection. The Israeli Jew might thus be viewed as more than an alien imperialist colonizer. Might the Palestinian narrative—within which more than 3,000,000 descendants of 750,000 refugees from the 1948 War are entitled to return to live within Israel's pre-1967 borders—be complicated by Israel's fear of the loss of a Jewish state? In a post-Holocaust world, how might Palestinians rethink their narrative to address the existential anxiety of Jewish Israelis regarding a need for majority status in a nation of their own? Might aspects of the Palestinian story be reshaped in response to Jewish concerns—rooted in two thousand years of oppression—regarding not having a state of their own and thus not being able, in some significant sense, to take responsibility for their own destiny? Finally, it goes without saying that the visceral fears of Israelis—triggered anew by suicide bombings—regarding the possibility of a new Holocaust in the Middle East need to be addressed in an ongoing and explicit rejection of that extremist Palestinian rhetoric within which Jews are threatened with extinction. That such existential anxiety may have little or no basis in reality does not allow for its dismissal out of hand. These fears—rooted as they are in the history of the Jewish people—must be fully encountered by Palestinians if authentic dialogue between co-claimants to the land is to be sustained.

How might the Jewish Israelis come to see their Palestinian counterparts anew? A set of queries must now be posed to Israeli Jews, calling into question the traditional Zionist narrative, and thus the lenses through which the Palestinian other has been viewed. Although I have argued above that just reconciliation must be fully dialogical, it is not the case here—and, I would argue, it is not the case in any conflict—

that the two sides bear equal measures of responsibility for initiating the breaking of the chain of violent action / reaction. I believe that the burden of responsibility for moving toward reconciliation in the Middle East lies with Israel. There exists an asymmetry between Israelis and Palestinians with regard to the arms possessed by each and the moral weight of past deeds. Such an asymmetry demands that Israel initiate movement toward reconciliation.

That Israel is now a major force in the Middle East is beyond question. Even when the danger of a regional conflict is taken into account, it still must be recalled that Israel possesses an army that is among the most powerful in the region and the most superior in the world.

That there exists a disparity in the moral weight of past actions on the part of the parties to a conflict is a far more complex issue. Although, as I have argued, both sides are guilty of injustices, in the struggle for a land to which two peoples have claims, it is certainly the case that hundreds of thousands of indigenous Palestinians have either been displaced from their native soil or continue to live as substantially less than full citizens within Israel. Although the controversy over Israel's exact measure of responsibility for the creation of the Palestinian refugee problem continues to rage, most scholars of the Middle East emphasize the fact that the vast majority of Palestinians were either expelled by force or became victims of the inevitable displacement occasioned by war.[8] Although European Jews "leaped from the burning buildings"—initially pogroms, later full-fledged genocide—it is also true, as peace activist and philosopher Michael Lerner has argued, that "they landed on the backs of Palestinians."[9] The Palestinians on whose backs they landed belonged to those predominantly Muslim peoples who have constituted a majority on the land for almost the entirety of the previous thirteen centuries. How, then, we must ask, could it be the case that many early Jewish leaders returning to Zion spoke of the alleged fact of a "people without a land" coming to a "land without a people"?[10] How did it come to pass that the Zionist narrative has often failed, even to this day, to recognize the fullness of the presence of an indigenous people living on the land and longing to exercise sovereignty in an independent, viable state? Although both sides to the conflict have demonstrated intransigence with regard to taking and sustaining initiatives toward reconciliation, what, we must ask, lies behind the intransigence of the more powerful party, Israel?

To seek some responses to these questions, we must once again turn to the Holocaust in whose shadow this conflict rages. As we noted earlier, post-Holocaust Israel is driven in substantial measure by the notion that Jewish blood will never again be shed with impunity. The trauma of the Holocaust permeates the consciousness of Israeli Jews. Israel appears not to be able to abandon a central aspect of its self-definition: its status as victim. Forged through two thousand years of persecution and finally sealed—seemingly indelibly—at Auschwitz, this part of Israel's self-understanding is not at all impressed by statistics detailing its military might. As sociologist and Holocaust scholar Zygmunt Bauman puts it, "victimization breeds more victimization." Hitler may yet have his (posthumous) victory in the war against the Jews: "What . . . [the designers of the Final Solution] failed to accomplish when alive, they may yet hope to achieve in death. They did not manage to turn the world against the Jews, but in their graves they can still dream of turning the Jews against the world, and thus—one way or another—to make the Jewish reconciliation with the world . . . all that more difficult, if not downright impossible."[11]

Yet the die has not been cast. The Holocaust offers us unlimited lessons; indeed, Bauman's account is restricted to just one way memory of the Holocaust has, in fact, been utilized. Other and very different responses have already come forth, and, what is more important for our purposes, other ways of memorializing six million murdered Jews can certainly be envisioned for the future. Indeed, the Holocaust must be mined for the vast array of teachings that can be extracted from it. Although Jewish pain was so great that relief—a secure future—seemed to lie solely in building a fortress state, the Holocaust also teaches the lessons of respecting the sacredness of each individual being, most especially the other who is oppressed. What we learn is that the downtrodden in one's midst must be protected. The notion that we must not abandon all considerations of power in the endeavor to preserve human dignity is thus immediately counterbalanced by a notion that dignity rests fundamentally in welcoming the one in need.[12] Both are teachings of the Holocaust; neither is to be neglected.

With these points in mind, a series of questions needs to be addressed to Israeli Jews: How might the traditional Zionist narrative be demythologized so as to include the Palestinian other as co-subject? Might Palestinians be viewed as other than, at best, less-civilized natives, and, at worst, those inclined to terrorism? Concretely, how might the dominant narrative be rendered more complex by an explicit acknowledgment of Israel's substantial responsibility for the creation of the Palestinian refugee problem? Although such a statement of accountability does not necessarily entail an acceptance of a literal right of return of all Palestinians to pre-1948 borders, it does mean that the displaced and dispossessed are called by their proper name. As a result, it means, further, that genuine negotiations can now take place for determining how many refugees will return and on what basis they will be chosen. The lessons of the Holocaust regarding the provision of hospitality for the other—in this case the Palestinian refugee—must be heeded.

Further, how might Zionism be reconfigured to embrace the creation of two viable states, linked both in economic confederation and in the confederation of mutual regard for the sacredness of the other? The dream of a Greater Israel must be explicitly disowned. Just as the deep-seated fears of Israelis must be taken into account by Palestinians, so must Israelis address the existential anxiety of Palestinians: How might Israel rethink its history of alleged justifications for the ongoing construction of settlements on the West Bank and Gaza, together with the creation of the massive bypass roads which link them? Such construction must be reconsidered in the process of encountering the fear of Palestinians that in the end negotiations will yield nothing more than a series of cantons divided by Israeli checkpoints—this posing as the "generous" offer of a so-called state? Such fears continue to be triggered among Palestinians by often arbitrary home demolitions and land appropriations carried out by Israeli forces.

And then, Jerusalem. How might the place of Jerusalem in Zionist ideology be reconsidered so that the City of Peace can be shared by both claimants? How might sharing Jerusalem be distinguished from some mechanical dividing of the city that may not address the spiritual and physical needs of both peoples? Must not the descendants of Holocaust victims—victims of the glorification of racial categories—reexamine any unthinking "veneration of rocks" in the name of which genuine reconciliation between conflicting parties is sacrificed? Although the hallowing of soil in accord with historical memory constitutes a vital element of authentic national self-awareness, how easily does the sacralization of land become sacrilege! Must the heirs of a prophetic tradition—chastising idolaters at every turn—not reject any idolatrous worship of land at the expense of a dialogical embrace of the Palestinian, now, paradoxically, an alien in a land to which he / she has such substantial claim? If, as I argue, the Holocaust teaches that power exercised without consideration of justice leads inevitably to the dehumanization of the other, then it is certainly the case that Israel's power must be employed in the name of just reconciliation with its Palestinian partners.

Having argued for Israeli initiative in creating a just resolution to the conflict, I wish to sound a cautionary note.[13] The asymmetry between Palestinians and Israelis which I have noted does not mean that largely dispossessed Palestinians are freed from the responsibility of exercising their own initiatives toward achieving just reconciliation. Victimhood—to which many peoples can appeal—does not mean that one is automatically released from what I would term a moral imperative to engage the other in genuine dialogue. Nor does the asymmetry imply that the new possessors of might—Israeli Jews—need banish from memory that dimension of their narrative which tells of an oppressed people yearning for self-determination in a land to which it has been tied for millennia, both in matter and spirit.[14] In the endeavor to achieve just reconciliation, each side must embrace its history while at the same time overcoming the temptation to read that history as something static, a given.

A final note: A post-Zionist movement, originally consisting largely of Israeli "new historians," has attracted other Israeli Jews who embrace the notion of a one-state solution to the Middle East conflict.[15] This solution—also advocated by large numbers of Palestinians—calls for one democratic state of all its citizens within the boundaries of pre-1948 Palestine. Such a state would clearly host a Palestinian majority within a short period of time. Although the demythologizing of the Zionist narrative would now seemingly be complete, I would argue that a newly mythologized entity would come to serve in its stead: a state created largely without reference to any weighing of the history of one of its peoples. While I believe strongly that the ultimacy of all national boundaries must be called into question in an ongoing movement toward internationalization, two thousand years of Jewish history, culminating in the Holocaust, prompts me to argue that in the dismantling of nation-states, Israel should not be among the first to relinquish sovereignty. Although I yearn for a time when dialogue among nations will lead to new and different understandings of borders, I contend that the specter of Auschwitz renders premature a fundamental reconsideration of those borders whose demarcation would allow for two viable states in the Middle East. It is a task demanding enormous moral courage to achieve a just reconciliation between two sovereign states committed to living as neighbors in confederations grounded and sustained in genuine dialogue. It is to this end that I believe all efforts in the Middle East should be dedicated. The Holocaust teaches us the perils that we face when we fail to acknowledge the other as co-subject. The extent to which that lesson is heeded will be revealed perhaps nowhere more clearly than in the degree and quality of reconciliation achieved in the Middle East. Just reconciliation in this part of the world will constitute a veritable "light unto the nations."

NOTES

1. The term *ghost of the Holocaust* is taken from Zygmunt Bauman's "The Holocaust's Life as a Ghost," *Tikkun: A Bimonthly Jewish Critique of Politics, Culture, and Society,* July–Aug. 1998.

2. See, for example, the charges detailed in the Palestinian Authority newspaper *Al-Hayat Al-Jadidah,* Sept. 3, 1997, quoted, in English translation, in the Israeli information sheet entitled "Holocaust-Denial Statements by Palestinian Authority Figures," Arutz Sheva News Service, Jan. 19, 1998. Online at http://www.geocities.com/CapitolHill/Senate/2396/quotes/hlcstden.htm.

3. Yair Sheleg, "A Very Moving Scenario," *Haaretz,* Mar. 23, 2001.

4. It should be noted that we must be cautious not to assume that there is only one Palestinian narrative or one Zionist narrative. In fact, there are

many Palestinian nationalisms and many Zionisms. My discussion attempts to speak, at least in broad outline, to a dominant or master narrative told by mainstream leaders through generations of conflict, and retold by a majority of both peoples.

5. I am indebted for the term *brokenness* in this context—as well as for the concept of the manner in which brokenness and wholeness relate—to Rabbi Irving Greenberg's keynote address to the 31st Annual Scholars' Conference on the Holocaust and the Churches, St. Joseph's College, Philadelphia, Pa., Mar. 4, 2001.

6. I am indebted for comment regarding turning to the other person's story to Rabbi Michael Lerner's address as a panelist at a conference entitled "The Middle East Peace Process: Political and Spiritual Dimensions," Nassau Community College, Garden City, N.Y., Apr. 25, 2001.

7. I am indebted for a deepening of my insight regarding reconciliation as process to Dr. Richard Rubenstein's presentation on the panel "Confronting Complicity" at the 31st Annual Scholars' Conference on the Holocaust and the Churches, St. Joseph's College, Philadelphia, Pa., Mar. 4, 2001. See also my own work in this regard in "Buberian Peace Education in the Mideast: A Buberian Critique," *Educational Theory* 35, no. 4 (Fall 1985): 423–32.

8. See, for example, Israeli historian Benny Morris's very early "revisionist" account of the refugee problem in *The Birth of the Palestinian Refugee Problem* (Cambridge: Cambridge University Press, 1987).

9. Michael Lerner, *Jewish Renewal: A Path to Healing and Transformation* (New York: G. P. Putnam's Sons, 1994), p. 219.

10. This saying—by now a canard—is often attributed to Prime Minister Golda Meir.

11. Bauman, "The Holocaust's Life as a Ghost," p. 37.

12. Richard Rubenstein stresses this point in the course of his critique of Martin Buber in "Buber and the Holocaust: Some Reconsiderations on the 100th Anniversary of his Birth," *Michigan Quarterly Review* 18, no. 3 (Summer 1979): 397. Rubenstein would certainly agree that this is but one teaching of the Holocaust.

13. I am indebted for this insight regarding a cautionary note to Mark Rosenblum in his address as a panelist at the conference "The Middle East Peace Process: Political and Spiritual Dimensions," Nassau Community College, Garden City, N.Y., Apr. 25, 2001.

14. Although never a majority in the land the Romans named Palestine, Jews have maintained a continuous presence there since the second century B.C.E.

15. A good description and analysis of post-Zionist thought is to be found in Lawrence J. Silberstein, *The Postzionism Debates: Knowledge and Power in Israeli Culture* (New York: Routledge, 1999).

In Response to Leonard Grob

HENRY F. KNIGHT

LEONARD GROB TAKES on the intractable problem of Israeli-Palestinian conflict and the seemingly impossible task of reconciliation between the estranged parties. Beginning as most analysts do, he cites the recovery of Jewish power embodied in the state of Israel and questions how the "reins of power" will be wielded by a previously oppressed and victimized people. Stating that "there are no innocent parties in this conflict," Grob recognizes that the Holocaust's shadow hovers over this conflict in a double way. He adds that genuine transformation of the conflicted relationship must occur at the structural or ontological level. In making this assertion, Grob moves beyond the view that one may incorporate the other into a new relationship within existing mythic structures. He explains that "each side must radically call into question the dominant story or narrative" that funds each one's conflicting identity. The place of the other must be reconfigured into a more inclusive relational framework. Since the conflict is mythic, any substantive healing must be mythic as well. Therefore, Grob calls for "breaking" the absolute hold our dominant narratives have on our collective imaginations. In other words, idolatry is not just an external threat, it is an internal one as well—for both Israelis and Palestinians.

The conflicts between Israelis and Palestinians are not simply political or historical, or emotional confusions of the two. They are mythic struggles for an encompassing view of one's world and every other in that world. And in this case, each views the other with negative mythic power. Grob underscores that the absoluteness of these mythic structures must be broken. But how does one break a myth? Even to suggest such a need will raise the defenses of those dwelling securely within their mythic structures. Furthermore, we must ask if it is within the power of any single individual to produce such myth-breaking. Or do myths "break" in other ways, ones that are much less intentional?

Paul Tillich's work from the 1950s and 1960s may be instructive. In *Dynamics of Faith,* his classic study of symbols and mythic structures, he maintains that one neither creates nor breaks symbols as an act of will.[1] That process is organic and rooted in a larger cultural ecology. In this regard, one can argue that the Shoah was a watershed event that broke the covenantal mythic structures of Judaism and Christianity. Those structures could not contain the experiences of the Shoah. Consequently, they were broken. This point is one that Irving Greenberg emphasizes in his seminal essay "Cloud of Smoke, Pillar of Fire."[2] The Shoah is a time of reorientation. Of course, one might also argue that allegiances to our myths are not so easily undone. While a myth may no longer be experienced in a way that is wholly consistent, many persons will still act with allegiance to many parts of the myth that have gone unchallenged or unnoticed as components of the problematic character of one's world. Greenberg speaks to this feature as well, distinguishing the Shoah as an orienting event but not a new moment of revelation.

Tillich also argues that one cannot "make" myths or symbols. Rather they are born out of shared cultural experiences where immanent and transcendent meanings converge in their own time. If so, then one does not simply rebuild the mythic structures of Israeli and Palestinian worldviews by fiat. They will emerge in reconfigured form, if they do so at all, as new forms of relationship emerge. Over time, new experiences call forth new ways of seeing and relating to each other. In other words, even when our mythic worlds are broken, we cannot intentionally rebuild them by acts of will alone. Experiences must call forth new articulations of the relationships that express new possibilities for shared life. Recognizing that we cannot control them, we may call these new opportunities mythic moments to distinguish them from myths per se. We can provide possibilities for their occurring, but we cannot assure their happening—otherwise they would not be mythic, transcending our own experience.

Grob's analysis is instructive. Nevertheless, it leads me to worry about the intractability of the Palestinian-Israeli conflict. Can the mythic structures of Israeli and Palestinian worldviews be recast? That question is the really significant one to ask. Recognizing the power of myth, the dynamics of symbols, and the ways we dwell in our myths—these are steps forward. How one sees and frames every step of the way increases in significance.

One strategy for moving forward in this manner grows out of Tillich's recognition that we do not break our myths. Instead, we respond to myths that have already broken. If one of the problems is the need to challenge the absolute form in which our myths are cast, then one strategy is to respond to the ways the absolutes in our myths have already shattered, making this response from within the mythic structures themselves. That is, one may confess that hitherto secure identities and relationships are broken and that a new configuration begins with that reality. After the Shoah, we may argue that the Shoah has broken the conventional mythic view of the covenantal world of scripture. But one cannot force that view. If one tries to do so, often the attempt to break a myth only strengthens its mythic hold, hardening the resolve of the one who dwells in it. Rather, one may proceed not by attacking another's mythic view but by confessing the brokenness of one's own and the need to seek a new one. Emil Fackenheim makes this point in proposing midrash—the seeking of new meaning in scripture—as the appropriate interpretive strategy for working with our root (or mythic) experiences after the Shoah.[3] That is, as one confesses the broken places in one's own worldview, one resists the myth by bringing its broken, problematic points to bear on the myth itself. Although this approach does not ensure that subsequent demythologization will occur, its confessional, first-person voice removes the threat of accusation and allows others to wrestle with the mythic structures in their fashion—if they so choose.

Of course, where Palestinian-Israeli relations are concerned, security as well as meaning is at stake, and security is not simply mythic. That is a critical part of the problem. Were the situation only mythic (a problematic statement in itself), then the experiences of estrangement between Palestinians and Israelis would be less difficult to resolve. However, the conflict is intensely political and personal as well as mythic. In particular, the matter of place is literal as well as figurative. The vulnerability called for in rethinking the mythic recasting of mortal foes entails serious risk for anyone who embraces it.

Consequently, any healing must be relational as well as mythic. Healing must be rooted in real relationships if it is ever to develop mythic dimensions. The experience of healing must be significant enough that a reconfiguration of mythic structures is necessary because new experiences require and produce new narrations of meaning. To complicate matters further, Grob calls for including the other as a "co-subject" or fellow agent in the reconfigured narrative. That is, one must give reconfigured place to others in one's own story, which, in turn, can bestow new positive significance on that place. Such moments and movements begin by discovering the displacement of the other, confronting it, and reconfiguring it, but within the overall spirit of the new narrative that is under way. We should ask, however, whether these developments require a new "meta-narrative," as Grob contends. If so, there are problems, for who will tell this meta-story? Whose will it be? Why not search instead for a reconfiguration of one's narrative that does not require its being a new meta-story or the only reconfiguration?

Responses to such questions may be glimpsed through the biblical narrative of a limping Israel (Genesis 32:22–32). After his long night at the Jabbok, Jacob's encounter with the quintessential other in his life gives him a new identity as well as a limp. The new identity and the limp are given together. Could this be a suggestion that the unfolding mythic story that follows throughout the scriptures is one that recalls the walking of the way of covenant fidelity as an imperfect walk? Would this image not be one that fits Micah's call to "walk humbly" with God and that is capable of articulating the imperfect though nonetheless steadfast possibilities of human fidelity?

While I am instructed by Grob's analysis of the mythic dimensions of the Palestinian-Israeli conflict, his analysis leads me to consider its intractability more seriously. That is, the hope of finding common ground for negotiation appears more problematic, not less. Grob argues that the way forward must include mythic adjustment with regard to how Palestinians and Jews are portrayed in their mythic worldviews of the other. But such changes cannot be forced. They must accompany experience that occasions enough mythic dissonance that the narratives are reconfigured on account of new gestalts of meaning and relation. And in this regard, the stakes as well as the problems are increased, not diminished, by these insights. Consequently, Grob's proposed adjustments, while essential for future healing, may be significantly more difficult to achieve than hitherto imagined.

NOTES

1. See Paul Tillich, *The Dynamics of Faith* (New York: Harper & Row, 1957), p. 43.
2. See Irving Greenberg, "Cloud of Smoke, Pillar of Fire," in Michael Morgan, ed., *A Holocaust Reader: Responses to the Nazi Extermination* (New York: Oxford University Press, 2001), pp. 102–14.
3. See Emil L. Fackenheim, *The Jewish Return into History* (New York: Schocken Books, 1978), pp. 252–72.

In Response to Leonard Grob

JOHN K. ROTH

IN ALL THE best senses, Leonard Grob is an idealist. Challenging individuals, groups, and nations to make the world more hospitable, he makes one think about the ideal and the real. That difference raises the question I want to ask him: What would he have done regarding the turbulent World Conference against Racism, Racial Discrimination, Xenophobia and Related Intolerance held in Durban, South Africa, only a few days before the terrorism of September 11, 2001?

To clarify why I pose this specific question, note, first, that I typically begin my workday by accessing the *New York Times* online. The news I seek includes reports about the Holocaust. In recent years, scarcely a day passes without the appearance of relevant articles. As my Holocaust-scholar friend Michael Berenbaum points out, the number of Holocaust-related articles published in the *Times* during an eighteen-month period from the beginning of 2000 to mid-2001 far exceeded the coverage that paper gave to the catastrophe when it happened.

The Holocaust remains newsworthy. Current news about it sometimes focuses on the past. Those reports may deal with new archival findings or historical interpretations that require fresh thinking about what took place between 1933 and 1945, when Nazi Germany unleashed its genocidal campaign against European Jewry. Frequently, however, current news about the Holocaust focuses on the present and the future. That disaster's impact does more than linger. It gnaws as an unmastered trauma still capable of straining crucial relationships to the breaking point.

In early September 2001, as I studied Grob's reflections on reconciliation in the Middle East, the *New York Times* confirmed that judgment. When I used its search engine to find Holocaust-related articles, many of those that surfaced referred to the UN's World Conference against Racism, which initially included delegations from more than 160 countries. Arguably doomed from the beginning, the conference nearly self-destructed because of Muslim-inspired anti-Semitic allegations that Israel is a racist nation whose practice of a so-called new form of apartheid has subjected the Palestinian people to foreign occupation and violated their inalienable right to self-determination and an independent state.

A last-ditch South African effort eventually proposed softer language, which became the basis for the declaration adopted by the conference on September 8. Using a concept that emerged from the Nuremberg Trials at the end of World War II, it stated that "slavery and the slave trade are a crime against humanity and should always have been so." Although the declaration contained no rhetoric about Israel as a racist nation, it still placed a singular onus on Israel by expressing concern about "the plight of the Palestinian people under foreign occupation." In addition, the declaration's anti-Israeli spin implicitly recognized that Palestinians have the right to return to "their homes and properties" in Israel, a claim that has long been a sticking point in Israeli-Palestinian negotiations.

Whatever agreement was reached on statements about the Middle East, the declaration produced no reconciliation of consequence on that topic because earlier debate had been so hostile and hypocritical that the American and Israeli delegations departed in protest midway through the conference. Even at the last minute, delegates from Syria and Pakistan insisted on branding Israel a racist state. That view did not prevail, but the Durban conference did little to silence such canards. On the contrary, they are likely to intensify, pouring more fuel on Palestinian-Israeli hatred. Meanwhile, the European Union and several nations—Australia, Iran, Canada, and Britain—immediately lodged objections about the declaration. The conference satisfied very few. Qualms and misgivings were its predominant final product.

Meanwhile, Grob's essay correctly argues that "the specter of the Holocaust haunts, unrelentingly, the turmoil in the Middle East." Confirmation of that judgment is not hard to find, and the Durban conference helped to provide it. Early on, its final declaration recalled that "the Holocaust must never be forgotten," but not before some Muslim states demanded that the word *European* should be inserted to modify *the Holocaust,* an obvious attempt to relativize and diminish the event's significance even as the qualification implied—inaccurately—that Europeans alone were implicated in or affected by that unprecedented genocide. A major problem at Durban was not that the Holocaust was forgotten but rather how Israel's anti-Semitic critics "remembered" it. For them, the Holocaust is primarily the pretext for Israeli oppression of dispossessed Palestinians.

The immediate outcomes of this conference were not causes for encouragement, let alone celebration. The worst was prevented, but the best did not prevail. Insofar as its objective included the development of honest and constructive responses to racism's multiple forms of destructiveness, the conference may prove to be an exercise in futility or it may be a first, lurching step toward something better. Be that as it may, I found it instructive to consider Grob's post-Holocaust reflections about reconciliation in the Middle East while I was following the reports from Durban in September 2001. The appearance of the final conference declaration notwithstanding, the daily reports from Durban, which were more telling than the agreement contentiously patched together in the final hours before the delegates went their separate and often divided ways, seemed a far cry from Grob's ideal of "genuine reconciliation—reconciliation within a commitment to justice." Some of the rhetoric in the run-up to Durban sounded similar to Grob's ideals, but Durban's results—at least in the short run—seem to have done little to increase *tikkun olam* or respect for the other, two of Grob's persistent concerns.

A huge gap yawns between Grob's idealism and the realities that so ironically revealed themselves in South African conference halls where people had purportedly gathered to discuss ways to cope better with injustice than humankind has done in the past. Given that human beings are frail, finite, and fallible creatures who are prone to folly and corruption on all sides, the gap between the ideal and real will never be totally closed. Indeed, as Grob suggests, we should be wary of human efforts to close it completely. For even if those aims are well intentioned, and by no means do all of them fit that description, they are likely to harbor totalizing impulses that would dominate and oppress those who hold justifiably different views. On the other hand, if the gap between the real and the ideal remains as vast as it is, then the outcome is likely to be more racism, anti-Semitism, violence, killing, and suffering in a world that has already been massively, woefully, shamefully scarred by them all.

Grob concentrates on what he calls the Israeli-Palestinian conflict, a term too gentle to identify what escalated into a low-level war as the first anniversary of Intifada II came and went in late September 2001. The Durban conference ran aground largely because it concentrated on that same struggle. Grob hopes that, somehow, the Israeli-Palestinian labyrinth can yield a "just reconciliation," which would "constitute a veritable 'light unto the nations.'" The Durban conference, let alone the on-the-ground realities in Israel, Gaza, and the West Bank, still offer scant support for such hope.

Reasons for that pessimism include the fact that what Grob preaches has been too little practiced—either in Durban or among the powers that may continue to dominate Israeli and Palestinian politics. As one reads Grob's essay, it is hard to quarrel with his idealism as idealism. Grob is right: In the Middle East, and in every human conflict, self-critique is crucial for healing resolutions; what he calls "dominant narratives" ought to be questioned; dialogical efforts that make people and groups "fully present" to one another are vital; respect for "the sacredness of each individual being, most especially the other who is oppressed" should be deepened. Yet the problem remains: How can the gap between the ideal and the real be meaningfully narrowed, not so the ideal dies the death of a thousand qualifications but so the real is transformed in the direction of the ideal?

Before the actual conference took place, it may have seemed to some that Durban's UN meeting provided a hopeful venue for reconciliation within a commitment to justice. Elie Wiesel, however, was not among them. The Holocaust survivor and Nobel Peace Prize recipient had a different view, as he explained on September 5 in an essay published in *Yedioth Ahronoth,* an Israeli newspaper, while the conference was still in session. Noting that he had originally been part of a small group that the UN established to prepare the meeting, Wiesel quit when he saw how anti-Israeli and anti-Jewish the proceedings were going to become. Kofi Annan, the UN secretary general, and Mary Robinson, the UN high commissioner for human rights and the conference organizer, urged Wiesel to change his mind, but he did not go to Durban.

Grob and Wiesel share many of the same ideals, but I wonder how Grob would have faced decisions about going to Durban if they had been his to make. Wiesel's option, of course, was not the only one. If the opportunity had presented itself, Grob might have gone to Durban as a delegate and then left in protest midway, as the Americans and Israelis did. Or he might have found a way to stay to the stormy end, hoping that something good would come from sustaining discussion, if not dialogue, rather than breaking it off or never engaging in it.

I sketch these scenarios not to put Grob in a hypothetical dilemma but rather as a way of asking my friend to say more about how the gap between the ideal and the real might be narrowed. At first glance, a World Conference on Racism seemed like a place to start some significant gap-bridging by putting many of Grob's ideals into practice. Unfortunately, this did not happen at Durban. Arguably, the gap between the ideal and real yawns even more widely than it did before the UN conference.

Leonard Grob's ideals are good and right, but what must happen for them to be better practiced than they were at the World Conference on

Racism? Emphasizing more ideals will not answer that question, at least not sufficiently. Grob's reflections on reconciliation need to bear down on the places where, as we sometimes say, the rubber hits the road.

In Response to Henry F. Knight and John K. Roth

LEONARD GROB

THE CRITIQUES OF John Roth and Henry Knight speak pointedly to the intractability of the Israeli-Palestinian conflict. Explicit in Roth's critique, more implicit in Knight's, is the challenge to find ways to realize *in practice* the vision of reconciliation in the Middle East that I sketch in my essay. Roth charges me "to say more about how the gap between the ideal and the real might be narrowed." Knight recalls that we have before us a *mythic* conflict of opposing narratives. He speaks to the need to provide possibilities for the occurrence of "experience that occasions enough mythic dissonance that the narratives are reconfigured on account of new gestalts of meaning and relation." The tasks set forth by both colleagues are daunting.

Roth's words prompt me to think harder. There are few lines of critique so challenging to the philosopher as those which summon him or her to come down to the earth we share. Folded within Roth's entreaty is a more pointed query as to what decision I might have made regarding attendance at Durban. Rather than speaking to the issue of my attendance at Durban—Roth agrees that there are arguments to be made for several positions—I will address his underlying concern that words be offered which will help us "bear down on the places where . . . the rubber hits the road."

Knight's critique is equally challenging: As he suggests, to address a mythic conflict, nothing short of a healing of mythic proportions must be proposed. In the context of political realities within which lives have been and continue to be lost, Knight ponders how entire worldviews might effectively be reconfigured. The summons in his critique is to probe more deeply, keeping in mind both the mythic dimensions of the narratives and the grave realities of the conflict at hand.

Throughout my essay, I worked to keep in mind the pressing need to address that disparity between ideal and real to which Roth points. Indeed, the very articulation of what he calls "ideals" *is itself* part and parcel of what I believe constitutes a "real" enterprise: As an educative offering—albeit one that only well-schooled participants in the conflict might ever read—my essay stands as a call to parties to the conflict to step back from expressions of radical hatred, such as have been exhibited at Durban, in the process of learning to listen to the other's story.

Let me illustrate. As both Knight and Roth agree, the Holocaust forms the backdrop of the Palestinian-Israeli conflict. Although, as Roth points out, it is not the case that the Holocaust has been forgotten by enemies of just reconciliation—instances of Holocaust denial in some Palestinian media as well as the rhetoric at Durban certainly attest to that—this is most certainly not the kind of "remembering" that either Roth or I have in mind. Both Palestinians and (seemingly paradoxically) Israelis themselves need to remember the Holocaust in vitally *new* ways in order for just reconciliation to occur. My essay is a call to very real transformation insofar as it summons an (admittedly small and select) audience of readers to rethink *how* it remembers.

For Palestinians, the call is to remember the Jewish encounter with the Holocaust as *the ground of Israel's existential anxiety,* and not merely as an instance of the other's suffering that would compare (unfavorably) with its own. With regard to Israel, my intent was to help alert Israeli Jews to new possibilities that might emerge from their collective trauma. Too little attention has been paid to the myriad lessons that the Holocaust offers—fundamental among them the teaching of the brokenness of all ideologies, including traditional forms of Zionist thought. A call to reconfigure Holocaust-related narratives on both sides is an endeavor not at all removed from the realm of *praxis;* it is part of the path by means of which we reach that place where "the rubber hits the road."

Yet when all is said and done, essential elements of the critiques advanced by both Roth and Knight remain to be addressed. The exercise of setting forth ideas in a philosophic essay—even if scholarly writing is dialogical and thus to be understood in some significant sense as *praxis*—is unlikely to shake the foundations of entrenched hatreds in an often all too "real" world. Although I argue that ideas in my essay may serve an important educative function, I do not believe that I have yet satisfied Roth's contention that ideals must be translated into *praxis* in a world beset by the kind of rhetoric manifest at Durban. I well understand that what is at issue here is not *whether or not* to attempt to educate, but rather *how* to educate inflamed parties to conflict.

Further, although my enterprise is a "call," a "summons"—and thus a "lived logos"[1] that offers itself to potential partners in dialogue—I do not believe I have fully addressed Knight's contention that changes in mythic worldviews require that parties to conflict encounter an altered *Lebenswelt* or lifeworld. Even then, it should be noted, the parties may or may not rethink reified mythic structures: Changes in worldview, Knight reminds us, can only be offered; offers can be avoided or refused. I agree with Knight that, in addition to discursive arguments, what is needed in the Middle East are opportunities for the emergence of experiences that *may,* if embraced existentially, lead to a much-needed reconfiguration of mythic structures. It is one thing to receive didactic instruction about the other, quite another to experience, in a moment of genuine encounter, an opening in what has hitherto been a closed system of fixed narrative. Experiencing the latter, each party opens itself to the possibility of standing in that sacred spot where the "inter-myth" resides.[2]

I will speak here more personally. At the same time I will present a case study of an "offering" of the kind that Knight might have in mind; it is also one that may bring us closer to the "real" world to which, Roth reminds us, we must always return. I have complemented my scholarly work on the Israeli-Palestinian conflict with the creation (along with my Palestinian partner) of a set of grassroots opportunities for new experiences which may lead to healing. The Palestinian-Israeli Oral History Project, Inc., offers elementary school–age children in Israel and in the territory under the control of the Palestinian Authority the opportunity to view videotaped accounts of ordinary life experiences of both peoples. With an eye toward creating an opening for de-demonizing the other, the Project will move from schoolyard to schoolyard, showing videotapes and, ultimately, bringing Israeli and Palestinian children—the generation currently growing toward political and moral agency—together in live dialogue.

The subject matter of the filmed material is the common experiences of both peoples. Some examples: the celebration of engagement and marriage; a child's first day of school; pregnancy and birth. Encountering the other in these contexts will hopefully provide an opening for the reexamination of one's own story, as one sees ways in which elements of one's ordinary life narrative are shared in some substantial measure by the other. Meeting the other who occupies a lifeworld in essential ways common to both parties may help each wrestle with those fixed modes of objectifying the other, which thus far have served as defining moments of its story. In the telling and listening to stories, the authentic power of narrative-in-process may prompt each party to acknowledge the limitations of those reified narratives formerly deemed absolute.

The Palestinian-Israeli Oral History Project is but one of many so-called dialogue projects already existing in the Middle East. (I now prefer to call them opportunities to experience inter-mythic space.) All root themselves in common existential concerns: for example, with the arts (a joint Israeli-Palestinian puppet theater); with disease prevention (a Palestinian-Israeli organization devoted to saving the eyesight of diabetic patients); with women's issues (a joint women's leadership development program). These are but a few of myriad projects that will be needed to provide openings toward rethinking the dominant narratives of Israelis and Palestinians, thus creating the potential for healing. It is my hope that such eminently *praxis*-oriented endeavors will blossom and open the path to genuine reconciliation in the Middle East.

NOTES

1. Discussion with Ernest Sherman, Oct. 2001.

2. I do not believe that my introduction of the concept of a "meta-narrative" is at odds with Knight's suggestion that each party to a conflict should search for a reconfiguration of its own narrative. Knight seems to imply that a meta-narrative would be a new, and perhaps superfluous, story. As I employ the term, *meta-narrative* is no substantive, no literally "new" or counter narrative

in its own right; rather the concept denotes the *process* of the meeting of peoples that may result in the reconfigured narratives to which Knight alludes. In this sense *meta-narrative* is akin to Martin Buber's use of the term *the Between* or, as I use the term, *the space of the inter-myth* as the locus of genuine, transformative encounter.

9

The Post-Holocaust Jewish Heart

RACHEL N. BAUM

ON MAY 15, 2001, the United Jewish Appeal-Federation honored Thomas Middelhoff, head of the Bertelsmann Music Group, for his commitment to Jewish causes and for his efforts in publishing the testimonies of Holocaust survivors. One significant fact made this event especially remarkable: the Bertelsmann Music Group is a German company that had Nazi ties during the Holocaust. In fact, Bertelsmann was the largest supplier of published material, including Nazi propaganda, to the German military. The event produced a maelstrom of controversy, with some calling it disgraceful while others praised UJA's courage and vision in honoring someone who is trying to take responsibility for his company's role in the Holocaust.

Those who argued against UJA's decision clearly saw the issue as one of memory. Critics accused the UJA of forgetting history—selling out the memory of the dead—for the sake of fund-raising. The *New York Times* quoted Melvin Jules Bukiet, the child of Holocaust survivors, as saying, "Try me in 5,000 years, and maybe we'll be ready to start talking. They should be ashamed of themselves at UJA. Are we allowing ourselves to be purchased? Of course we are, and it's an outrage."[1] Bukiet went on to say that healing is another word for forgetting, and that many in the second generation "prefer the open wound to closure." For these critics, it was an additional disgrace that the keynote address would be given by Holocaust survivor Elie Wiesel, arguably the most influential Holocaust writer in the world.

For others, however, the issue was not one of forgetting, but of learning how to move forward after the Holocaust. Middelhoff was born in 1953, after the war, supporters argued, and has made sincere efforts to advance Holocaust memory and to acknowledge his company's role in the Holocaust. Bertelsmann pledged one million dollars to the Holocaust Survivors' Memoir Project, and Middelhoff appointed an independent commission to look into the company's Nazi past. After the commission confirmed Bertelsmann's connection to the Nazis, the company announced that it would contribute to the German fund to compensate slave laborers. The supporters of UJA's decision argued that while no one can change the past, we need to acknowledge those who are making real efforts to create a different future.

In the editorial pages of the *New York Times,* Elie Wiesel reminded critics that "only the guilty are guilty, not their sons."[2] That this needed to be said is, in some sense, surprising, if not shocking. It seems irrational to equate forever young Germans with the perpetrators of the Holocaust, and, as Wiesel argued, those who have been the victims of discriminatory thinking should well understand its dangers.

The problem is that the issue is not purely an intellectual one. While Wiesel's arguments were intelligent and thoughtful, they centrally argued the issue as a cognitive one, whereas the expressions of outrage and dissent were largely emotional. Even if Wiesel's words managed to convince some that they *ought to* support the UJA's decision, their internal sense of there being something wrong with a Jewish organization honoring a Germany company would probably remain. I imagine that there are many intelligent, thoughtful Jews who still bristle at a German accent, just as there are many thoughtful Jews who will extend a plane trip rather than have a layover in Germany. As these Jews know, today's Germans are not, by and large, the perpetrators of the Holocaust. Nevertheless, many Jews remain uncomfortable in their relationships with Germany and Germans.[3] While this behavior is understandable among the generation who lived through the Shoah, it is more complicated when seen in their children and grandchildren, young men and women born after the Holocaust. Such Jews may feel shame at their behavior, because they *know* better, and yet their emotional blueprint remains unchanged.

Wiesel is right to condemn the behavior of those who damn an entire people for the actions of their ancestors, but I suggest we need to go further. We need to understand the pain that fuels such behavior and consider what we, the American Jewish community, can do with our profound pain, anger, and grief about the Holocaust. We cannot simply "get over it," but neither can we let our pain guide us into the future.

This question—what will we do with our suffering?—is fundamentally a spiritual question. It touches upon the deepest issues of our Jewish existence, both as individuals and as a community: How will we respond to the world that hurt us so deeply? Can we hope and trust again, after having been so wounded? How will our painful experiences affect who we are?

At the heart of these questions is an even deeper one: What happens to the soul of a murdered people? The survivors went on and built, many of them, awe-inspiring new lives, but it is clear that there is a legacy of loss that continues through the generations, even where we are unaware of it. While this legacy may be most acute in the children and grandchildren of survivors, it extends, I want to argue, to the entire American Jewish community. It is, as the title of this essay reveals, a matter of the post-Holocaust Jewish heart.

It is difficult to talk about the heart of a community. Two Jews, three opinions, the old joke goes, but it is a joke saturated with pain today, as Jews find themselves divided over so many issues. While my comments focus on the American Jewish community, the community with which I identify and that I call home, even this community is so diverse that it feels risky to talk about *a* community, let alone its heart.

Yet surely it is also dangerous *not* to talk about the heart of a community. Indeed, what happens to a community that stops talking about its heart, its soul, its pain, its joy? That which holds a community together cannot be simply intellectual belief, but must also be affective. Certainly, there is evidence that this sense of a Jewish soul, of a commonplace of affective experience, continues to bind many people to their Jewish identities. Even those who do not identify religiously with the tradition often feel a common sensibility with other Jews, a concern for Israel, for the Holocaust, for a shared tradition despite the fact that they may not fully identify with that tradition.

So, let me ask again: What happens to the soul of a murdered people? What happens to those who remain, those who are given the honor and burden of carrying the memories of the murdered? What happens to the pain of loss, of violence? What happens to the cries of mothers and fathers, viciously taken from their children? Where do these cries go, more than fifty years later?

Many contemporary scholars have answered this question by pointing to the ways in which memory of the Holocaust has become incorporated into Jewish ritual and narrative. In these accounts, Jewish pain over the Holocaust becomes channeled into ceremonies of memorialization, fund-raising efforts, and even religious identity. Such activities give voice to inarticulate emotions by making them useful, drawing on them for productive ends. In this way, Jews draw upon their pain over the memory of the Holocaust to serve the needs of their community—needs such as continuity, affiliation, and identification. In this scholarship, the needs of the community are understood largely as political and social. Thus, as scholar James Young has chronicled in *The Texture of Memory,* Holocaust memory is shaped differently in Israel than in New York City, differently in Germany than in France, because of the differences in their political and social contexts.[4] In many ways, this process of turning pain into action has been at the heart of the success and survival of the Jewish people after the Holocaust; without it, the Jewish community would surely have been paralyzed by the sheer devastation of its loss.

A community has spiritual needs as well, however—particularly a religious community. While turning pain into action may serve the political and social needs of the Jewish community, it may not serve the spiritual needs of the community. Arguably, the Holocaust presents the most significant spiritual challenge for the American Jewish community today. Yet while Jewish writers have grappled with the theological ramifications of the Holocaust for Jews, too few have engaged directly with the matter of the Jewish heart, asking what the Holocaust means for us spiritually.

This lack of attention to the Holocaust as a spiritual issue is surprising, given the proliferation of spiritual concerns in contemporary popular culture. There is a thirst for spirituality in America today, and liberal Jewish communities have contributed actively to this contemporary concern for spirituality. The Judaica section of any major bookstore reveals many titles on Jewish spirituality, renewal, meditation, and prayer. In large numbers, Jews are drawing upon both their own religious tradition and the traditions of Eastern religions to deepen their relationship to themselves, other people, and the divine. This contemporary focus on spirituality makes it surprising that Jews, by and large, have not focused on the Holocaust as a spiritual issue. Indeed, some Jews report that this lack of attention to the spiritual in Judaism has led them to turn to other traditions such as Buddhism. Yet surely the Holocaust presents Jews with the most profound of spiritual challenges—how to acknowledge pain and suffering without becoming over-identified with it or subsumed by it.

In considering the Holocaust as a spiritual issue, I seek to focus attention on the fact that the issues raised by the Holocaust are soul issues, issues that call upon and challenge our deepest capacities for love, connection, trust, and openness. If a primary goal of spiritual practice is the experience of the divinity of all existence, we must acknowledge as Jews that our collective memory of the Holocaust at times stands in our way of experiencing a deep affective connection with others and, subsequently, with God and the divine. It is one thing to believe that we are all God's children; it is quite another for a Jew to embrace her new German-Catholic acquaintance with an open heart.

It would be naive to think that history will not intervene between Jews and Germans. Without question, the Holocaust provides a backdrop to everyday life that affects our sense of ourselves and the world around us in both subtle and unsubtle ways. This is not always a problem; indeed, it is appropriate that contemporary Jewish identity be fundamentally shaped through our memory of the Holocaust. However, when Holocaust memory holds us back from connecting openly with the people and world around us, we need to ask whether this response serves us well spiritually.

Many Jews have become interested in Buddhist practice as a way to learn how to deepen their spiritual connection to the world, but surely it is impossible for Jews to leave the Holocaust behind, even in the meditation hall.[5] Imagine, for example, a Jew practicing the traditional Buddhist loving kindness meditation: *May all beings be happy.* She starts with herself, and moves to her family and friends, spreading loving kindness to them. *May I be happy; may my family be happy.* Now she expands the circle to her community, her country, the world. Does the meditation break down at the border of Germany? Poland? At the image of the perpetrators, or at the image of the broken, emaciated bodies of her people?

Indeed, Buddhism recognizes this difficulty and embraces it as part of spiritual practice. In the loving kindness meditation, the circles move outward until they encompass a difficult person, an enemy, someone who presents the meditator with negative emotions. But who is the enemy for our Jewish meditator? The perpetrators of the Shoah, without a doubt, but most of them are now long gone. So her rage and grief over the terrible deaths of her people have no satisfying object. She needs a way to bring those emotions into the present moment, to let her people know that she remembers them and that their lives will not be forgotten. And so, perhaps, against her better judgment, she finds herself feeling animosity toward Germans, because it is a way to keep memory alive in the present moment.

This analysis lacks a certain sophistication, to be certain. In actuality, the process of creating the heart of a community is much subtler. It would be wrong to suggest that most contemporary Jews are walking around thinking regularly about Auschwitz. Yet it is clear that the Holocaust has left its scar on the Jewish community. How could it not? Many of the issues that most concern the American Jewish community—continuity, assimilation, intermarriage, education, the survival of Israel—are particularly forceful because of the Holocaust. We are afraid of the destruction of our community, through the long-term effects of intermarriage and assimilation, or through the violence in the Middle East. These issues are inextricably connected with our memory of the Holocaust, with our knowledge that our community was decimated only fifty years ago. In this context, not being on guard for destruction can appear ignorant. It seems too early to trust the world community that, by and large, stood aside while our people were massacred.

Clearly, Jews have legitimate reasons to be concerned with the survival of their community, yet at times the fear seems out of concert with contemporary Jewish life. Even as a tiny minority, American Jews have become a powerful political force. Israel remains under attack, but Germany and Israel are allies. The situation is quite different now than it was in 1942. So it can be difficult to know exactly what to do with our memory of the Holocaust and with the emotions it raises. There is a tension between our need to honor our tremendous pain and our desire to move on with our shared lives. I am teaching my young son not to prejudge people, to meet them as they are, without bias. But can I do the same?

Jews are the people of memory, but it is not an easy responsibility to keep both memory and compassion alive at the same time. Memory can bring us closer to others, as in the Passover story, when we remember to be kind to the stranger "because we were strangers in Egypt," but it does not always bring us closer to others. Remembering the Holocaust does not bring me closer to humanity, but puts me in utter despair. If I am able to move beyond that condition, it is by effort alone, not because the narratives bear any deeper truth. This effort is at the heart of spiritual practice, which demands that we soften the parts of us that have been hardened through pain and hurt, and that we open our souls, despite all the reasons to leave them closed.

Learning about the Holocaust cannot help but throw the learner into spiritual despair. I leave it to other communities to explore what this means to them, but for my community, I want to say that if we yearn for a dynamic, vibrant Judaism of the twenty-first century, we must be honest about the parts of our own hearts that hold us back from others, the parts that are hardened, angry, hurt, aggrieved. We must be honest that there is part of us (part of me, I will be honest) that is not ready to give up our anger and hurt, that nurtures it as a source of our ethical compass. We need not be proud of our discrimination against Germans, but we can do the work to understand how it serves us and what it would take to let it go.

What are we holding onto with our anger? What are we keeping alive? I think we are keeping alive memory itself. This is not to defend discrimination, but rather to suggest that the anger and even hatred have a function for the community, and that if we want to let go of the anger and hatred, we must have those needs met in another way.

Our memory of the Holocaust *should* make us look differently at contemporary life. If nothing has changed, then how will we remember the murdered? If Germans and Jews will now be drinking in the local pub together, then isn't it as if the Holocaust never happened? I think these are some of the fears that drove the protesters at the Middelhoff event. When one's life has been ruptured, it is painful to think that the world is simply moving on. So let's be honest that many of us do have complicated feelings about Germany and Germans and that we are not always proud of these feelings. And let's be honest that many of us are not necessarily ready to give up these feelings, because we believe that these feelings kindle our memory of the Holocaust.

At the same time, we can admit that anger and hatred are ultimately unsatisfying roads to Jewish memory. Are the murdered honored by our bitterness, by our hardness to others? Such emotions ultimately limit our ability to connect not only to other people but also to God. Is this how we honor our murdered brothers and sisters, by closing off our own souls?

So the spiritual question for Jews must be one of memory: How do we remember without becoming embittered? How do we remember our suffering without being defined by it? How do we carry memory into the present while also recognizing that today is not yesterday?

These are questions for the spiritual path; they are not questions that have easy answers, and different people will find different ways down this path. My purpose in this essay is not so much to provide answers as to suggest questions and ways of thought that might suggest a path. One such example comes from Sylvia Boorstein, a Buddhist teacher and an observant Jew. In drawing upon Boorstein's words, I do not mean to promote Buddhism as a model spiritual practice. Rather, I hope that Boorstein's thoughts will resonate in ways that enable each of us to confront the complexity of these issues.

Like others, Boorstein was initially attracted to Buddhism because it offered a way to deal with suffering. While suffering is an inherent part of existence, Buddhism explains that we often deepen our suffering needlessly. Our minds hold on to our suffering, fight against it, magnify it.

Buddhism's response to this tendency is the clarity of mind achieved through meditation. Meditation allows us to experience things as they are and to approach the world with an open heart and clear mind. While some fear that Buddhism does not allow for taking a passionate stand against injustice, Boorstein disagrees:

> A concern of some new meditators is that a peaceful heart doesn't allow for taking a stand, or acting decisively against injustice. This is particularly true for Jews, for whom the prophetic vision of social justice is a cornerstone of religious practice. My father, for instance, thought that a peaceful heart precluded forceful action. He used to say, "I *need* my anger. It obliges me to take action."
>
> I think my father was partly right. Anger arises, naturally, to *signal* disturbing situations that might require action. But actions initiated in anger perpetuate suffering. The most effective actions are those conceived in the wisdom of clarity.[6]

I think Boorstein's distinction can help us understand better the anger many felt at Thomas Middelhoff's receiving the UJA award. Melvin Jules Bukiet and others seem to feel that they need to hold on to their anger as a way of remembering the past, but perhaps Boorstein is right that we can see such anger as a *signal* that something needs to change. Perhaps we are not remembering well enough; perhaps we need more communal places to share our pain; perhaps we have moved too quickly toward reconciliation.

The "soft mind" of Buddhism will not end the pain that comes from the destruction of our community, but it may help us see more clearly what it means to live with that pain in the present. We do not need to pass our anger at the Germans from one generation to another; perhaps we can find other ways to be with our pain, to acknowledge and express it. Can we imagine, for example, a critic of the UJA's decision saying "I feel betrayed by my community"? Can we envision the conversation that might follow such an expression, a conversation about what it means to belong to a community and about what we owe each other? For it seems to me that this is precisely what was behind Bukiet's words. His anger, I believe, was the anger of betrayal, of feeling unsupported by his people.

In this way, we can see Bukiet's feelings of anger and betrayal as the expression of legitimate needs, even if we do not agree with his conclusions.

Boorstein goes on to say:

> We need to feel safe enough to remember. We need to be able to remember without fear, in the space of clear mind, so that we remember as witnesses rather than as victims. As a victim, I become frightened and then confused and angry. I perpetuate suffering. As a witness, I can testify to the terrible, evil consequences of ignorance and vow to end it. As a witness, I can also swear that my experience of clear mind is one of boundless love and I can teach it. I can respond to suffering, and my response can be compassionate. I can say—with perfect faith—that my contribution to *tikkun olam* (the repair of the world) begins with my dedication to maintaining a loving heart. I can only transform myself. It is all any of us can do. If we all do it, it will be enough.[7]

Boorstein's distinction between remembering as a witness and remembering as a victim is both difficult and instructive. What she is suggesting is that although we were victims in the past, our present-day memory of our victimization can be founded on love and openness, rather than on anger and hostility. Opening our hearts to others need not signal the death of Holocaust memory; on the contrary, our memory of destruction can open our hearts further to the desperate need for healing. For this to happen, though, we need to feel safe enough to remember. We need to feel that our open hearts will not be trampled upon, that we are not exposing ourselves to more devastation. Perhaps we are not yet there in the global community, but perhaps we can create islands of safety in our own community where we can honor our pain in ways that encourage the wholeness and openness of our hearts.

What I am suggesting is quite different from the spiritual view of some that we need to forgive those who have hurt us, lest our lack of forgiveness hurt ourselves. I cannot comprehend the term *forgiveness* in the context of the Holocaust, and I know that it is not my place to forgive the murder of another human being. Nor do I feel the need to "forgive" contemporary Germans for the behavior of their ancestors. No, forgiveness is not what is needed here. Rather, with Boorstein, I suggest that the issue is one of memory and how we will remember the Holocaust. Will our memory serve both the memory of the dead and *tikkun olam,* or will it harden our hearts? Can we envision a memory that is clear and morally right and that does not perpetuate suffering? For when we judge others based on their ancestry, when we distrust Germans simply because they are German, surely we perpetuate the suffering of the world.

Some have worked on their emotions about the Holocaust in connection with other communities. Young Jews and young Germans have engaged in encounter groups that encourage them to express their complex feelings and, over time, hopefully to move toward some kind of reconciliation. These groups are important and I support those who are doing this kind of work, but I want to be clear that what I am speaking about is a bit different. I am suggesting that the Holocaust has wounded the Jewish heart and that we need to attend to our pain *as* a spiritual community. While some Jews may find healing in connection with other communities, such as Germans or Christians, others will feel more comfortable in conversations that include only Jews. What I am calling for, however, is a sustained conversation within the American Jewish community, one that honors the spiritual questions that lie at the heart of Holocaust memory.

Perhaps we have moved too soon in transforming our pain into action. Perhaps now is the time to learn as a community how to sit with our pain, how to talk about our prejudices without holding on to them, how to talk about the role the Shoah will have in our sense of ourselves as Jews. This is particularly important as the Holocaust recedes further into history, for Holocaust memory will very soon be held entirely by those who were not there. It is crucial that those of us who remain consider how Holocaust memory will shape who we are as individuals and as a community. We sponsor community trips to the United States Holocaust Memorial Museum so that our young people will learn about the past, but we have not yet attended carefully enough to what the story has done to us, as a people. We have not yet focused intently enough on the spiritual lessons our young people draw from the Shoah. What will they do, spiritually, with the crisis of faith that learning about the Holocaust must bring? What will they do, existentially, with their doubts about human nature, about a loving God, about themselves, and their own capacity for evil? What will they do with the feelings about Germans, Christians, and non-Jews that learning about the Holocaust may raise in them? And how will *we* as a community help them resolve those issues in a way that promotes their wholeness as human beings and their connection to other people and perhaps to God? How will we nurture the part of them that desires connection and wholeness, without erasing the memory of our own suffering?

These are huge issues, of course, and each of us will struggle with them in his and her own way. But it is time to begin the conversation, to explore our hearts with honesty and compassion, and to pay attention as a community to what remains of the Holocaust within us. The challenge is to keep the memory of the Shoah alive while creating a Jewish community of compassion, love, and openness. The challenge is to carry a heart that is both wounded and open, full of the pain of memory, and vulnerable to the hope of tomorrow. This is my sincerest prayer: May it be so, speedily and in our day.

NOTES

1. Tamar Lewin, "Past Collides with Closure as Jewish Gala Honors German," *New York Times,* Apr. 30, 2001.

2. Elie Wiesel, "Only the Guilty Are Guilty, Not Their Sons," *New York Times,* May 5, 2001.

3. See, for example, the Associated Press's account in "Religion in the News," *New York Times,* Dec. 28, 2001. In this article, Harriet Mandel of the Jewish Community Relations Council of New York is quoted as follows: "Sentiment to continue boycotting Germany is quite deeply embedded. Second- and third-generation American-born Jews are the most reluctant to move on." The article goes on to report that "even American Jews not directly touched by the Holocaust say they are expressing a tribal solidarity with the victims and their offspring by refusing to buy German or visit the country."

4. James E. Young, *The Texture of Memory: Holocaust Memorials and Meaning* (New Haven: Yale University Press, 1993).

5. For more about the high percentage of Jews involved in American Buddhism, see Rodger Kamenetz, *The Jew and the Lotus* (San Francisco: HarperSanFrancisco, 1994), and Alan Lew, *One God Clapping: The Spiritual Path of*

a Zen Rabbi (Woodstock, Vt.: Jewish Lights Publishing, 2001). Interestingly, Kamenetz's book begins with the author's narration of his intense discomfort in Germany, imagining the Holocaust as a "grainy newsreel" superimposed on the scene before him.

6. Sylvia Boorstein, *That's Funny, You Don't Look Buddhist* (San Francisco: HarperSanFrancisco, 1997), p. 23.

7. Ibid., pp. 125–26.

In Response to Rachel N. Baum

LEONARD GROB

RACHEL BAUM'S THOUGHTFUL essay poses a vital question for all who live in the post-1945 world: "What happens to the soul of a murdered people?" Vital as it may be, this query has often escaped the attention of philosophers and theologians who write in the Holocaust's aftermath. Touching the heart of the issue of "heart" in the post-Holocaust Jewish community, Baum raises not just one penetrating question but a host of them. For example, how do we post-Holocaust Jews face up to our pain "without becoming over-identified with it"? How do we "carry a heart that is both wounded and open?" Each query tears at us, challenging and provoking us to reexamine our remembering.

Baum believes that the American Jewish community has often failed to remember well. Memory of the Holocaust has seldom led to the openness and hopefulness that she emphasizes. On the contrary, memory has frequently led to attitudes and actions that evidence a hardened, angry heart. The dangers of retaining such anger are grave. Baum makes a valuable contribution to post-Holocaust ethics by arguing that we must achieve that clarity of mind which will allow us to come to grips with our pain and anger—and thus renounce acts that have sometimes perpetuated suffering.

Baum offers an explanation for why "the hardened heart" has persisted: holding on to anger has become a way to preserve the memory of six million murdered Jews. If anger is abandoned, there is fear that memory itself will die. Yet Baum argues astutely that we can remember differently, that clarity of mind regarding our anger can be (progressively) attained. If American Jews can succeed in living lives in authentic community, a community in which they feel safe enough to examine their remembering in the course of sharing one another's pain, then perhaps they can break the cycle of a perpetuation of suffering. New modes of remembering may be created: the angry victim may be transformed into the indignant but clear-minded witnesses of injustice. As Baum says, we may learn, "as a community how to sit with our pain, how to talk about our prejudices without holding on to them."

For Baum, a major impediment to sitting with our pain has been the productive action of the post-Holocaust American Jewish community. Transforming pain into action has been one highly effective way of avoiding "soul issues." Pain, Baum points out, has often been channeled into "doing." Rather than dealing openly, dialogically, with their pain, American Jews have often sublimated rage and grief by building memorials, constructing museums, providing monetary assistance for Israel, and solidifying religious identity.

Such doing has served a vital function for the Jewish community in the United States. As Baum acknowledges, it has helped the Jewish people survive the Holocaust's trauma. Nevertheless, the dangers implicit in "doing" loom large for her: "Perhaps," she argues, "we have moved too soon in transforming our pain into action." Our doing, she implies, may have led to the neglect of a spiritual need, the need to experience "a deep affective connection with others and, subsequently, with God and the divine."

Ideally, no divide would exist between our doing and our soul-searching. Yet, as Baum asserts, many forms of doing in the post-Holocaust world are devoid of spiritual content. As such, I add, they may not merit the name "doing" at all. In my view, doing is informed by spiritual concern or it is little more than the mechanical movement of limbs. "Ceremonies of memorialization, fund-raising efforts, and even religious identity"—cited by Baum as examples of post-Holocaust "doing"—*may or may not* merit that name. Serving what Baum terms "the political and social needs of the Jewish community" *may or may not* be genuine service. It depends on whether such service is rendered through what the philosopher Martin Buber calls "holy intercourse with all existing beings," the hallowing of everyday existence through full engagement with the other.[1]

Just as I share Baum's concern about action that fails to be imbued with the spiritual, I am also troubled by something that she does not seem to criticize enough, namely, uses of the word *spirit* that might place it outside the context of doing. Addressing *spiritual* needs, I contend, must ultimately mean addressing *social* and *political* needs. If there is danger in engaging in an (alleged) doing bereft of the spirit, there is also danger of embracing an (alleged) spirituality that might spurn the political. Although Baum's essay entreats us to confront our post-Holocaust spiritual needs, it pays less attention to the dangers of a spirituality removed from praxis.

To engage in spiritual pursuits is precisely to remain within the world as a doer. As Buber puts it, true spiritual relationship "does not involve ignoring everything . . . not renouncing the world but placing it upon its proper ground."[2] It is this relation to divinity, I believe, that Baum properly celebrates. For Buber, spirituality, cut off from engagement with the world, is pseudo-spirituality. Ours is the task of consecrating the everyday world: "Our concern," writes Buber, "is with this world in order to let the hidden life of God shine forth. . . . One eats in consecration, and the table becomes an altar. One works in consecration . . . and a splendor radiates over the community. . . ."[3] Understood as something ecstatic—something lived outside of history, something experienced by me in isolation from genuine encounter with the other—the spiritual dries up and loses all connection with the divine. Thus sitting with our pain—which Baum argues constitutes a neglected spiritual element of our post-Holocaust existence—is authentic sitting only when it is realized, ultimately, in dialogical engagement with the world.

An example of dangers inherent in *any* discussion of spirituality: Boorstein, cited by Baum, proclaims that "my contribution to *tikkun olam* (the repair of the world) begins with my dedication to maintaining a loving heart. I can only transform myself. It is all any of us can do." One danger in this discourse on spirituality is that of introducing a dichotomy between me and my relating-to-the-other. Transforming myself cannot be done in isolation from my engagement with the other. For Buber, becoming who I am as a whole (and thus loving) person is inextricably bound up with entering into authentic dialogue with that other whom Buber names my "Thou." Buber puts the point as follows: "Concentration and fusion into the whole being can never take place through my agency, nor can it ever take place without me. I become through my relation to the *Thou;* as I become *I,* I say *Thou.*"[4] My becoming whole and my engaging the other in dialogue thus constitute a circle that I can enter at any point.

This is not to say that all points within this circle are interchangeable. There are moments of differing emphasis within it.[5] As we are reminded by Baum's essay, the "I" needs to gather itself, to regroup, as it were: in the post-Holocaust period, this sitting with oneself assumes special significance. However, I contend that this gathering and regrouping of the "I" will be authentic *only* if effected within a larger movement, one that is ultimately dialogical.

Given my argument thus far, it may not be the case, as Boorstein suggests, that transforming myself is all that I can do; this is not my limit. Ultimately, I can transform myself *only in the process of working (in concert with the other) to transform the world.* My authentic "I" is integrally and inextricably linked to the other. A "dedication to maintaining a loving heart" takes place solely in the realm of the inter-subjective, what Buber calls "the Between." When Boorstein suggests that *tikkun olam* "begins" with self-transformation, she introduces a consideration of before and after that gives the lie to the inextricable nature of the link between work on the self and work with the other. Neither work can claim temporal or ontological priority over the other. Spiritual activity is fundamentally dialogical.

Having sounded my note of caution, I wish to reaffirm my view that Baum's essay sounds a clarion call for the Jewish community to remember its pain in newly creative ways. In spiritual / political engagement with the other, we can (progressively) rid ourselves of that specter of Auschwitz that would keep us subsumed by our anger. In so doing, we can renew an authentic commitment to *tikkun olam* in the post-Holocaust era.

NOTES

1. Martin Buber, *Hasidism and Modern Man,* trans. Maurice Friedman (New York: Horizon Press, 1958), p. 176.

2. See Martin Buber, *I and Thou,* trans. Ronald Gregor Smith (New York: Charles Scribner's Sons, 1958), pp. 78–79.

3. Martin Buber, *The Origin and Meaning of Hasidism,* trans. Maurice Friedman (New York: Horizon Press, 1960), pp. 55–56.

4. Buber, *I and Thou,* p. 11. The italics are mine.

5. On this point, I am indebted to discussion with Ernest Sherman, Aug. 25, 2001.

In Response to Rachel Baum

HENRY F. KNIGHT

IN HER REFLECTIONS on Jewish heart after the Shoah, Rachel Baum offers a bold and vulnerable challenge. As a Jew, she raises issues that are difficult for a Christian to criticize without feeling impertinent or arrogant. Consequently, as her Christian dialogue partner, I am compelled to ask myself, What can I provide that helps each of us, as well as both of us together, increase our understandings and capacities for justice, reconciliation, and forgiveness in a world still deeply wounded by the institutionalized hatred and violence of the Third Reich?

At first glance, the most important response I can make is to provide hospitable space for a difficult conversation. While this offer may seem simple, it has dimensions that are essential for the work of reconciliation to occur, particularly if it is to take place in ways that are not determined beforehand by one party or the other. After the Shoah, any Christian attempt to foster reconciliation by Jews, among Jews, for Jews, or with any so-called non-Christian other must be wary of covert attempts to lead the final outcome to an already disclosed Christian answer. In matters like this one, the first task of participating in a conversation with a Jewish partner is to provide genuine hospitality, room to engage the issues as she or he determines and for the resulting conversation to unfold on its own terms.

One of the key components of hospitality is that its recipients are provided safety and rest in the context of their host's home or familiar domain. If I am to participate as a host to the conversation begun by Baum, then I should provide her a safe place in which to pursue it. Likewise, if I am a fellow guest or her guest, I am called to acknowledge the safety provided for me and to extend it to others as the conversation unfolds. Furthermore, if the conversation occurs within the context of hospitality, it will also provide nurture and delight—food and drink, for example, welcoming guests to the host's table for nurture, and enjoying each other's company. In the context of Baum's paper and this book's dialogue, such hospitality means being nurtured by her words while at the same time offering substantive words of my own—along with those of others, all in the context of conversation and critique among colleagues bound together in a covenant of dialogue.

As a Christian, I begin with the awareness that the typical way for Christians to proceed is to applaud Baum's concerns. But after Auschwitz, should I not be alert to ways in which concerns for forgiveness and reconciliation can be an easy seduction for avoiding the more difficult matter of relating to others with integrity and understanding? If I honor such suspicions, my responsibility is to share these same concerns with Baum, inquiring of her whether she thinks she is asking too much from the survivor generation. Yet, as I raise this issue, I am also mindful of the summons to attempt to do as Baum has done, even when we are unable. So, while I ponder the possibility that she may be asking for more than anyone can give, I must still support her asking and seeking.

Baum risks being accused of abandoning or betraying memory by others who do not wish to provide her room to wrestle with her issues. If there is to be any movement in the direction she champions, it will undoubtedly come with courageous efforts like hers, with others choosing to follow her lead. Consequently, Christian friends must provide understanding and support with the full recognition of the significance of what she is doing, lest we undercut her efforts and break her trust that we, who are outsiders to her struggle, are worth the risk she is taking.

Still, even though it is important that Christian conversation partners provide safe, hospitable space for a colleague to raise the questions she does, it is equally important not to withhold any cautionary words we might offer regarding her project. Not to respond can inadvertently create the impression that my Jewish friends should be protected from my questions. Even worse, a failure to respond could convey an arrogant disdain.

Baum has raised spiritually significant issues for herself as well as for other Jews. She has done so, moreover, in a positive, non-accusatory way. Importantly, her voice is confessional. She asks, "What will we do with *our* suffering?" This point is significant. By avoiding the accusative voice she invites others to consider her concerns without having to defend their own. Too often the accusative voice is used, with one person pointing fingers at another by saying "you" or "they" did this or that. The wisdom of conflict management suggests that first-person language be employed for negotiating our ways through conflict. Furthermore, Baum asks in the future tense, pondering not so much the past but the present and the future. In addition, she extends the matter for herself along with others who share her identity, asking a second, more haunting question: "What happens to the soul of a murdered people?"

Here I must question her use of the phrase "a murdered people." During the Holocaust, nearly six million Jews were murdered. However, the ones about whom she raises her questions are not only survivors and their children but all Jews who live in a post-Holocaust world. These facts bear on the questions Baum raises. During the Holocaust, all Jews were targeted. Millions were actually attacked, killed, and degraded beyond the imagination of anyone who has not undergone such experience. Jewish existence has been traumatized by terror, by what might have been, by what nearly happened. During the Holocaust, all Jews lived on the threshold of murder. This recognition redefines Jewish existence and its world. It is this feature, surviving an attempted murder—not murder, per se—that stalks Holocaust survivors, their children, extended kin, and, indeed, Jews everywhere in a post-Holocaust world. It is the near experience that lingers and remains, attacking the heart and soul long after the body is spared.

Raising her questions, Baum opens an important door for dialogue, but she is less alone than she sometimes suggests. Consider once more the case with which her reflections begin. When the United Jewish Appeal decided to honor Thomas Middelhoff, head of the Bertelsmann Music Group, for his efforts to face up to the problematic history of the German people with regard to their embedded anti-Semitism, the UJA appeared to embody the very values that Baum promotes. In fact, her reflections are in some measure a defense of the UJA's actions. In other words, the UJA's attempt to recognize Middelhoff signals the very promise of the heart and soul that she seeks.

At another place in her essay, Baum states that "it would be naive to think that history will not intervene," but that statement is problematic. We compose history. Although Baum may mean that history resists human control, it is still true that we compose history, even as it resists our control. Her basic point, however, is well taken: How we compose our history matters deeply. How we compose it, if I read Baum correctly, is a matter of soul. This point is the heart of her critique. She suggests that people may not be remembering well enough. Indeed, she recommends taking the grieving process more seriously. Will it be wrapped in bitterness or clothed in grief fully expressed? If clothed in grief, it may begin in bitterness; still, it must move through lament, often expressing deep anger, toward something more. The bitterness and anger are understood to have their place in a larger context and thereby do not determine all that can and should happen.

Surely Baum is correct to assert that this movement is not simply a matter of the human will, but an indication of how people, consciously and unconsciously, lean into the future, turn toward each other, and engage the unknown. For this reason, she suggests that forgiveness may not necessarily be what is needed to recover fully one's heart and soul. That recovery, if it takes place, comes not so much through rational intention and willpower, but by attending to a wounded spirit that has made its way through the wounds to some measure of healing and wholeness.

By raising these concerns, particularly in the way I have, I hope I have offered some measure of hospitable resistance as well as solidarity in the struggle Baum describes. At the same time, I realize that I can also engage similar matters in my own tradition, matters where I need to do comparable work and to raise similar questions with Christian colleagues. If I can do this work with regard to Christian complicity and violence toward others who do not fit our way of holding the world, I can demonstrate that, as a Jew, Rachel Baum and others taking similar risks can do so with the knowledge that they have Christian colleagues engaging related issues. We help our Jewish colleagues by doing our own work, not by attempting to do theirs for them. In each case, we do our best work when we avoid easy responses and face up to the blind spots in our own identities.

In Response to Leonard Grob and Henry F. Knight

RACHEL N. BAUM

SINCE I WROTE my main essay for this book, thousands of people lost their lives in the September 11, 2001, attacks on the United States. I have written this response under the weight and grief of those losses. It has been a difficult doubling, writing my initial essay in the shadow of one world tragedy and responding in the shadow of another.

It is with new ears that I hear the concerns of my friend Henry Knight when he wonders if I am asking too much from the survivors and their descendants. My commitment to an open heart is difficult to reconcile with the images of burning buildings, men and women jumping from the World Trade Center's twin towers, rescue workers buried alive. Surely it is also difficult to speak of an open heart with the Holocaust's images of starvation, torture, and murder burning one's eyes.

It is with new ears that I hear my friend Leonard Grob emphasize the importance of connecting the world of spirit to the world of action. That an open heart can contribute to the peacefulness of the world, we can all agree, but surely it is not enough. Surely, in the real world, a world too often marked by hatred and violence, an open heart provides only part of the story.

If there is one thing that all this has shown me—the responses of my colleagues, the complexities of my own heart after September 11—it is the significance of time. As I write these words, very little time has passed since September 11, 2001, but already, one can discern a difference among the American people. Already, the anger and grief of the first days have changed, if only into a differently textured anger and grief.

My contribution to this volume could not have been written ten years after the Holocaust. It could not even have been written twenty years after. My essay is very much the product of a woman born a quarter century after the destruction, a woman who not only was not there, but who was born into a different world, with a different set of responsibilities. What remains unchanged throughout history is *that* we must remember; *how* we remember, however, will change over time. The shape of memory changes over time because *we* change.

Knight is right to emphasize the difference between being murdered and being *almost* murdered. He is correct that the hardening of the Jewish heart is to be expected, given how the Jewish people have suffered. Yet it is also true that Jews today live in an essentially different world than that of the Jews of fifty years ago. We live with the knowledge that our ancestors were murdered and that there are those who still desire our annihilation. At the same time, we have substantial social power as a group. It is the necessity to hold both of these things simultaneously that makes the issue so complex and delicate.

In writing of the soul of a murdered people, I seek to emphasize the Jewish soul that links contemporary Jews to the murdered Jews of the Holocaust. Yet I write—perhaps too narrowly—for Jews like myself, Jews who live with a cultural memory of the Holocaust, not an actual memory of that event. The struggles for the survivors have been entirely different. Simply to survive after the Shoah, to build lives and perhaps even to find some joy in life—surely this is enough for those who experienced the horror firsthand. The historical moment I am trying to touch in my essay is precisely the moment *after*, the moment when the survivors are no longer with us and we must decide how we will honor, hold, and shape the memory of the Shoah.

Knight's concerns raise questions about the children and grandchildren of Holocaust survivors—the second and third generations—and whether my words have as much relevance for them. I feel unequipped to make such a determination, as I am neither child nor grandchild of survivors. I want to be sensitive to this difference, for I recognize the specificity of knowing that *one's own family* was tortured, humiliated, murdered. Yet I also know, and respect, that much of the work of reconciliation has been borne by the second and third generations, men and women who are trying to build a different world than the one that victimized their families. I hope that these men and women hear my words not as critique but as part of the dialogue.

Leonard Grob reminds me of the dangers of speaking of spirituality without speaking as well of praxis. His words highlight the difficulty of using the term *spiritual,* which may imply a distinction between spirit and earth, being and doing. I share his discomfort with the term, which can be used to justify a withdrawal from the world.

Yet I sense that the danger is not so much spirituality removed from action as it is a particular kind of spiritual practice. Prayer is praxis, as are meditation, creating petitions, and building museums. If there is a danger in a spirituality removed from praxis, there is also a danger in too narrowly defining what counts as praxis.

Jewish tradition teaches that if all Jews observe the Sabbath in a single week (some say in two consecutive weeks), the Messiah will come. There are several ways to understand this. One reading might suggest that if Jews behave correctly toward God, they will be rewarded with the coming of the Messiah. Another way of understanding this teaching, however, is to suggest that observing the Sabbath is an activity that changes Jews and the world so profoundly that we will be ready for the time of peace ushered in by the Messiah. Spiritual practice, however defined, changes us—creates and defines us—and changes the world. It is not that spirituality must come before action, as Grob notes, but that our values and spirituality are inextricably part of our very existence.

The choice is not one between spirituality and praxis, as both Grob and I realize. The choice is between competing values at the heart of our actions. Committees of Holocaust memory (resource centers, museums, educational facilities) often see their work in terms of *protecting* Holocaust memory, rather than *creating* it. Once we acknowledge that our actions give shape to Jewish memory, our responsibility to articulate our values becomes much clearer.

Through my dialogue with Grob, I have come to understand that what really concerns me is the space where spirit and praxis combine—the space we call identity. What I am really trying to get at in my essay is the complexity of post-Holocaust Jewish identity. Who will we *be*, after the Holocaust? This *being* is shaped through our values, our practices, and, most essentially, through the stories we tell about ourselves. Like Grob's contribution to this volume, my essay suggests that Jews must reshape the stories they tell about themselves. The story of the Holocaust is a story of Jewish victimization, and it is right that it be told in such a way, but we as a community must decide if that is the only story we have to tell about ourselves. Do the stories we tell about ourselves as Jews bring us fully into the world, or do they separate us from it? Do the stories we tell about ourselves as Jews bring us closer to the stranger, the orphan, the widow, as our tradition commands, or do they estrange us? Do the stories we tell about ourselves as Jews sustain Judaism as a religion of joy, compassion, and love, or do they limit our expression of such a Judaism?

I feel as if I owe my friend Hank Knight and my other Christian dialogue partners a bit of an apology. I knew when I wrote my essay that it was largely directed to my own community, and that it was, in many ways, an odd contribution for a project focused on dialogue between Jews and Christians. Knight has been gracious in his intellectual hospitality, and in his commitment to promoting similar work in his own community. The significance of this kind of doing needs to be underscored even further.

The writers of this book are part of a somewhat larger international community of Holocaust scholars that meets biennially in Wroxton, England. It was at our gathering in June 2000 that the thoughts of my essay began, as I really *saw* the German participants for the first time, and imagined how difficult our meeting might be for them. It was there that I recognized the power of my own hospitality, my responsibility to extend a warm word, to foster an environment of openness and trust. And so, my essay was not written in the ivory tower, but in the world, in confrontation with my own complex feelings toward Germans and Christians, and in my desire to live up to the ideals of dialogue and reconciliation upon which the Wroxton gathering was founded. Leonard Grob and Henry Knight were at the center of that community's creation. They have indeed contributed to a spiritually informed praxis. For that, and for their thoughtful responses to my work, I thank them.

POSTSCRIPT

An *After* That Is *Yet to Be*

DAVID PATTERSON AND JOHN K. ROTH

Man lives in the spirit when he is able to respond to his You.
—Martin Buber, *I and Thou*

REACHING THE END of these dialogical encounters, we come to no closure. Indeed, the aim of dialogical encounter is not to have the last word but to summon a latent word, an after-word, that might take the word to deeper levels of meaning by taking human beings to deeper levels of relation. As its title implies, this book is itself made of after-words whose "before" is the Holocaust. And a defining feature of the Holocaust is an assault on the word, a tearing of word from meaning in a tearing of human from human. In the Holocaust Kingdom, words "had meanings totally different from their usual ones," as Primo Levi has said,[1] "meanings" that rendered each person "desperately and ferociously alone."[2] In her memoir, Sara Nomberg-Przytyk writes that the new, twisted meanings of words "provided the best evidence of the devastation that Auschwitz created."[3] And in *Star of Ashes,* Ka-tzetnik cries out, "Words are no more!"[4]

What, then, is the devastation that is Auschwitz, where words have been swallowed up in the Kingdom of Night? One answer to this question can be found in the *Muselmänner,* those whom a radical evil rendered radically silent and infinitely distant from the rest of humanity. They are the camp incarnate, the ones Levi describes as "the backbone of the camp, an anonymous mass, continually renewed and always identical, of *non-men* who march and labor *in silence, the divine spark dead within them,* already too empty to really suffer. One hesitates to call them living: one hesitates to call their death death."[5] Where words are no more, the divine spark that sanctifies the human image is no more, and men are made into non-men. Thus, coming to the end of these reflections, we realize what is at stake in the post-Holocaust struggles with these after-words: it is the restoration of a sacred likeness to the human image. Therein lies the urgency surrounding the three words that have guided our dialogical encounters: *forgiveness, reconciliation, justice.*

These three words are essential to the restoration of the divine spark to the human being because they are essential to restoring human relation. And fundamental to a mending of human relation is a mending of the relation between word and meaning. Adopting a dialogical method, this book has aspired to approach such a mending by wrestling with these after-words. Numerous levels of tension and contention have emerged in the process: tensions between Jew and Christian, between Christian and Christian, between Jew and Jew. And yet those tensions have emerged precisely because beneath the surface something as meaningful as it is dear is at work. It turns out that in the post-Holocaust era, the mending of relation—between human and human or between word and meaning—lies not in settling matters but rather in a certain strife of the spirit, which is a struggle with the word.

For "spirit is word," as Martin Buber has said. "It is not in the I but between I and You. It is not like the blood that circulates in you but like the air in which you breathe. Man lives in the spirit when he is able to respond to his You."[6] The speaking and responding that comprise this book unfold in the between space that Buber describes as the realm of word and spirit. It has been necessary to open up this between space because, like word and spirit, questions of forgiveness, reconciliation, and justice unfold in a space between human beings. And they involve what Buber describes as an I-Thou relation, that is, a relation of the whole being. Forgiveness, reconciliation, and justice may be subjects of argumentation and reflection, but they cannot be subject to manipulation or exploitation if they are to have meaning.

In the post-Holocaust era, however, the embrace between an I and a Thou has assumed the form of a wrestling match. Like the relation between human and human, meaning cannot simply be reattached to the word—it must be wrestled back into the word. To be sure, the example of Jacob at Peniel teaches us that only in such wrestling can we hope to find blessing. Our engagements with each other throughout this book suggest that, like truth, such blessing is forever sought but never quite found. It recedes even as we approach it, at times revealing its back but always concealing its face. And yet a face is precisely what we seek in these post-Holocaust struggles with forgiveness, reconciliation, and justice: it is the face of our fellow human being.

When we seek the face of our fellow human being, that seeking is a kind of turning, as one may gather from Peter Haas's discussion of *teshuvah* or repentance, since *teshuvah* is a return or turning about—a turning to *face* our fellow human being. Without that facing, we realize, there is no forgiving. Whether reconciliation requires forgiveness, as Didier Pollefeyt argues, or is possible without forgiveness, as Haas maintains, it entails a turning toward one another in such a way that one person does not presume to define the other. Such a turning is needful to a mending of word and relation in the post-Holocaust era, even though—or especially because, as Henry Knight has shown—forgiveness is in abeyance: when it comes to turning to face our fellow human being, we have never turned far enough. If that is the case, then it would seem that reconciliation is also forever yet to be realized, even if Christians and Jews should manage to cooperate in various efforts to alleviate suffering in the world, as Haas rightly urges.

This problematic nature of forgiveness, as well as the equally problematic issue of justice, leads John Roth to maintain that neither should stand in the way of reconciliation. It may be the case that much of the frustration surrounding matters of forgiveness and justice is due to what Roth identifies as the "useless experience" that only widens the distance separating human beings from one another. What one sees in the dialogical encounter with Roth, moreover, is that dialogue is not enough—hence his concern with the opening of the Vatican's Holocaust-related archives. Roth also enables us to see that reconciliation is not only an interfaith issue; it is also an intrafaith concern facing the Christian community.

Further expanding the scope of the issue, Britta Frede-Wenger has shown that reconciliation is a matter that concerns not only the self-to-other relation but also the self-to-self relation, particularly for the younger generation of Germans. While her respondents warn against lay-ing the burden of forgiveness and reconciliation on the victim, Frede-Wenger brings to light the complex nature of the relation between history and identity. One implication of Frede-Wenger's insight is that forgiveness, reconciliation, and justice decide something very significant not only about our relation to one another but also about who we are. Juergen Manemann takes this insight even further with his thinking on the "unencumbered self" that threatens human presence and the responsibility that defines who we are. From the interaction between Manemann and his respondents—as well as from the essays on reconciliation by Roth and Frede-Wenger—it becomes evident that responsibility is a key component of reconciliation.

David Patterson also emphasizes a responsibility to and for the other human being in matters of justice, over against notions of justice as getting even or imposing penalties. Whether or not a concept of justice as righteousness can be retrieved from Jewish thought, it seems clear that the post-Holocaust pursuit of justice requires rethinking certain categories that were operative prior to the Holocaust. One can see from the responses to Patterson's essay that such a process of rethinking is neither easy nor comfortable. And implementing a renewed notion of justice is even more difficult, as Leonard Grob demonstrates in his essay on the Israeli-Palestinian conflict. Here too it becomes evident that the responsibility necessary to reconciliation is equally necessary to the attainment of justice in the post-Holocaust era. What we learn from Grob's essay is this: If the restoration of the divine spark to the human image requires a mending of the link between word and meaning, then it also requires a renewed effort to *listen to the other human being.* And the truth of this matter pertains not only to the Israeli-Palestinian conflict but to every human conflict, from the personal to the global.

Similarly, what Rachel Baum writes about the post-Holocaust Jewish heart has implications for the heart of all humanity. Baum leads us to realize something about the truth of the Jewish teaching (based on Psalms 51:17) that there is nothing as whole as a broken heart. For the broken heart in this instance is the heart broken by the suffering of the *other* human being. In order to attain this wholeness, Baum enables us to realize, the Jewish people must seek ways of remembering that do not eat away at the Jewish soul—a soul that, like any human soul, finds the wholeness of its presence in the world through its heart-wrenching concern for the other person. Without placing all the burden of forgiveness, reconciliation, and justice on the shoulders of the Jews, Baum reminds them that their role in this difficult process is not a passive one. And, just as the Christians have their intrafaith issues, so do the Jews. The questions Baum leaves us with are: What are the limits and the possibilities of Jewish spirituality in the post-Holocaust era? And what is the role of that spirituality in the struggle for forgiveness, reconciliation, and justice?

Of course, as this book demonstrates, one question leads to another. Just as each word summons an after-word, the truth we seek in these post-Holocaust struggles abides in an *after* that is forever *yet to be.* In that *yet to be* lies the dimension of time that underlies senses of meaning and mission in life. If we set out to restore a broken human image by mending the link between word and meaning, then, through these after-words, we set out to recover this *yet to be.* Thus, we seek a recovery of the human being—of the *ben adam* or "child of Adam," to use the Hebrew expression—in an age characterized by a new after-word: *September 11.* It is a word that returns us to the beginning, where we must once again make the movement of return by responding to the questions put to the first child of Adam: "Where is your brother?" and "What have you done?"

NOTES

1. Primo Levi, *Moments of Reprieve,* trans. Ruth Feldman (London: Michael Joseph, 1986), p. 93.

2. Primo Levi, *Survival in Auschwitz: The Nazi Assault on Humanity,* trans. Stuart Woolf (New York: Simon & Schuster, 1986), p. 88.

3. Sara Nomberg-Przytyk, *Auschwitz: True Tales from a Grotesque Land,* trans. Roslyn Hirsch (Chapel Hill: University of North Carolina Press, 1985), p. 72.

4. Ka-tzetnik 135633, *Star of Ashes,* trans. H. Zeldes and Nina De-Nur (Tel Aviv: Hamenora, 1971), p. 69.

5. Levi, *Survival in Auschwitz,* p. 90, italics added.

6. Martin Buber, *I and Thou,* trans. Walter Kaufmann (New York: Charles Scribner's Sons, 1970), p. 89.

BIBLIOGRAPHY

Abel, O. *Le pardon: Brisser la dette et l'oubli.* Paris: Autremont, 1998.

Adorno, Theodor W. *Gesammelte Schriften.* Vol. 10. Frankfurt am Main: Suhrkamp Verlag, 1977.

———. *Negative Dialektik.* Frankfurt am Main: Suhrkamp Verlag, 1966.

Améry, Jean. *At the Mind's Limits: Contemplations by a Survivor on Auschwitz and Its Realities.* Trans. Sidney Rosenfeld and Stella P. Rosenfeld. New York: Schocken Books, 1986.

Anderson, Herbert, and Edward Foley. *Mighty Stories, Dangerous Rituals: Weaving Together the Human and the Divine.* San Francisco: Jossey-Bass, 1998.

Arendt, Hannah. *The Human Condition.* Chicago: University of Chicago Press, 1958.

Barkan, Elazar. *The Guilt of Nations: Restitution and Negotiating Historical Injustices.* New York: W. W. Norton, 2000.

Barnett, Victoria J. *Bystanders: Conscience and Complicity during the Holocaust.* Westport, Conn.: Praeger, 2000.

———. "Provocative Reconciliation: A Jewish Statement on Christianity." *The Christian Century,* Sept. 27–Oct. 4, 2000.

Bauer, J. B., ed. *Entwürfe der Theologie.* Graz, Vienna, and Cologne: Styria Verlag, 1985.

Bauman, Zygmunt. "The Holocaust's Life as a Ghost." *Tikkun: A Bimonthly Jewish Critique of Politics, Culture, and Society,* July–Aug. 1998.

———. *Modernity and the Holocaust.* Ithaca, N.Y.: Cornell University Press, 1989.

Beck, Ulrich. *Die Erfindung des Politischen.* Frankfurt am Main: Suhrkamp Verlag, 1993.

Bendersky, Joseph W. *Carl Schmitt: Theorist of the Reich.* Princeton, N.J.: Princeton University Press, 1983.

Benjamin, Walter. *Gesammelte Schriften.* Ed. R. Tiedemann and H. Schweppenhäuser. Vol. 1. Frankfurt am Main: Suhrkamp Verlag, 1980.

Berger, Alan, and Naomi Berger. *Second Generation Voices: Reflections by Children of Holocaust Survivors and Perpetrators.* Syracuse, N.Y.: Syracuse University Press, 2001.

Bieringer, R., Didier Pollefeyt, and F. Vandecasteele-Vanneuville, eds. *Anti-Judaism and the Fourth Gospel: Papers of the Leuven Colloquium 2000.* Assen: Van Gorcum, 2001.

Blet, Pierre. *Pope Pius XII and the Second World War: According to the Archives of the Vatican.* Trans. Lawrence J. Johnson. New York: Paulist Press, 1999.

Blumenberg, Hans. *Legitimität der Neuzeit.* Frankfurt am Main: Suhrkamp Verlag, 1996.

Blumenthal, David. *Facing the Abusing God: A Theology of Protest.* Louisville, Ky.: Westminster John Knox Press, 1993.

———. "Repentance and Forgiveness." *Cross Currents* 48 (Spring 1998).

Bonhoeffer, Dietrich. *The Cost of Discipleship.* New York: Macmillan, 1995.

Boorstein, Sylvia. *That's Funny, You Don't Look Buddhist.* San Francisco: HarperSanFrancisco, 1997.

Boszormenyi-Nagy, Ivan, and Barbara R. Krasner. *Between Give and Take: Clinical Guide to Contextual Therapy.* New York: Brunner / Mazel, 1986.

Boszormenyi-Nagy, Ivan, and Geraldine M. Spark. *Invisible Loyalties: Reciprocity in Intergenerational Family Therapy.* New York: Harper & Row, 1973.

Braiterman, Zachary. *(God) after Auschwitz.* Princeton, N.J.: Princeton University Press, 1998.

Buber, Martin. *Hasidism and Modern Man.* Trans. Maurice Friedman. New York: Horizon Press, 1958.

———. *I and Thou.* Trans. Walter Kaufmann. New York: Charles Scribner's Sons, 1970.

———. *Israel and Palestine: The History of an Idea.* Trans. S. Goodman. London: East and West Library, 1952.

———. *Israel and the World: Essays in a Time of Crisis.* New York: Schocken Books, 1963.

———. *A Land of Two Peoples: Martin Buber on Jews and Arabs.* Ed. and trans. Paul Mendes-Flohr. Magnolia, Mass.: Peter Smith, 1994.

———. *The Origin and Meaning of Hasidism.* Trans. Maurice Friedman. New York: Horizon Press, 1960.

Camus, Albert. *Der Mensch in der Revolte.* Trans. Justus Streller. Reinbek: Rowohlt, 1964.

Cargas, Harry James. *Reflections of a Post-Auschwitz Christian.* Detroit: Wayne State University Press, 1989.

———. *Shadows of Auschwitz: A Christian Response to the Holocaust.* New York: Crossroad, 1990.

Carroll, James. *Constantine's Sword: The Church and the Jews, a History.* Boston: Houghton Mifflin, 2001.

Cassirer, Ernst. *Kant's Life and Thought.* Trans. James Haden. New Haven: Yale University Press, 1981.

Cornwell, John. *Hitler's Pope: The Secret History of Pius XII.* New York: Viking, 1999.

Davis, Stephen T., ed. *Encountering Evil: Live Options in Theodicy.* 2d ed. Louisville, Ky.: Westminster John Knox Press, 2001.

De Visscher, James. "Over het vergeven van het nooit te rechtvaardigen kwaad." *Wijsgerig pespectief op mens en maatschappij* 33 (1992–93): 113–17.

Delbo, Charlotte. *Auschwitz and After.* Trans. Rosette C. Lamont. New Haven: Yale University Press, 1995.

———. *Convoy to Auschwitz: Women of the French Resistance.* Trans. Carol Cosman. Boston: Northeastern University Press, 1997.

———. *Days and Memory.* Trans. Rosette C. Lamont. Marlboro, Vt.: Marlboro Press, 1990.

Derrida, Jacques. "Jacques Derrida im Gespräch mit Michel Wieviorka: Jahrhundert der Vergebung. Verzeihen ohne Macht—unbedingt und jenseits der Souveränität." *Lettre international* 48 (2000): 10–18.

———. *On Cosmopolitanism and Forgiveness.* Trans. Mark Dooley and Michael Hughes. New York: Routledge, 2002.

Dillen, Annemie. "Vergeving of exoneratie? Kritische kanttekeningen vanuit en bij de theorie van Ivan Boszormenyi-Nagy." *Tijdschrift voor theologie,* no. 1 (2001): 61–84.

Ellis, Marc H. *Revolutionary Forgiveness: Essays on Judaism, Christianity, and the Future of Religious Life.* Waco, Tex.: Baylor University Press, 2000.

Enright, Robert D., and Joanna North, eds. *Exploring Forgiveness.* Madison: University of Wisconsin Press, 1998.

Fackenheim, Emil L. *Encounters between Judaism and Modern Philosophy.* New York: Basic Books, 1973.

———. *God's Presence in History: Jewish Affirmations and Philosophical Reflections.* Northvale, N.J.: Jason Aronson, 1997.

———. *The Jewish Bible after the Holocaust.* Bloomington: Indiana University Press, 1990.

———. *The Jewish Return into History.* New York: Schocken Books, 1978.

———. *To Mend the World: Foundations of Future Jewish Thought.* New York: Schocken Books, 1982.

———. *What Is Judaism?* New York: Macmillan, 1987.

Farina, John, ed. *Beauty for Ashes: Spiritual Reflections on the Attack on America.* New York: Crossroad, 2001.

Fleischner, Eva, ed. *Auschwitz: Beginning of a New Era?* New York: KTAV, 1977.

Ford, David F. *Self and Salvation: Being Transformed.* Cambridge: Cambridge University Press, 1999.

Friedlander, Albert H. *A Thread of Gold: Journeys towards Reconciliation.* Trans. John Bowden. Philadelphia: Trinity Press International, 1990.

Friedländer, Saul. *Memory, History, and the Extermination of the Jews of Europe.* Bloomington: Indiana University Press, 1993.

Fuchs, Ottmar, Reinhold Boschki, and Britta Frede-Wenger, eds. *Zugänge zur Erinnerung: Bedingungen anamnetischer Erfahrung, Studien zur subjektorientierten Erinngerungsarbeit.* Münster: LIT-Verlag, 2001.

Geras, Norman. *The Contract of Mutual Indifference: Political Philosophy after the Holocaust.* London: Verso, 1998.

Giordano, Ralph. *Die zweite Schuld oder Von der Last Deutscher zu sein.* Munich: Knaur, 1990.

Glover, Jonathan. *Humanity: A Moral History of the Twentieth Century.* New Haven: Yale University Press, 1999.

Goldhagen, Daniel J. *Hitler's Willing Executioners.* London: Little, Brown, 1996.

———. "Modell Bundesrepublik: National History, Democracy, and Internationalization in Germany." *Blätter für deutsche und internationale Politik* 42 (1997).

———. *A Moral Reckoning: The Role of the Catholic Church in the Holocaust and Its Unfulfilled Duty of Repair.* New York: Knopf, 2002.

———, ed. *Briefe an Goldhagen: Eingeleitet und beantwortet von Daniel Jonah Goldhagen.* Berlin: Siedler, 1998.

Golinkin, David. *Responsa in a Moment: Halakhic Responses to Contemporary Issues.* Jerusalem: Institute of Applied Halakhah at the Schechter Institute of Jewish Studies, 2000.

Gordon, Haim, and Leonard Grob, eds. *Education for Peace: Testimonies from World Religions.* Maryknoll, N.Y.: Orbis Books, 1987.

Govier, Trudy. *Forgiveness and Revenge.* New York: Routledge, 2002.

Graham, Robert A. *The Vatican and Communism in World War II: What Really Happened?* San Francisco: Ignatius Press, 1996.

Greenberg, Irving. "Cloud of Smoke, Pillar of Fire." In Michael Morgan, ed., *A Holocaust Reader: Responses to the Nazi Extermination.* New York: Oxford University Press, 2001.

Grob, Leonard. "Buberian Peace Education in the Mideast: A Buberian Critique." *Educational Theory* 35, no. 4 (Fall 1985): 423–32.

Haas, Peter J. *Morality after Auschwitz: The Radical Challenge of the Nazi Ethic.* Philadelphia: Fortress Press, 1988.

Hallie, Philip. *Tales of Good and Evil, Help and Harm.* New York: HarperCollins, 1997.

Hargrave, Terry D. *Families and Forgiveness: Healing Wounds in the Intergenerational Family.* New York: Brunner / Mazel, 1994.

Hartman, Geoffrey H. *Holocaust Remembrance: The Shapes of Memory.* Oxford: Blackwell, 1994.

Hayner, Priscilla B. *Unspeakable Truths: Confronting State Terror and Atrocity.* New York: Routledge, 2000.

Haynes, Stephen R. *Reluctant Witnesses: Jews and the Christian Imagination.* Louisville, Ky.: Westminster John Knox Press, 1995.

Hegel, G. W. F. *Vorlesungen über die Ästhetik.* Vol. 1. Frankfurt am Main: Suhrkamp Verlag, 1975.

———. *Vorlesungen über die Philosophie der Geschichte.* Frankfurt am Main: Suhrkamp Verlag, 1970.

Heil, J., and R. Erb, eds. *Geschichtswissenschaft und Öffentlichkeit: Der Streit um Daniel J. Goldhagen.* Frankfurt am Main: Fischer, 1998.

Heschel, Abraham Joshua. *Man's Quest for God.* New York: Charles Scribner's Sons, 1954.

Hillesum, Etty. *Etty: De nagelaten geschriften van Etty Hillesum 1941–1943.* Amsterdam: Balans, 1991.

Jacob, Walter, ed. *Questions and Reform Jewish Answers: New American Reform Responsa.* New York: CCAR, 1992.

Jankélévitch, Vladimir. *L'imprescriptible: Pardonner? Dans l'honneur et la dignité.* Paris: Éditions du Seuil, 1986.

———. *Le pardon.* Paris: Aubier, 1967.

Jaspers, Karl. *The Question of German Guilt.* Trans. E. B. Ashton. New York: Fordham University Press, 2000.

Jonas, Hans. *Mortality and Morality: A Search for the Good after Auschwitz.* Ed. Lawrence Vogel. Evanston, Ill.: Northwestern University Press, 1996.

Jones, David H. *Moral Responsibility in the Holocaust: A Study in the Ethics of Character.* Lanham, Md.: Rowman & Littlefield, 1999.

Jones, L. Gregory. *Embodying Forgiveness: A Theological Analysis.* Grand Rapids, Mich.: Eerdmans, 1995.

Kamenetz, Rodger. *The Jew and the Lotus.* San Francisco: HarperSanFrancisco, 1994.

Kaplan, Chaim A. *Scroll of Agony.* Ed. and trans. Abraham I. Katsh. Bloomington: Indiana University Press, 1999.

Ka-tzetnik 135633. *Star of Ashes.* Trans. H. Zeldes and Nina De-Nur. Tel Aviv: Hamenora, 1971.

Kellenbach, Katharina von, Björn Krondorfer, and Norbert Reck, eds. *Von Gott reden im Land der Täter.* Darmstadt: Wissenschaftliche Buchgesellschaft, 2001.

Khalidi, Rashid. *Palestinian Identity.* New York: Columbia University Press, 1997.

Kirschner, Robert, ed. *Rabbinic Responsa of the Holocaust Era.* New York: Schocken Books, 1985.

Knight, Henry F. *Confessing Christ in a Post-Holocaust World.* Westport, Conn.: Greenwood Press, 2000.

———. "From Shame to Responsibility and Christian Identity: The Dynamics of Shame and Christian Confession Regarding the Shoah." *Journal of Ecumenical Studies* 35, no. 1 (Winter 1998): 41–62.

Koetschau, Paul, ed. *Origenes Werke.* Vol. 5, *De Principiis.* Leipzig: J. C. Hinrichs'sche Buchhandlung, 1913.

Krondorfer, Björn. *Remembrance and Reconciliation: Encounters between Young Jews and Germans.* New Haven: Yale University Press, 1995.

Kushner, Harold S. *How Good Do We Have to Be? A New Understanding of Guilt and Forgiveness.* New York: Little, Brown, 1997.

Kushner, Lawrence. *River of Light: Spirituality, Judaism, Consciousness.* Woodstock, Vt.: Jewish Lights Publishing, 1991.

Lang, Berel. *The Future of the Holocaust: Between History and Memory.* Ithaca, N.Y.: Cornell University Press, 1999.

Lanzmann, Claude. *Shoah: An Oral History of the Holocaust.* New York: Pantheon, 1985.

Lerner, Michael. *Jewish Renewal: A Path to Healing and Transformation.* New York: G. P. Putnam's Sons, 1994.

Levi, Primo. *The Drowned and the Saved.* Trans. Raymond Rosenthal. New York: Summit Books, 1988.

———. *Moments of Reprieve.* Trans. Ruth Feldman. London: Michael Joseph, 1986.

———. *Survival in Auschwitz: The Nazi Assault on Humanity.* Trans. Stuart Woolf. New York: Macmillan, 1976; Simon & Schuster, 1986.

Lévinas, Emmanuel. *Difficile liberté: Essais sur le judaïsme.* Paris: Albin Michel, 1963.

———. *Difficult Freedom: Essays on Judaism.* Trans. Seàn Hand. Baltimore: Johns Hopkins University Press, 1990.

———. *Entre Nous: On Thinking-of-the-Other.* Trans. Michael B. Smith and Barbara Harshav. New York: Columbia University Press, 1998.

———. *Ethics and Infinity.* Trans. Richard Cohen. Pittsburgh: Duquesne University Press, 1985.

———. *Of God Who Comes to Mind.* Trans. Bettina Bergo. Stanford, Calif.: Stanford University Press, 1998.

———. "La mémoire d'un passé non révolu." *Revue de l'Université de Bruxelles* 1–2 (1987).

———. *Outside the Subject.* Trans. Michael B. Smith. Stanford, Calif.: Stanford University Press, 1993.

———. *Die Spur des Anderen: Untersuchungen zur Phänomenologie und Sozialphilosophie.* Freiburg: Verlag Karl Alber, 1983.

———. *Time and the Other.* Trans. Richard A. Cohen. Pittsburgh: Duquesne University Press, 1987.

———. *Totalité et infini: Essai sur l'extéiorité.* The Hague: Nijhoff, 1992.

Lew, Alan. *One God Clapping: The Spiritual Path of a Zen Rabbi.* Woodstock, Vt.: Jewish Lights Publishing, 2001.

Littell, Franklin H. *The Crucifixion of the Jews: The Failure of Christians to Understand the Jewish Experience.* Macon, Ga.: Mercer University Press, 1975.

———, ed. *Hyping the Holocaust: Scholars Answer Goldhagen.* East Rockaway, N.Y.: Cummings & Hathaway, 1997.

Littell, Marcia, Eric Geldbach, and G. Jan Colijn, eds. *The Holocaust: Remembering for the Future II on CD-ROM.* Stamford, Conn.: Vista InterMedia, 1996.

Marchione, Margherita. *Pope Pius XII: Architect for Peace.* New York: Paulist Press, 2000.

Margalit, Avishai. *The Ethics of Memory.* Cambridge, Mass.: Harvard University Press, 2002.

McInerny, Ralph. *The Defamation of Pius XII.* South Bend, Ind.: St. Augustine's Press, 2001.

Metz, Johann Baptist. *Faith in History and Society: Toward a Practical Fundamental Theology.* Trans. David Smith. London: Burns and Oates, 1980.

———. "Im Eingedenken fremden Leids." In *Gottesrede.* Münster: LIT-Verlag, 1996.

———. *Jenseits bürgerlicher Religion: Reden über die Zukunft des Christentums.* Mainz: Grünewald, 1984.

Metzger, Alter B. Z. *Rabbi Kook's Philosophy of Repentance: A Translation of* Orot Ha-Teshuvah. New York: Yeshiva University Press, 1968.

Minow, Martha. *Between Vengeance and Forgiveness: Facing History after Genocide and Mass Violence.* Boston: Beacon Press, 1998.

Monbourquette, Jean. *Comment pardonner? Pardonner pour guérir. Guérir pour pardonner.* Ottawa: Novalis, 1992.

Monbourquette, John. *How to Forgive: A Step-by-Step Guide.* Ottawa: Novalis, 2000.

Moore, James F. *Christian Theology after the Shoah.* Lanham, Md.: University Press of America, 1993.

Morgan, Michael, ed. *A Holocaust Reader: Responses to the Nazi Extermination.* New York: Oxford University Press, 2001.

Morris, Benny. *The Birth of the Palestinian Refugee Problem.* Cambridge: Cambridge University Press, 1987.

Müller-Fahrenholz, Geiko. *The Art of Forgiveness: Theological Reflections on Healing and Reconciliation.* Geneva: World Council of Churches Publications, 1997.

Murphy, Jeffrie G., and Jean Hampton. *Forgiveness and Mercy.* Cambridge: Cambridge University Press, 1988.

Neher, André. *The Exile of the Word: From the Silence of the Bible to the Silence of Auschwitz.* Trans. David Maisel. Philadelphia: Jewish Publication Society, 1981.

Nomberg-Przytyk, Sara. *Auschwitz: True Tales from a Grotesque Land.* Trans. Roslyn Hirsch. Chapel Hill: University of North Carolina Press, 1985.

Nussbaum, Chaim. *The Essence of Teshuvah: A Path to Repentance.* Northvale, N.J.: Jason Aronson, 1993.

Patterson, David. *Along the Edge of Annihilation: The Collapse and Recovery of Life in the Holocaust Diary.* Seattle: University of Washington Press, 1999.

———. *The Shriek of Silence: A Phenomenology of the Holocaust Novel.* Lexington: University Press of Kentucky, 1992.

———. *Sun Turned to Darkness: Memory and Recovery in the Holocaust Memoir.* Syracuse, N.Y.: Syracuse University Press, 1999.

Peters, Tiemo Rainer. *Mystik—Mythos—Metaphysik: Die Spur des vermissten Gottes.* Mainz: Grünewald, 1992.

Phayer, Michael. *The Catholic Church and the Holocaust, 1930–1965.* Bloomington: Indiana University Press, 2000.

Pollefeyt, Didier, ed. *Incredible Forgiveness: Christian Ethics between Fanaticism and Reconciliation.* Leuven: Peeters, 2002.

Reck, Norbert. *Im Angesicht der Zeugen: Eine Theologie nach Auschwitz.* Mainz: Grünwald, 1998.

Reemtsma, Jan Philip. "Abkehr vom Wunsch nach Verleugnung?" *Blätter für deutsche und internationale Politik* 42 (1997).

Ricoeur, Paul. "Can Forgiveness Heal?" In H. J. Opdebeeck, ed., *The Foundation and Application of Moral Philosophy: Ricoeur's Ethical Order.* Leuven: Peeters, 2000.

———. *La mémoire, l'histoire, l'oubli.* Paris: Éditions du Seuil, 2000.

———. *Oneself as Another.* Trans. Kathleen Blamey. Chicago: University of Chicago Press, 1992.

———. *Das Rätsel der Vergangenheit: Erinnern—Vergessen—Verzeihen.* Göttingen: Wallstein Verlag, 2000.

Rittner, Carol, and John K. Roth, eds. *"Good News" after Auschwitz? Christian Faith within a Post-Holocaust World.* Macon, Ga.: Mercer University Press, 2001.

———. *Pope Pius XII and the Holocaust.* New York: Continuum Books, 2002.

Rittner, Carol, Stephen D. Smith, and Irena Steinfeldt, eds. *The Holocaust and the Christian World.* New York: Continuum Books, 2000.

Roiphe, Anne. *A Season of Healing: Reflections on the Holocaust.* New York: Summit Books, 1988.

Rosenbaum, Irving J. *The Holocaust and Halakhah.* New York: KTAV, 1976.

Rosenzweig, Franz. *Understanding the Sick and the Healthy.* Trans. Nahum Glatzer. Cambridge, Mass.: Harvard University Press, 1999.

Roth, John K. *Holocaust Politics.* Louisville, Ky.: Westminster John Knox Press, 2001.

———, ed. *Ethics after the Holocaust: Perspectives, Critiques, and Responses.* St. Paul, Minn.: Paragon House, 1999.

Roth, John K., and Elisabeth Maxwell, eds. *Remembering for the Future: The Holocaust in an Age of Genocide.* 3 vols. New York: Palgrave, 2001.

Rubenstein, Richard. "Buber and the Holocaust: Some Reconsiderations on the 100th Anniversary of his Birth." *Michigan Quarterly Review* 18, no. 3 (Summer 1979).

Rychlak, Ronald J. *Hitler, the War, and the Pope.* Columbus, Miss.: Genesis Press, 2000.

Sánchez, José M. *Pius XII and the Holocaust: Understanding the Controversy.* Washington, D.C.: Catholic University of America Press, 2002.

Schaeder, Grete. *The Hebrew Humanism of Martin Buber.* Trans. Noah J. Jacobs. Detroit: Wayne State University Press, 1973.

Schlink, Bernhard. *Flights of Love.* Trans. John E. Woods. New York: Pantheon, 2001.

Schmitt, Carl. *Der Begriff des Politischen: Text von 1932 mit einem Vorwort und drei Corollarien.* Berlin: Dunker & Humbolt, 1963.

———. *The Crisis of Parliamentary Democracy.* Trans. Ellen Kennedy. Cambridge, Mass.: MIT Press, 1986.

Schneider, Theodor. *Zeichen der Nähe Gottes.* Mainz: Grünewald, 1992.

Schupp, Franz. *Schöpfung und Sünde.* Düsseldorf: Patmos, 1990.

Schuster, Ekkehard, and Reinhold Boschert-Kimmig, eds. *Hope against Hope: Johann Baptist Metz and Elie Wiesel Speak Out on the Holocaust.* Trans. J. Matthew Ashley. New York: Paulist Press, 1999.

Segev, Tom. *The Seventh Million: The Israelis and the Holocaust.* Trans. Haim Watzman. New York: Hill and Wang, 1993.

Shiffman, Lisa. *Generation J.* San Francisco: HarperSanFrancisco, 1999.

Shriver, Donald W., Jr. *An Ethic for Enemies: Forgiveness in Politics.* New York: Oxford University Press, 1995.

Signer, Michael A. *Humanity at the Limit: The Impact of the Holocaust Experience on Jews and Christians.* Bloomington: Indiana University Press, 2000.

Silberstein, Lawrence J. *The Postzionism Debates: Knowledge and Power in Israeli Culture.* New York: Routledge, 1999.

Sold, Emil Georg, and Paul Friedhoff. *"That Time Cannot Be Forgotten": A Correspondence on the Shoah.* Trans. Ivan Fehrenbach. Bloomington: Indiana University Press, 2002.

Stendahl, Krister. *Paul among Jews and Gentiles.* Philadelphia: Fortress Press, 1976.

Suchocki, Marjorie Hewitt. *The Fall to Violence: Original Sin in Relational Theology.* New York: Continuum Books, 1994.

Taubes, Jacob. *Vom Kult zur Kultur: Bausteine zu einer Kritik der historischen Vernunft: Gesammelte Aufsätze zur Religions- und Geistesgeschichte.* Munich: Wilhelm Fink Verlag, 1996.

Tillich, Paul. *The Dynamics of Faith.* New York: Harper & Row, 1957.

Volf, Miroslav. *Exclusion and Embrace: A Theological Exploration of Identity, Otherness, and Reconciliation.* Nashville: Abingdon Press, 1996.

West, Cornel. *Prophetic Thought in Postmodern Times: Beyond Eurocentrism and Multiculturalism.* 2 vols. Monroe, Maine: Common Courage Press, 1993.

Wiesel, Elie. *Against Silence: The Voice and Vision of Elie Wiesel.* 3 vols. Ed. Irving Abrahamson. New York: Holocaust Library, 1985.

———. *One Generation After.* Trans. Lily Edelman and Elie Wiesel. New York: Avon Books, 1972.

———. *Paroles d'étranger.* Paris: Éditions du Seuil, 1982.

———. *Souls on Fire: Portraits and Legends of Hasidic Masters.* Trans. Marion Wiesel. New York: Simon & Schuster, 1982.

Wiesel, Elie, and Albert Friedlander. *The Six Days of Destruction: Meditations towards Hope.* Trans. Cynthia Lander and Evelyn Friedlander. Oxford: Pergamon, 1988.

Wiesel, Elie, and Philippe de Saint-Cheron. *Evil and Exile.* Trans. Jon Rothschild. Notre Dame, Ind.: University of Notre Dame Press, 1990.

Wiesel, Elie, and Richard D. Heffner. *Conversations with Elie Wiesel.* Ed. Thomas J. Vinciguerra. New York: Schocken Books, 2001.

Wiesenthal, Simon. *The Sunflower: On the Possibilities and Limits of Forgiveness.* Ed. Harry James Cargas and Bonny V. Fetterman. Rev. and enl. ed. New York: Schocken Books, 1997.

Wills, Garry. *Papal Sin: Structures of Deceit.* New York: Doubleday, 2000.

Young, James E. *The Texture of Memory: Holocaust Memorials and Meaning.* New Haven: Yale University Press, 1993.

Zank, Michael. "The Reception of Daniel Goldhagen's *Hitler's Willing Executioners* in Germany." *Religious Studies Review* 24 (1998): 231–40.

Zimmels, Hirsch Jacob. *The Echo of the Nazi Holocaust in Rabbinic Literature.* New York: KTAV, 1975.

Zuccotti, Susan. *Under His Very Windows: The Vatican and the Holocaust in Italy.* New Haven: Yale University Press, 2000.

ABOUT THE EDITORS AND CONTRIBUTORS

EDITORS

DAVID PATTERSON holds the Bornblum Chair of Excellence in Judaic Studies at the University of Memphis, where he directs the university's Bornblum Judaic Studies Program. In addition to lecturing at numerous universities and community organizations throughout the United States and Canada, as well as in Oxford, Berlin, Moscow, and Jerusalem, Patterson is a consultant for the Philadelphia Center for Holocaust and Genocide Studies and a member of the advisory board for the Annual Scholars' Conference on the Holocaust and the Churches. The author of scores of journal articles and book chapters, he has also published more than ten books, including, most recently, *The Shriek of Silence: A Phenomenology of the Holocaust Novel*; *Sun Turned to Darkness: Memory and Recovery in the Holocaust Memoir*; and *Along the Edge of Annihilation: The Collapse and Recovery of Life in the Holocaust Diary,* which received the 1999 Koret Jewish Book Award for Jewish Thought and Philosophy. He is also translator and editor of the English edition of *The Complete Black Book of Russian Jewry* and co-editor of the *Encyclopedia of Holocaust Literature.*

JOHN K. ROTH is the Edward J. Sexton Professor of Philosophy at Claremont McKenna College, where he directs the Center for the Study of the Holocaust, Genocide, and Human Rights. In addition to serving on the United States Holocaust Memorial Council and on the editorial board for *Holocaust and Genocide Studies,* he has published hundreds of articles and reviews and more than thirty-five books, including, most recently, *"Good News" after Auschwitz? Christian Faith within a Post-Holocaust World*; *Pope Pius XII and the Holocaust*; and *Holocaust Politics,* as well as major contributions to *The Holocaust Chronicle* and a revised edition of *Approaches to Auschwitz* (with Richard L. Rubenstein). Roth's Holocaust-related research appointments have included a 2001 Koerner Visiting Fellowship for Study of the Holocaust at the Oxford Centre for Hebrew and Jewish Studies in England. In 1988, Roth was named U.S. National Professor of the Year by the Council for Advancement and Support of Education and the Carnegie Foundation for the Advancement of Teaching.

CONTRIBUTORS

RACHEL N. BAUM is a lecturer in the departments of English and Hebrew studies at the University of Wisconsin-Milwaukee, where she has also directed the Edition Initiative, a program centered on improving undergraduate education. She has organized a Holocaust conference at the University of Wisconsin-Milwaukee for both college teachers and K–12 educators, and she has worked with groups such as the Milwaukee Area Teachers of English and the Holocaust Education and Resource Center to promote teaching about the Holocaust throughout the state of Wisconsin. Baum's research and published essays on the Holocaust concentrate on pedagogy, the role of the emotions in Holocaust memory, and narratives of the children of Holocaust survivors.

BRITTA FREDE-WENGER received a Ph.D. from the University of Tübingen, Germany, where her work has included studying and teaching theology. Her Holocaust-related publications have focused on issues of memory and on the post-Holocaust theology of Emil Fackenheim. She is involved in various national and international initiatives centering on Holocaust education and remembrance, including a project sponsored by the Canadian Centre for German and European Studies and the Centre for Jewish Studies at York University in Toronto, which brought together students from Canada, Germany, and Poland for field study and research on Holocaust education in the context of anti-racist education.

LEONARD GROB, cofounder with Henry Knight of the biennial Pastora Goldner Holocaust Symposium, is professor of philosophy and coordinator of philosophy studies at Fairleigh Dickinson University, where he also directs the university's Core Curriculum Program. His publications include numerous articles on the philosophy of dialogue and the thought of Martin Buber and Emmanuel Lévinas. Grob is the coeditor of *Education for Peace: Testimonies from World Religions* and *Women's and Men's Liberation: Testimonies of Spirit,* two anthologies based on Buber's thought, as well as a contributor to *Ethics after the Holocaust,* a 1999 book that resulted from work of the Goldner Holocaust Symposium. His memoir "Goodbye Father," which appeared in *Judaism,* describes his 1989 journey to Ukraine, which led him to the field of Holocaust studies when he uncovered the history of the destruction of his father's family during the Shoah. Grob's current work includes co-directing the Palestinian-Israeli Oral History Project, which educates children for peace in the Middle East.

PETER J. HAAS holds the Abba Hillel Silver Chair of Jewish Studies at Case Western Reserve University, where he also directs the Samuel Rosenthal Center for Judaic Studies. Ordained as a Reform rabbi, he served as an active duty chaplain in the United States Army for three years. That experience influenced his interests in moral philosophy and education. Haas's many publications include *Morality after Auschwitz: The Radical Challenge of the Nazi Ethic,* which studies the use of moral language in Nazi society, and, most recently, *Responsa: Literary History of a Rabbinic Genre,* which focuses on the moral discourse of classical Rabbinic Judaism. Haas has made presentations at numerous conferences in Israel, as well as in England, Italy, Germany, and Belgium. His current research interests include the relationship between science and religion in the contemporary world.

HENRY F. KNIGHT, cofounder with Leonard Grob of the biennial Pastora Goldner Holocaust Symposium, is university chaplain and associate professor of religion at the University of Tulsa, where he teaches courses on Christian theology, the Holocaust, and Jewish-Christian relations. An ordained minister in the United Methodist Church for more than twenty years, his research and publications have addressed two areas: ministry in higher education and the impact of the Holocaust on Christian faith and thought. Knight is the author of *Confessing Christ in a Post-Holocaust World: A Midrashic Experiment* and the coeditor with Marcia Sachs Littell of *The Uses and Abuses of Knowledge.* His articles have appeared in *The Journal of Ecumenical Studies, Quarterly Review, Shofar,* and *Encounter.*

JUERGEN MANEMANN, a Coolidge Fellow at Columbia University in 1997, teaches political theology at the Institute of Foundational Theology in the department of Catholic theology at the University of Münster, Germany. His teaching and research deal with topics such as theology after Auschwitz, post-humanism, and recent debates in Germany about the history and significance of the Holocaust. The founder and organizer of a biennial colloquium on political theology, Manemann is also the author or editor of numerous publications, including *"Weil es nicht nur Geschichte ist": Die Begründung der Notwendigkeit einer fragmentarischen Historiographie des Nationalsozialismus aus politish-theologischer Sicht*; *Demokratiefähigkeit*; *Christologie nach Auschwitz*; *Befristete Zeit*; *Politischer Anti-Monotheismus*; and *Religion und der Terror.* His current research includes a study of Carl Schmitt, the most important and influential German jurist during and after the Nazi period.

DIDIER POLLEFEYT teaches courses on religion, theology, Jewish-Christian relations, and religious education in the faculties of theology, the arts, pedagogy, and psychology at the Catholic University of Leuven, Belgium, where he also heads the Center for University Teacher Education and the Center for Peace Ethics. Pollefeyt is a member of Belgium's National Catholic Commission for Jewish-Christian Relations, and he also serves on the editorial boards for the journals *Ethical Perspectives* and *Bijdragen: Tijdschrift voor filosofie en theologie.* Pollefeyt's research, which includes studies of Emil Fackenheim and Richard Rubenstein, focuses on post-Holocaust religious life and thought. Among his publications are *Religious Teaching of the Holocaust,* which received the Belgian Peace Prize, and *Jews and Christians: Rivals or Partners for the Kingdom of God? In Search of an Alternative for the Christian Theology of Substitution,* as well as major contributions to *Ethics after the Holocaust.*

INDEX

Abraham, 29, 47, 173
Adam, 178, 185
Adorno, Theodor, 131, 140, 142
Amalek, 14, 17, 18, 161, 198
Amalekites. *See* Amalek
Améry, Jean, 85, 86–87, 90, 93, 101–2, 106–7, 110
Amos, 167
Anderson, Herbert, 31–32, 41
Annan, Kofi, 218
Apokatastasis, 73–74, 78, 131, 141, 149
Augustine, 185
Auschwitz Murder Camp, xiii, xv, 28, 93, 140, 179

Bauman, Zygmunt, 205
Beck, Ulrich, 147–48
Bendersky, Joseph, 151
Benjamin, Walter, 75, 126, 131–32, 142
Benz, Wolfgang, 117
Berenbaum, Michael, 215
Bertelsmann Music Group, 224–25, 243
Bible, 26–27, 150. *See also* Gospel; Torah
Blet, Pierre, 89, 97n5, 98n9
Blumenberg, Hans, 165
Blumenthal, David, 146
Bonhoeffer, Dietrich, 31, 56
Boorstein, Sylvia, 231–32, 238, 239
Borowi, Czeslaw, 102
Boszormenyi-Nagy, Ivan, 134–35
Buber, Martin, 22–23, 26, 193, 202, 209n12, 223n2, 238–39, 250
Buddhism, 228–29, 231–33
Bukiet, Melvin Jules, 224, 232–33
Bush, George W., 187

Cain, 180, 181
Camus, Albert, 57, 107, 152, 162, 165

Cassidy, Cardinal Edward I., 88
Christ. *See* Jesus
Christian theology, 19, 77, 142; and covenantal heritage, 28; as damaged, 39, 43; on original sin, 155–56; and reconciliation, 125–26, 129, 150, 152, 164; on redemption, 172–73, 184–85, 189
Christology, 146
Collective guilt, 65. *See also* Guilt
Confession, 7, 9, 30–39, 41–43, 45
Covenant, 37, 46–49
Crusades, 12

"Dabru Emet," 6, 14–15, 21, 23, 66–67, 72, 77
Death, 127
Delbo, Charlotte, xiii, xv, xviiin, 94–95
Diabolization, 59, 62
Dialogue, 22–23, 129, 201–4, 207, 239, 249
Divine commandment: as basis of freedom, 193; and ethics, 183, 196; and justice, 175, 177, 180, 190; as key to salvation, 195; as a manifestation of God, 174
Dogma, 22, 111
Durban. *See* World Conference against Racism
Dwelling, 177

Eucharist, 37–38, 48, 53
Evil, 57–61, 71, 75–76, 106, 134–36, 161
Ezekiel, 143–44, 148, 156

Fackenheim, Emil, 56, 76, 212
Feinstein, Moshe, 12
Fisher, Eugene, 24n1, 146–47
Fleischner, Eva, 88, 96n5, 97n6
Fogarty, Gerald, 96n5
Foley, Edward, 31–32, 41
Ford, David, 37
Friedhof, Paul, 109, 110–12

German churches, 126, 128, 160,
Giordano, Ralph, 143
Glover, Jonathan, 91
Goldhagen, Daniel, 116–17, 129, 135, 141n1
Gospel, 46
Grace, 124, 159–60, 185–86, 193, 195
Greenberg, Irving, 29, 36, 41, 51, 141, 209n5, 211
Guilt: and German identity, 122, 123–26, 130; inherited, 133–34, 139; and subjectivity, 143–44, 155–56, 158–59. *See also* Collective guilt; Original sin
Gumpel, Peter, 88, 89, 97n7, 97n9

Hanania ben Teradion, 13
Hegel, G. W. F., 130, 143, 165
Heidegger, Martin, 172
Herzog, Isaac Halevy, 11
Hillesum, Etty, 57, 107
Hitler, Adolf, 12, 56, 90, 149, 205
Holocaust Remembrance Day, 11–13
Holy Door, 100–101
Humility, 22

Jacob, 29, 175, 213, 251
Jacob, Walter, 13–14
Jerusalem, 160, 206–7
Jesus: covenantal heritage of, 28; death and resurrection of, 43, 76; and forgiveness, 30, 35–36, 39, 145, 146, 157; as means to salvation, 46–49, 161, 172–73, 176, 178, 181, 184, 186, 189, 193–94; teachings of, 44, 100–101
Joel, 74
John Paul II, Pope, 100–101
Judaism, 103, 160–61, 164–65, 230, 247

Kamenetz, Rodger, 235–36n5
Kant, Immanuel, 172, 175, 193
Kaplan, Chaim, 173, 190
Kasper, Cardinal Walter, 88–89
Katallage, 144, 163
Ka-tzetnik 135633, 249
Kierkegaard, Søren, 192, 193
Kushner, Lawrence, 32

Language, xiii-xiv
Lanzmann, Claude, 102
Lerner, Michael, 204, 209n6
Levi, Primo, xiii, xv, 93, 95, 180, 249–50
Lévinas, Emmanuel, 130, 179, 180, 189, 193; on evil, 57; on forgiveness, 55, 61, 149; on substitution, 146, 164; on suffering, 93–94, 95, 106
Locke, Hubert, 147
Lot, 122–23

Maimonides, 6–10, 21
Mandel, Harriet, 235n3
Manicheanism, 78–79
Marrus, Michael, 96n5
Mejia, Cardinal Jorge Maria, 97n9
Memory: and forgiveness, 125, 126; and the future, 60; and history, 58–59; of the Holocaust, 130, 227; and reconciliation, 144, 159, 227
Messiah, 27, 131–32, 246
Metz, Johann Baptist, 28, 44, 124, 126
Meyers, Joel, 89
Micah, 213
Middelhoff, Thomas, 224–25, 231, 232, 243
Modernity, 147–48
Monbourquette, Jean, 63
Moore, James, 55
Morley, John, 96n5
Moshe ben Nahman, 11
Muselmann, 179, 249–50
Mythic structure, 211–13, 219–20. *See also* Narrative structure

Nachmanides. *See* Moshe ben Nahman
Nachshon, 195
Narrative structure, 201–4. *See also* Mythic structure
National Socialism, 90–91, 93, 94, 98n14, 99n16, 201
Nietzsche, Friedrich, 193
Noahide covenant, 52
Nomberg-Przytyk, Sara, 249
Nuremberg trials, 215

Origen, 78, 149
Original sin, 70, 133–34, 139, 151, 156, 163, 184–85, 193. *See also* Guilt

Palestinian-Israeli Oral History Project, 221–22
Pascal, Blaise, 193
Pastora Goldner Holocaust Symposium, xvi, xvii, 38
Paul, 31, 35, 47, 49n1
Paul VI, Pope, 100
Pius XII, Pope, 85, 88, 89, 97n5, 100
Pollefeyt, Didier, 150
Post-traditional society, 147–48, 151, 160–61, 165
Post-Zionism, 207–8
Prayer, 174–75, 191
Protestant spirituality, 31

Reemtsma, Jan Philip, 116
Remembrance. *See* Memory
Resurrection, 76
Ricoeur, Paul: on forgiveness 60, 61; on historical guilt, 120–22; on reconciliation, 116, 117, 125, 128–29, 131, 135, 138
Righteous among the Nations, 161, 176, 196
Robinson, Mary, 218
Roman Catholic Church, 71–72, 76, 113n2, 164; and gnosticism, 151; and Jewish-Christian relations, 89, 100, 103, 104; and the "We Remember" document, 56, 65–66. *See also* Vatican
Romans, the, 14, 17, 18, 210n14
Rosenzweig, Franz, 172, 175, 193
Rubenstein, Richard, 52, 209n7

Schlink, Bernhard, 116, 118–20, 129
Schmitt, Carl, 151–52
Schneider, Theodor, 42
Schupp, Franz, 185
Secularism, 73–75
September 11, 2001, xiv-xv, 71, 109, 187–88, 214, 244–45, 253
Sherman, Ernest, 24n2
Signer, Michael, 15, 21, 67
Silberstein, Lawrence J., 210n15
Sold, Emil, 109, 110–12
Stalin, Joseph, 91
Steinberg, Elan, 89
Stendahl, Krister, 150
Suchecky, Bernard, 96n5

Tanakh. *See* Bible
Temple, 7
Theodicy, 126
Third Reich. *See* National Socialism
Tillich, Paul, 211, 212
Tolstoy, Leo, 193
Torah, 7, 46, 47, 161, 175, 195
Torture, 90–91

Unencumbered self, 147–48, 161
United Jewish Appeal, 224–25, 232, 243
United Methodist Church, 30, 41, 49–50, 54n1
Useless experience, 91–93
Useless suffering, 93–95, 106

Vatican, 85, 87–92, 95–96, 99–102, 103–5, 108–9, 113n2, 160. *See also* Roman Catholic Church
Victimism, 59–60
Volf, Miroslav, 37, 39, 48

Walzer, Michael, 152
Weinberg, Yehiel Jacob, 13
Weizsäcker, Richard, 125
"We Remember," 56, 65
West, Cornel, 142
Wiesel, Elie, xiv, 34, 175, 218, 225–26
Wiesenthal, Simon, 107
Wistrich, Robert, 96n5
World Conference against Racism, 214–18, 219, 220
World Jewish Congress, 89

Yom Kippur, 8
Young, James, 227

Zedong, Mao, 91
Zionism, 205–7, 220

LIBRARY OF CONGRESS CATALOGING-IN-PUBLICATION DATA

After-words : post-Holocaust struggles with forgiveness, reconciliation, justice / edited and introduced by David Patterson and John K. Roth.

p. cm.—(The Pastora Goldner series in post-Holocaust studies)

Includes bibliographical references.

ISBN 0-295-98371-X (cloth : alk. paper)

1. Holocaust, Jewish (1939–1945)—Moral and ethical aspects.

2. Holocaust, Jewish (1939–1945—Influence—Congresses.

3. Forgiveness—Religious aspects—Congresses.

4. Reconciliation—Religious aspects—Congresses.

5. Religion and justice—Congresses.

I. Title: Afterwords. II. Title: Afterwards.

III. Patterson, David. IV. Roth, John K. V. Series.

D804.3A38 2004 940.53'1814—dc22 2003061647